Fashioning Film Stars

Fashioning Film Stars

Dress, Culture, Identity

Edited by Rachel Moseley

 Publishing

First published in 2005 by the
BRITISH FILM INSTITUTE
21 Stephen Street
London
W1T 1LN

The British Film Institute's purpose is to champion moving image culture in all its richness and
diversity across the UK, for the benefit of as wide an audience as possible, and to create and
encourage debate.

Cover design by Ketchup
Cover image: *Breakfast at Tiffany's* (Blake Edwards, 1961, © Paramount Pictures Corporation)

Set by Fakenham Photosetting Limited, Fakenham, Norfolk
Printed in the UK by St Edmundsbury Press, Bury St Edmunds, Suffolk

British Library Cataloguing-in-Publication Data
A catalogue record for this book is available from the British Library

ISBN 1–84457–068–1 (pbk)
ISBN 1–84457–067–3 (hbk)

Contents

Acknowledgments

First, I must thank the contributors to this collection for their ongoing enthusiasm for the book's intellectual project, and for their hard work – often under great pressure. I am, of course, also very grateful to BFI Publishing for supporting the collection, and in particular to my editor, Andrew Lockett for continuing to support the project through the series of delays which have plagued it. In particular, my gratitude goes to Sophia Contento at BFI Publishing, for her invaluable contribution to seeing the book through its final stages. I would also like to thank Richard Dyer, for encouraging me in the first instance, and my friends Jacinda Read and Helen Wheatley, who have, as always, been a constant source of support and companionship.

Notes on Contributors

Kaushik Bhaumik is currently a research fellow at the Ferguson Centre for African and Asian Studies at the Open University, Milton Keynes. His research interests lie in the areas of early film history, twentieth-century cultural studies and South Asian cultural history. His forthcoming publications include *From the Bazar to the Nation: The Bombay Film Industry, 1896–1936* (Clarendon Press), *The BFI Indian Cinema Book* (BFI) and *Visual Cultures: An Alternative Reader* (Berg).

Stella Bruzzi is Professor of Film Studies in the Department of Media Arts, Royal Holloway, University of London. She is author of *Undressing Cinema: Clothing and Identity in the Movies* (Routledge, 1997) and *New Documentary: A Critical Introduction* (Routledge, 2000). She co-edited *Fashion Cultures: Theories, Explorations, and Analysis* (Routledge, 2000) with Pamela Church Gibson, and is currently completing *Bringing up Daddy: Fatherhood and Masculinity in Postwar Hollywood*.

Pamela Church Gibson is Senior Lecturer in Cultural Studies at the London College of Fashion. She has published essays on film, fashion, fandom, history and heritage. She has also co-edited three collections of essays including *Fashion Cultures: Theories, Explorations, and Analysis* (Routledge, 2000) with Stella Bruzzi, and *The Oxford Guide to Film Studies* (Oxford University Press, 1998). She is currently working on the relationship between cinema and consumption of the post-war era.

Pam Cook is Professor of European Film and Media at Southampton University. Her publications on British cinema include *Fashioning the Nation: Costume and Identity in British Cinema* (BFI, 1996) and *I Know Where I'm Going!* (BFI, 2002). Her most recent book is *Screening the Past: Memory and Nostalgia in Cinema* (Routledge, 2005), and she is currently working on a monograph about Baz Luhrmann.

Jane Marie Gaines is Professor of Literature and English and Director of the Program in Film and Video at Duke University. She is the author, most recently, of *Fire and Desire: Mixed Race Movies in the Silent Era* (University of Chicago Press, 2001). She is editor, with Charlotte Herzog, of *Fabrications: Costume and the Female Body* (Routledge, 1990).

Christine Geraghty is Senior Lecturer in Communications at Goldsmith's College, University of London. Her main interests lie in the analysis of film and television texts with particular regard for textual analysis and audience identification and involvement. She has a particular concern for gender issues and the social and historical context in which the pleasures of film/television can be understood. Her publications include *Women and Soap Opera* (Polity Press, 1991), *The Television Studies Book*, co-edited with David Lusted (Arnold, 1998) and *British Cinema in the Fifties: Gender, Genre and the 'New Look'*, (Routledge, 2000).

Joanne Hershfield is the author of *The Invention of Dolores Del Rio: Mexican Cinema/ Mexican Women*, 1940–1950 (University of Minnesota Press, 2000) and the co-editor, with David R. Maciel, of *Mexico's Cinema* (Scholarly Resources, 1999). She teaches Media Studies and Media Production at the University of North Carolina at Chapel Hill and is a documentary film-maker.

Charlotte Cornelia Herzog is Professor Emeritus of Art History at Harper College and has recently published articles in *Women's Art Journal* and the *Journal of the American Art Pottery Association*. She is editor, with Jane Gaines, of *Fabrications: Costume and the Female Body* (Routledge, 1990).

Claire Hines is a part-time lecturer in Film Studies. She completed her doctorate at the University of Southampton in 2005, with a thesis entitled 'Shaken, Not Stirred? James Bond, Playboy and Changing Gender Roles in the 1960s'.

Tamar Jeffers is a lecturer in Film Studies at Buckinghamshire Chilterns University College. She read English at Somerville College, Oxford, before receiving an MA in Film Studies from Westminster University. Her current research projects concern representations of female virginity in 1950s' Hollywood, costume, performance and romantic comedy.

Denise Miller received a PhD on the work of María Luisa Bemberg from the University of Warwick. She has taught Literature and Cultural Studies in Britain, Spain and Mexico. She has a particular interest in the interrelationship between film and Spanish American and Italian literatures, and is the author of 'María Luisa Bemberg's Interpretation of Octavio Paz's *Sor Juan*', in J. King, S. Whitaker and R. Bosch (eds), *An Argentine Passion: María Luisa Bemberg and her Films*, (Verso, 2000). She has organised an international conference on film stars outside Hollywood, focusing on South Asia and South America.

Rachel Moseley is a lecturer in Film and Television Studies at the University of Warwick. She is the author of *Growing Up with Audrey Hepburn: Text, Audience, Resonance* (Manchester University Press, 2002) and co-editor, with Joanne Hollows, of *Feminism in Popular Culture* (Berg, forthcoming 2006). She has published on popular film and television, and is currently writing a book on the history of television programming for teenagers in Britain.

Drake Stutesman is writing *The Emperor of Fashion*, a biography of Mr John. Her recent book, *Snake*, a study of snakes in culture, myth and science will be published by Reaktion Books in 2005. She is the editor of *Framework: The Journal of Cinema and Media*.

Ginette Vincendeau is Professor of Film Studies at the University of Warwick. She has published widely on French cinema, including articles in *Screen, Sight and Sound,*

Positif and *Iris*. Her books include *French Film, Texts and Contexts* (Routledge, 1990 and 2000), co-edited with Susan Hayward, *The Encyclopedia of European Cinema* (BFI/Cassell, 1995), *The Companion to French Cinema* (BFI/Cassell, 1996), *Pépé le Moko* (BFI, 1998), *Stars and Stardom in French Cinema* (Continuum, 2000) and *Film/Literature/Heritage* (BFI, 2001).

Russell White is lecturer in Media with Cultural Studies at Southampton Institute. His article on Samuel L. Jackson builds upon his long-standing research interests in post-soul African American culture..

Introduction

Rachel Moseley

What do you think of when you think of Marlene Dietrich, Audrey Hepburn, Gregory Peck or Samuel L. Jackson? First, probably, you bring to mind their face, and possibly their voice, those key aspects of performance which made them a star. Second, you think clothes. It is difficult to imagine conjuring up the image of any of the stars mentioned above without thinking in general terms of their style, and indeed, often, the specific modes of dress with which they were associated: Dietrich in top hat and tails, Hepburn in Givenchy or dancer's black, Peck in a suit, Jackson in a Kangol beret. Surprisingly, then, given the centrality of dress to our commonplace understandings of stars, a scant amount of scholarly attention has been paid to the importance of the relationship between stars and their fashioning: the role played, in the constitution of their stardom, by clothes, dress, fashion, costume. While 'coffee table' books on stars and style have always highlighted the significance of dress in star-making, academic work on stars and stardom, while sometimes acknowledging costume, has rarely devoted space to its extended analysis. As Elizabeth Wilson has noted, dress is always 'unspeakably meaningful' (1985, p. 3), and as Jane Gaines has discussed at some length, Hollywood film costume has, historically, had to both disappear and speak simultaneously (1990, pp. 195–6). As Bruzzi and Church Gibson suggest in their introduction to *Fashion Cultures* perhaps it has been the case that fashion in academia has been seen largely as 'too trivial to theorise, too serious to ignore' (2000, p. 2). The aim of this collection, then, is to begin to redress that balance. The essays collected here extend the small body of scholarship which does exist and bring together a range of scholarly approaches and methodological frameworks. The key questions which have guided the writing of the essays in *Fashioning Film Stars* have been: how does dress operate in relation to stardom to articulate particular identities – gendered, national, classed, ethnic, sexual? How, precisely, does film costume operate, and how is it understood, semiotically, socially, culturally? Does star dress 'disappear' against the body as 'clothes', or speak out performatively as 'costume' or 'spectacle'?

The Oxford English Dictionary (2nd edn, 1989) gives the following definitions:

Clothes
1. Covering for the person; wearing apparel; dress, raiment, vesture (p. 355).

Dress
2.a. personal attire or apparel: orig. that proper to some special rank or order of

person, or to some ceremony or function; but, in later use, often merely: clothing, costume, garb, esp. that part which is external and serves for adornment as well as covering.

2.b. a suit of garments or a single external garment appropriate to some occasion when adornment is required; now spec. a lady's robe or gown made not merely to clothe but also to adorn (p. 1044).

Fashion

3.b. esp. with reference to attire: a particular 'cut' or style.

8.a. a prevailing custom, a current usage; esp. one characteristic of a particular place or period of time.

8.c. spec. with regard to apparel or personal adornment (p. 743).

These definitions are useful, because they allow us to tease out some of the important distinctions between terms which, frequently, are used interchangeably – especially 'clothes' and 'dress'. 'Clothes', then, are a way of describing body coverings which are just that – there primarily to cover the body rather than to adorn it, and which therefore are functional rather than decorative. Dress, by contrast, I would argue, does in fact retain a little of its earlier usage – the sense that it is adornment, but with a purpose – that it may indicate something quite specific about both the person who wears it or the occasion for which it is worn – be that in terms of gender, class, ethnicity, nationality, sexuality. Definitions of costume, interestingly, secondary to those referring to clothes worn for theatrical (or cinematic) performances, carry similar connotations of a specificity of identity: social, cultural or temporal. The term fashion, finally, indicates a mode of adornment tied to a particular moment. The essays in this collection consider the relationship between stars and their clothes in ways which address their function as dress, costume and fashion, and sometimes as all three. It is hoped, then, that this book represents an attempt to further carve out in the field of film studies an interdisciplinary niche which looks at the significant role played by clothes in constructing and inflecting star images, and in producing meaning as a significant element of the total signifying system of the cinema.

The Fields

The work in this collection is formed at the intersection of several fields of social, historical, critical and textual scholarship, which, broadly, can be grouped as follows. First, there has been the study of stars, both that founding theoretical and critical work in the field (for example, Dyer, 1979a and 1986) and the work of scholars such as Barry King, Richard de Cordova and others, exemplified by in Gledhill's 1991 collection, *Stardom: Industry of Desire*. There is also that body of more recent work which addresses stars from an historical, nationally specific or sociological/cultural studies perspective, such as Jackie Stacey's work on Hollywood stars and female spectatorship (1994), Vincendeau (2000), Babington (2001) and my own work on Audrey Hepburn (Moseley, 2002). Second is the small but significant set of texts which has sought to address directly the relationship between dress (or, more commonly, costume) and the cinema, including Sue Harper's work on costume in Gainsborough melodrama (1987), Pam Cook's *Fashioning the Nation* (1996), Stella Bruzzi's *Undressing Cinema* (1997), Sarah Berry's *Screen Style* (2000), Christine Geraghty's *British Cinema in the Fifties* (2000), Sarah Street's *Costume and Cinema* (2001) and, of course, Gaines and Herzog's germinal collection, *Fabrications* (1990). While, of course, some of this work has looked at the importance of the relationship between fashion and stars (for instance, Berry, 2000) in the main it has looked at costume as a signifier not specifically linked to the star who wears it. To my delight, then, a number of these key scholars agreed to contribute to this book, and here offer new work focused specifically on the relationship between stars and their clothes. Third is work on fashion history and theory, for example Laver (1983), Wilson (1985), Evans and Thornton (1989), Craik (1994), Ash and Wilson (1992), Entwhistle (2000) and Bruzzi and Church Gibson (2000). Fourth, and finally, is the body of scholarship attending to dress, clothes and the body, including Roach and Eicher (1965), Barnes and Eicher (1993), Garber (1993), Hollander (1993), Warwick and Cavallaro (1998) and Entwhistle and Wilson (2001). My aim, then, in this introduction, is to offer a brief overview of some relevant aspects of this divergent field and to position the book within it.

Stars and Stardom

In his 1979 book *Stars*, Richard Dyer considers the meanings made by stars from both semiotic and sociological perspectives, and argues that star images are 'a complex configuration of visual, verbal and aural signs' and that they 'function crucially in relation to contradictions within and between ideologies, which they seek variously to "manage" or "resolve" ' (p. 38). Dyer goes on to use the example of Gloria Swanson to discuss the ways in which women stars might function ideologically in relation to fashion, and as I have argued here and elsewhere in relation to Audrey Hepburn, fashion and dress can play an important role in the way that stars are able to manage and resolve those ideological contradictions, particularly through their reception and appropriation by audiences in their own practices (Moseley, 2002; see also Stacey, 1994). Despite this early acknowledgment of the role that fashion and dress play in relation to stars and stardom in perhaps the seminal theoretical work on stars (and indeed later too in *Heavenly Bodies* [1986] in the analysis of the star images of Marilyn Monroe, Paul Robeson and Judy Garland), the baton has rarely been taken up as the field of study has expanded.

To take a well-known instance, Christine Gledhill's 1991 collection, *Stardom: Industry of Desire*, contains some of the most influential work in the field; however, there is little detailed consideration of clothes, whether as dress, fashion or costume, in this volume, with the exception of Charles Eckert's reprinted 1978 essay "The Carole Lombard in Macy's Window", Herzog and Gaines' ' "Puffed Sleeves Before Tea-Time" ', (originally published in 1985) on Gilbert Adrian's designs for Joan Crawford in *Letty Lynton* (Clarence Brown, 1932), and Jackie Stacey's 'Feminine Fascinations'. All three essays concentrate on processes of consumption around the star–fashion relationship, with

Eckert looking specifically at the cinema tie-up; significantly, given the direction their work would take later, it is only Herzog and Gaines' essay which links costume and dress directly to star image. Jackie Stacey's work on stars investigated the relationship between Hollywood stars and the female spectator, and in *Star Gazing* (1994), she investigates the practice of 'copying' star styles, including hair, make-up and fashion, by young women in the movie audience in post-war Britain; while *Star Gazing* is thus concerned with the relationship between stars and dress, then, it is at the point of reception, rather than production of meaning making, that Stacey approaches that relationship, and the book does not address the relationship between dress and star image in any extended way.

Ginette Vincendeau's *Stars and Stardom in French Cinema* (2000) is one of the few scholarly works in this area of the field to attend to the operation of fashion and dress in relation to stardom. In considering French stars, including Alain Delon, Catherine Deneuve and Jeanne Moreau, she investigates the way in which clothes function both as part of the star image, but also their diegetic significance within the films she examines; in her essay for this collection, Vincendeau extends her existing work on Bardot, and looks at the impact of Bardot's 'clothes grammar' across her career.

Film Costume

It is in the body of scholarship which looks at film costume, however, that we find the most extended discussion of the significance of the relationship between stars and dress. It was the publication of *Fabrications* (Gaines and Herzog, 1990) which opened up the debate significantly for the first time, with Jane Gaines' introduction to the volume, 'Fabricating the Female Body' and her own essay, 'Costume and Narrative: How Dress Tells the Woman's Story', which offered a detailed analysis of the way in which costume functions in classical Hollywood narrative and in relation to star image, becoming formative for the emerging field of scholarship on film costume. Gaines' observation that the term 'fetish' might be used in its original, rather than the psychoanalytic sense which had become almost hegemonic in film studies by that point, freed up the discussion of costume, looking and desire. At the same time, her reminder that 'the *fetish* in history has been used to dismiss the ritual practices of the cultural other' (1990, p. 23) suggested that there was more to the pleasure invoked by fashion, dress and film costume than those which were perceived as somehow merely trivial because largely perceived to be within the province of the feminine. This might be seen as indicative of the shift in critical and theoretical approaches towards what might be described as a 'post-feminist' position and historical periodisation in which, as Charlotte Brunsdon (1997) and others have argued, the relationship between feminism and fashion is no longer one primarily of contradiction. While some of the essays in *Fabrications* are concerned with dress and the body more generally, those which look at the place of fashion and costume in cinema, such as Maureen Turim's piece on the 'New Sweetheart Line' (first published 1984), film costume and stardom have provided a model for future scholarship.

Pam Cook's *Fashioning the Nation* (1996) offers a rich analysis of the construction of national identity through costume, fashion and the designs of Elizabeth Haffenden in a number of British historical romance films of the 1940s. While Cook's analysis here is not concerned with the intersection of costume and stardom, she offers a clear account of film and cultural studies' complex relationship with fashion and costume, and goes on to explore the way in which costume in the Gainsborough dramas of the 1940s contributed to the construction of a complex, fluid and hybrid notion of national identity which has impacted on the positioning of that body of work in the British cinema canon. In *Undressing Cinema* (1997), Stella Bruzzi offers an analysis of the operation of fashion in cinema and the construction of generic and gendered identities through clothes, in the process challenging understandings about the relationship between costume and narrative through an interdisciplinary approach which brings clothes and fashion theory to the study of cinema. *Undressing Cinema* does not explore the relationship between stars and dress, but is revolutionary in its address to questions of fashion in contemporary cinema (of the 80s and 90s), and further in that it considers this subject in relation to masculinity and race. Bruzzi's work has thus paved the way for more recent work such as Sarah Street's *Costume and Cinema: Dress Codes in Popular Film* (2001), and indeed for the work collected in this volume. Such work includes Sarah Berry's *Screen Style: Fashion and Femininity in 1930s Hollywood* (2000), which offers a socio-historically situated analysis of the relationship between fashion, Hollywood cinema, femininity, stardom and consumption in the 1930s. Perhaps the first work to bring together the range of methodological approaches of work on stars from Dyer (1979) to Herzog and Gaines (1991), *Screen Style* draws on sources including women's and film fan magazines of the period to address questions of class and gender in relation to fashion and spectacle, focusing on the role played by stars such as Greta Garbo, Joan Crawford and Marlene Dietrich in that dynamic. It is perhaps Berry's *Screen Style*, then, which is the most direct predecessor of *Fashioning Film Stars*, along with a group of essays exploring the relationship between fashion and the icon which appear in Part Three: 'Images, Icons and Impulses' of Bruzzi and Church Gibson's recent collection *Fashion Cultures* (2000).

Fashion, Dress and the Body in Cinema

Without the shift indicated in Elizabeth Wilson's comment in *Adorned in Dreams*, that 'the most important thing about fashion is not that it oppresses women' (1985, p. 13), this book would not have been possible. It has been the change in feminist critical and cultural studies' relationship with fashion and its theorisation which has enabled an opening up of the field, and allowed a growing body of work on the meanings articulated through fashion, dress and the body to emerge (see, for instance, Evans and Thornton (1989), *Women and Fashion: A New Look* and Ash and Wilson (1992), *Chic Thrills*).

In *Vested Interests: Cross-Dressing and Cultural Anxiety* (1993), Marjorie Garber, in her consideration of the meanings and implications of cross-dressing, examines the ways in which dress constructs social and national identities; the essays in this collection are indebted to cultural studies work of this kind which has unpicked the commonplace assumptions we hold about the meanings of dress, and teased out the precise semiotics of clothing. In their *Fashioning the Frame: Boundaries, Dress and the Body* (1998), Alexandra Warwick and Dani Cavallaro ask a series of questions about the relationship between dress and the biological and social body which strike me as eminently applicable to the investigations of the relationship between stars and their dress undertaken in this anthology. In their preface to the book, they ask:

> Should dress be regarded as part of the body, or merely as an extension of, or supplement to it? Even confining dress to the apparently secondary status of supplement hardly resolves the problems inherent in the assessment of the relationship between dress and the body, since, as indicated by Derrida's analysis of supplementarity, the supplement operates simultaneously as an optional appendix and as a completing and hence necessary element. (Ibid., p. xv)

This deliberation, it seems to me, goes right to the heart of the relationship between stars and dress, and is suggestive of the way in which film costume both speaks – and sometime shouts – for itself, but may also operate simultaneously as an inextricable part of the complex system of cinematic signification, and particularly in relation to stardom and performance. In this volume, Drake Stutesman's analysis of Mr John's hats for Dietrich in chapter two, Christine Geraghty's analysis of Kay Kendall's relationship to fashion in chapter ten and Denise Miller's discussion of Luisina Brando's performance in chapter thirteen indicate precisely this complexity in the relationship between body and clothes around the film star.

Warwick and Cavallaro continue with a discussion of the way in which dress operates as both boundary and margin; dress, they suggest,

> *frames* the body and insulates private fantasies from the Other, yet it simultaneously connects the individual self to the collective Other and fashions those fantasies on the model of a public spectacle, thus questioning the myth of a self-contained identity . . . Dress, then both defines and de-individualizes us. . . . Dress as boundary is meant to trace a neat line between self and other: the limitation of physical visibility via clothing, for example, parallels metaphorically an intended limitation of psychological accessibility. As margin, on the other hand, dress connects the individual to other bodies, it links the biological entity to the social ensemble and the private to the public. This cohesive action holds the advantage of releasing the individual subject to the possibility of collective interactivity and communication, yet it erases its very individuality. (Ibid., pp. xvi–xvii)

Especially interesting for the analysis of the relationship between stars and clothing in this anthology, is the suggestion that dress is more than one thing at once. On the one hand, it is separating and defining; fashion and dress, in relation to stars, can become the supreme marker of their identity – indeed the uniqueness of their persona. It can make them seem special, unreachable and untouchable. At the same time, however, dress and fashion are also part of the connective tissue of the social, allowing us to make judgments – and even sartorial choices – based upon our ability to read their articulations in relation to that identity. My own work on Audrey Hepburn and the significance of her style for young British female fans in chapter nine indicates this connectivity, and a number of the essays in the collection – for instance, Tamar Jeffers' discussion of Doris Day's white dress in *Pillow Talk* (Michael Gordon, 1959) in chapter four, Pam Cook and Claire Hines' work on Sean Connery's James Bond (chapter twelve) and Ginette Vincendeau's work on Bardot (chapter eleven), suggest a similar relation. I want to argue, then, that it is precisely the possibility that dress might operate simultaneously as boundary and margin, as barrier and connection, that is at the heart of the power of the fashionable star.

The interdisciplinary essays in this anthology bring the insights, methodologies and historical understandings of such work in the field of fashion, dress and the body to bear on film studies' discussion of costume and stardom; it is hoped, then, that this anthology will begin to extend the existing literature in those areas of the discipline. Analysis of stars, stardom and film costume has remained, with a few significant exceptions (see, for example Alexander, 1991; Bruzzi 1997; Dwyer, 2000), largely white, Hollywood and Eurocentric, while work on dress and the body has always been more concerned with the ways in which clothing constructs identities, be they gendered, sexual, national or ethnic. Accordingly, in bringing together work on fashion and dress with work on stardom, this book was conceptualised with the precise intention of addressing the existing structure of the field and making an intervention within in it; essays were commissioned in order to address questions of stardom outside as well as within the Hollywood system, and to address issues of race and ethnicity as well as gendered and sexual identities. While a range of methodologies are employed across the anthology, the use of close textual analysis of the film as a primary source, in conjunction with concretely situated contextual analyses which draw on theoretical work on dress and fashion, is common to many of the essays. It is indicative too of the shift in film studies methodologies, that the work here relies much less on cine-psychoanalytical frameworks than previous work on stars and costume has tended to do, preferring to root the analyses it offers in the socio-cultural and historical moment, and through recourse to more 'cultural studies' notions of representation.

The essay which opens the anthology, Jane Gaines and Charlotte Herzog's discussion of the fashioning of Norma Shearer as Marie Antoinette, looks at the relationship between stars, character, and the costume designs of Gilbert Adrian. Their chapter draws analogies between the production of *Marie Antoinette* (W. S. van Dyke, 1938) at MGM and the French court of Louis XVI, producing a detailed and insightful critique. Also concerned with the importance of the relationship of star and costume designer, Drake Stutesman's detailed analysis of Mr John's designs for Dietrich in chapter two reveals the stories eloquently told through hats in *Shanghai Express* (Josef von Sternberg, 1932) and *Morocco* (Josef von Sternberg, 1930). The two following essays use detailed textual analysis to examine the work done by dress in producing meanings in relation to star personae, but also situate their discussions theoretically and historically in relation to the broader understandings of the clothes they discuss: Stella Bruzzi

considers Gregory Peck as an 'anti-fashion' icon in chapter three, and in chapter four
Tamar Jeffers looks at the use of dress to manipulate Doris Day's star image in *Pillow
Talk*. Chapters five and six are the last to consider stars specifically in the context of Hollywood. Pamela Church Gibson highlights two key types of Hollywood masculinity – the
'rough' and the 'smooth', embodied in contemporary stars Brad Pitt and George
Clooney, and traces their development from the 1950s to the present day. In chapter
six, Russell White looks at Samuel L. Jackson's articulation of the 'post-post-soul male'
through style in *Pulp Fiction* (Quentin Tarantino, 1994), *Jackie Brown* (Quentin Tarantino, 1997) and *Shaft* (John Singleton, 2000). Part Two, which looks at stars in Asia and
Latin America, opens with Kaushik Bhaumik's analysis in chapter seven of the Indian film
star Sulochana and the sartorial significance of the 'modern Indian woman' of the Bombay cinema in the 1920s. In the following chapter, Joanne Hershfield follows a similar
line of investigation in relation to the Mexican *chica moderna*, and suggests the role
played by Hollywood and Mexican stars in producing a model of modern femininity in
Mexico in the 1930s. In chapter thirteen, Denise Miller explores the function of the costume designs of Graciela Galán for Argentine actress Luisina Brando in the films of María
Luisa Bemberg, and shows how performance and fashion operate powerfully together
as 'excessive femininity'. Turning to European stars, Christine Geraghty explores the significance of fashion to star image and performance in Kay Kendall's films for MGM, *Les
Girls* (George Cukor, 1957) and *The Reluctant Debutante* (Vincente Minnelli, 1958) in
chapter ten. My own chapter on Audrey Hepburn appears in the section on Europe
rather than Hollywood, because it focuses on the meanings and uses made of the star's
powerfully European style by young British women growing up and shifting class in the
1950s and 60s. Ginette Vincendeau considers the significance of Brigitte Bardot's fashionable and individual style across her career in chapter eleven and, in chapter twelve,
Pam Cook and Claire Hines consider the fashioning of Sean Connery's James Bond,
offering an illuminating analysis of the significance of this star and his dress in relation
to changing modes of masculinity and style in the 1960s. *Fashioning Film Stars* deliberately brings together established and emerging scholars in the field, and it is hoped that
the lively and engaged work in this volume will spark further debate and exploration of
what promises to be a very rich seam of investigation.

PART ONE

Hollywood

1

Norma Shearer as Marie Antoinette: Which Body Too Much?

Jane Marie Gaines and Charlotte Cornelia Herzog

In popular fashion culture, the word 'revolution' is commonly used in relation to changes in women's dress. This popular usage, of course, exaggerates the cataclysmic effects of style, but may at the same time dilute the significance of genuine political revolt. The idea that fashion in women's clothing could be explosive, world-transforming or radical cuts two ways. It raises women's 'insignificant' interests to a higher plane of importance while confirming the triviality of these interests. The concept of 'revolutionary fashion' further satirises the way the apparently inconsequential becomes exceedingly consequential. In order to probe this further, we want to look at a key moment in the history of fashion, but a moment as told by Hollywood, with the 'as told by' as interesting to us as the history itself. In *Marie Antoinette* (W. S. van Dyke, 1938), the Hollywood studios at their apex attempted to tell a story of the triumph and failure of fashion, the grandeur of its reign and finally the tragedy of its demise. This story, it turns out, is about a taste revolution that pales in comparison with the story of real social transformation and revolutionary circumstances. But in the case of the French Revolution of 1789, the two revolutions were intertwined and linked to the degree that one may be led to think that the extremes in women's fashion actually caused the political uprising. To some degree, they did.

This would be an appropriate subject for Metro-Goldwyn-Mayer in its most profitable period and in the glory of its supremacy as the fashion leader of the major studios and glamour capital of the world. The life of Marie Antoinette was an old subject for the American film industry, which had banked its success so many times on stories of the individual woman about whom everything revolved as played by actresses about whom everything revolved, given to understand the power of personal appearance – but above all given the power of clothes.[1] It would be an MGM studio covenant that great design was essential to every scene and that great star designers such as Gilbert Adrian literally made stars, a restatement on a higher plane of a truism to which many ordinary women subscribed. MGM mega star and clothes horse, Norma Shearer articulated this commonsense knowledge for both constituencies, real women and female stars, when she said: 'The right dress can triumph over any situation, build any mood, create any illusion, and make any woman into the sort of person she most desires to be' (Gutner, 2001, p. 173).

But with the big-budget spectacular *Marie Antoinette*, the studio was in a sense playing with fire. If it looked too closely at the premises of the film it was producing, it might have found that the triumph of dress was only a Pyrrhic victory. It had in fact produced a film in which the eccentricities of fashion exemplified the very dangers that the detractors (fashion moderates) predicted. The right dress was the wrong dress in the end. In the case of Marie Antoinette, Queen of France, the woman who most understood revolutions in style least understood the political revolution that she herself set in motion. Her story is the story of the consequences of what her biographer Stefan Zweig called 'riotous luxury', the luxury that enacts, while it prefigures, the dangers of excess (1933, p. 113). Already it should be clear that two historical registers have become entwined. The historical moment is now impossible to extricate from the contemporary 'making of' that moment in a medium that would claim always to have a special relation to the historical real. Our alternation between these two historical registers emphasises a relation of imperfect analogy, but, however imperfect, suggesting comparisons that worked for creative personnel as well as for audiences: 'Queen of the Lot' and 'Queen of France' and the 'world of the court' in contrast with the 'world of MGM'.

Queen of the Lot/Queen of France

The story of the making of *Marie Antoinette* is the story of the relationship between top studio star, Norma Shearer and MGM head of production, Irving Thalberg. Shearer secured her position as Queen of the Lot when she married the legendary creative genius Thalberg in 1927. Like the marriage between Marie Antoinette and Louis XVI of France, the marriage was understood as politically convenient, a marriage designed to shore up a dynasty by producing symbolic stability and real heirs. Both were alliances of no passion and little sex but great affection and loyalty. Also, somewhat like the liaison between Marie Antoinette and Louis XVI, the union between Shearer and Thalberg was doomed, although unlike the union of the French king and his Austrian bride their tragedy was known early, even in advance of their wedding. It was commonly understood in Hollywood circles that Irving Thalberg, who had a congenital heart defect, was not expected to live past the age of thirty. Thus his wedding to Shearer on 29 September 1927, at twenty-eight, was a gamble for her. But in marrying her boss, Shearer would not only reinforce her star status at MGM but might rise to new heights. However, if Thalberg were to die, she could lose her guarantee, the primary source of her power. As we will see, Shearer would eventually do battle on her own with the rulers of the studio, a battle over the very role in which she played a parallel life – the role of a queen in constant danger from scheming courtiers.

The part of Marie Antoinette was written for Norma Shearer. Travelling in Europe after Thalberg's first heart attack, the couple bought the rights to the Zweig biography and visited the palace at Versailles. When then they returned, as early as 1933, Thalberg ordered research and scriptwriting to begin. It is thus no surprise that of all of her parts, even that of Juliet which won her an Academy Award in 1936, Shearer saw herself most thoroughly in the role of the French queen. We would stress here the not insignificant difference between speaking of 'Norma Shearer as Marie Antoinette' and representing that 'Norma Shearer is Marie Antoinette', the former suggesting the way in which a role is put on and taken off and the latter the indistinguishability between star and role that the star system held out as an ideal that it never could achieve. This indistinguishability is seen in the publicity convention advertising 'Norma Shearer is Marie Antoinette'. Paradoxically, the complete 'disappearance' of the actor into the role produced a condition inimical to the star system. Shearer could not become the queen so successfully that the viewer completely forgot the star. As Marie Antoinette, Norma Shearer had to be seen as Norma Shearer (see King, 1985, p. 41).

Which Body?

Some aspects of this paradox have been addressed by Jean-Louis Comolli in his 'Historical Fiction: A Body Too Much', an essay on the problem of belief in the fiction film made problematic by the historical film, where the success or the failure of the illusion depends upon the eclipse of the body of the actor by the character he or she plays (1978, pp. 41–53). The creation of the illusion is somewhat more complicated, the argument goes, in the historical fiction film. In the historical epic based on the biography of the real historical figure, there are two rival bodies, the memory image made up of the residue of recollected images, and the body of the actor, the image we see on screen. Comolli's example, conveniently for us, is Jean Renoir's La Marseillaise (1937), in which actor Pierre Renoir portrays Louis XVI. In his play with the concept of the body-in-excess, Comolli first suggests that the body of the actor Pierre Renoir is the body 'too much'. Later, it seems that the memory image is the 'body too much', the body that the film needs to 'obliterate' in order to produce the illusion. What we would take from Comolli is the competition between the memory traces of the body of Marie Antoinette and the body of Norma Shearer as used to represent the body of her rival. Without a doubt, the unending publicity around the film made this implicit comparison, particularly with its emphasis on historical accuracy.[2] But we will want to know which body is the more excessive and troublesome in the end in terms of an aesthetics of costume and body. Comolli's interest in the extra body of Louis XVI turns out to be an interest in the alienation effect produced by Pierre Renoir the actor (Ibid., p. 53). In an echo of his earlier 'Cinema/Ideology/Criticism', Comolli suggests that La Marseillaise is almost a case of the famous auto critique, where the film is able to comment on itself (Comolli and Narboni, 1971). Pierre Renoir's performance makes the audience see the body of the king as too much, seeing it as his eighteenth-century contemporaries saw it, as a body too much that had to be condemned to disappearance.

Our modification of Comolli's argument here has to do with which body: 'Which body is too much?' Although Comolli may seem to be arguing that the actor's body is in excess of that of the historical personage, there is a way in which the body of the real historical person is also too much to be represented, is over and above representation. Since it is impossible finally to replicate, it is always left standing outside the star image – too much even to approximate. The real historical Marie Antoinette would in this case be the 'body too much'. To Comolli's considerations we would add those of the studio, ever confused as to whether it should pick up the straggling ends of the star actor and fold them into the character (actor's body 'too much') or to emphasise them as they extended beyond the role (to counter the memory image 'too much'). But there is also the case of the star who identifies so completely with a character itself that the character through her extends beyond the life of the performance. Since there is evidence that Norma Shearer identified herself with Marie Antoinette for much of the rest of her life, we have to take seriously such incidents as her decision not to go to the Astor Theatre for the opening of the film because of the picketing. In defending her decision, Shearer compared herself to the historical person who had made the fatal mistake of attending the opera on the evening that the verdict against her by a corrupt court was announced. In French history, the crowd turned on the queen, marking a turning point in the events that led to the revolt against the crown. In the contemporary moment, however, Shearer failed to realise that by deciding to forgo the theatre appearance she revealed not the parallel between herself and Marie Antoinette but how different she was from the wilful and headstrong French queen. 'I'm not one to chance trouble,' Shearer is reported as saying in a very un-Marie Antoinette-like way (Jacobs and Braum, 1977, p. 42). Thus the degree of differentiation between star actor and character (in this case an historical person) is always an issue. Difference is an issue because the requisite illusion requires that there be little or no distance, hence the idealisation of what Richard Dyer once called the 'perfect fit', the goal of casting in realist cinema (1979, pp. 145–6). Dyer, as well, has given us the theory of stardom's ideological work, alerting us to the way in which the star image functions within a culture at the level of the superstructure.

Functioning in a way similar to the smoothing feature of ideology, the star functions to unify the contradictory versions of the way things are in the society (Ibid., pp. 72–98). Yet it seems to us that Norma Shearer's star image, infused as it was with the character of a real historical queen whose legacy has been in dispute, may not have functioned to smooth over the contradictory aspects of the expectations placed on women in history. What star theory may not have addressed sufficiently are the cases of failure to unify where popular culture becomes interested in real historical exceptions. We want to know if the 'true story' ingredients of the real historical narrative are here 'too much' for the star image to integrate. Eventually we will want to connect the 'too much' of the life of the historical figure with the aesthetic excess of the historical epic, as our readers may wonder about the degree to which we will want to attribute a critical dimension to these two aspects of excess.

Which History?

Following Vivian Sobchack's theorisation of the aesthetic excess and the superlative aspirations of the Hollywood historical epic, we understand this genre as having a particular relation to the extra-textual accounts of its own undertaking. There will thus be another way in which the excess and excesses outside the film itself become significant – particularly as the production process produces its own simultaneous understanding or 'reading' of the historical epic. Sobchack sees this reading in formal terms. In its production of the 'history effect' (White, 1987, pp. ix–xi), the historical epic as genre 'formally repeats the surge, splendor, and extravagance, the human labor and capital cost entailed by its narrative's historical content in both its production process and its modes of representation' (Sobchack, 1995, p. 287). In short, there is a parallel between the 'history of production' and the 'production of history', that, as she says, is perfectly reversible (Ibid., p. 289). Or, as we are arguing, there are apparently symmetrical operative analogies governing the production as well as the reception of *Marie Antoinette*. But we would go further, for our account of the making of *Marie Antoinette* negotiates between that lived history which is known first through the written accounts of it, then the 'history of the production', really the history of the production of history, and the final work, that 'production of history' which is really the production of history produced. And between the question of the 'production of history' and the 'history of production' is also the question of 'which history', that always ideological question.

What interests us is the difficulty MGM had with the production of a history that they were in the process of rewriting; how the studio went about representing their film as true to a history that they were engaged in radically revising – thus the strategy of basing their version of the queen's life on another new version found in a recent biography. In preparation for the role of Marie Antoinette, Shearer is said to have read and re-read the Stefan Zweig biography several times. Understood by critics at the time as a breakthrough in historical research, Zweig's book was based on sources in the Austrian Library never before used by scholars, accessing letters that would produce a significantly modified picture of the queen who had been vilified for over a century. Following the Zweig book closely, the MGM film was intent on rehabilitating the image of Marie Antoinette. But in order to rehabilitate her, she had to be made not only innocent but psychologically comprehensible to viewers. And it is questionable whether the premise of the book, summarised in Zweig's subtitle, *The Portrait of an Average Woman*, achieved its goal of conveying her motivations and her make-up as typical. Indeed, the thesis, on which Norma Shearer must have dwelled, proclaims the queen's exceptionality all the while it protests her typicality:

> Marie Antoinette was neither the great saint of royalism nor yet the great whore of the Revolution, but a mediocre, an average woman; not exceptionally able nor yet exceptionally foolish; neither fire nor ice; devoid of any vigorous wish to do good and of the remotest inclination to do evil; the average woman of yesterday, today, and tomorrow; lacking impulse toward the daimonic, [sic], uninspired by the will of heroism, and therefore (one might fancy) unsuited to become the heroine of a tragedy. (Zweig, 1933, pp. xi–xii)

The problem here is that while the queen may be said to be mediocre, by virtue of her sovereignty she is actually and always the antithesis of mediocrity and smallness. A queen is by definition elevated above others. An ordinary woman who is queen is no longer ordinary. To some degree, this was the premise underlying Norma Shearer's own strategy. Although a rising star when she married Thalberg, her distinguishing qualities were undramatic and colourless: 'niceness', 'graciousness', 'dutifulness' and 'thoughtfulness'. As Mrs Irving Thalberg and Queen of the Lot she particularised and coloured herself by assuming the extravagant role and persona of Marie Antoinette. In addition, it could be said that in defining herself Shearer also re-defined the popular image of the queen. Perhaps Shearer's achievement as an actress, then, if it can be called an achievement, was in her modification of the excesses of the queen's personality. Where, for instance, Marie Antoinette was said to have been self-indulgent and scatter-brained, Shearer plays her as good-humoured and slightly flighty, a portrayal designed to excuse the indulgence and defuse the criticism.

We must not underestimate the magnitude of work that needed to be done to rehabilitate Marie Antoinette. After all, this is the woman who was characterised in vicious political pamphlets during the height of the revolution as 'mauvaise fille, mauvaise épouse, mauvaise mère, mauvaise reine, monstre en tout' (bad daughter, bad wife, bad mother, bad queen, monster in everything) (Hunt, 1992, p. 123). Historical records tell us that not only was she accused of poisoning her first son, the Dauphin, but of having had incestuous relations with the second (Louis XVII) and of having had a lesbian relationship with her close friend Madame de Polignac. At her trial in 1793, sexual crime was added to the list of the charges against her which, in addition to high treason, included 'depleting the national treasury' (Lever, 2000, p. 300). Shearer was used to rehabilitate Marie Antoinette for history, portraying her as innocent and naive, her only failing a tendency in early life towards tastes that were too extravagant. Unchecked, the film says, these tastes led to her ruin. Shearer's portrayal thus exonerated the queen from the sin of excess. She is patient with the husband that history remembers as petulant and impotent, and, towards the end of her life, concerned above all for the welfare of her two remaining children.

The portrayal is developed ingeniously (and the part written) to supplement aesthetic excess with emotional excess so that the tendency towards extravagant dress finds an extra outlet in feeling. One is struck, on viewing this film, how the sparkling brilliance of jewels and glittering gowns of the first two-thirds are gradually replaced by glittering tears in the eyes of Shearer's suffering monarch. The effect is striking since Shearer's beady eyes are so unusually close together that she sometimes appears nearly cross-eyed and almost crazed towards the end of the film, her eyes like cat's eye marbles. She manufactures her glistening tears on cue. It could not be said that there was much natural resemblance between Shearer and the queen, but the one feature both shared was small blue eyes. Both women had flaws that were supposedly minimised or eclipsed by redeeming features, this tactic detailed in the description of Marie Antoinette provided by her favourite painter, the official court portraitist, Madame Elizabeth Vigée-LeBrun:

Marie Antoinette was tall, very statuesque and rather plump, though not excessively so. She had superb arms, small perfectly formed hands and dainty feet. ... Her features were not all that regular; she bore the long, narrow, oval face of her family, typical too of the Austrian race. Her eyes were not particularly large and a shade approaching blue. Her expression was intelligent and sweet, her nose fine and pretty, her mouth was not wide, although her lips were rather full. Her most outstanding feature, however, was the clarity of her complexion. (Vigée-LeBrun [trans. Evans], 1989, p. 32)

It is tempting to compare the work of the court portraitist to that of the studio publicist whose job it was also to obfuscate, manage and flatter. Madame LeBrun's portraits were distributed as gifts to the loyal nobility, to embassies and foreign courts. There is no doubt that the image of Marie Antoinette helped to consolidate the power that queens of France had not historically been able to claim, but it could also be argued that the image campaign back-fired, leading eventually to charges that the queen had usurped the French throne. With no means of mass image management to counter the spurious charges of their enemies, both king and queen between 1787 and their execution in 1793, were easily villainised and consequently convicted in the public imagination.

Clearly we also want here to compare Gilbert Adrian and Madame Vigée-LeBrun as image-makers, analogising costume design with painting. Curiously, however, the professional image-maker (like Adrian, Vigée-LeBrun and the queen's *modiste*, the exceedingly entrepreneurial Mademoiselle Rose Bertin), reinforces not a theory of the constructed persona but the doctrine of divine right – the monarch or star born, not made. Such production erases its signs of manufacture by means of the theory and practice of entitlement. Marie Antoinette may have been produced as queen by an alliance between France and Austria masterminded by her mother, Empress Maria Theresa, but she lived in the religion of divine right that guaranteed the rule of her husband and which appeared to be extended to her by the rituals, the trappings and the privileges bestowed upon her by virtue of her position. Consistently, the discourse of and around her dress and its portrayal raised the issue of divine right as opposed to human failing. To summarise the discursive functions of court painting which are also the functions of costume: to achieve likeness while camouflaging flaws, to represent the queen/star as sovereign and superlative, to testify to the largeness of the treasury, and to locate the source of entitlement in and on the natural body of the queen/star thus reinforcing an idea of divine right. What would become historically important would be, as we have been arguing, the failures of (ideological) representation: the historical failure of the attempt to make the queen into an undisputed monarch, and the failure of sartorial representation, evident in the way she is costumed as queen but toppled as unfit ruler. As we will see, the historical memory image 'too much' was a difficult problem for the studio.

The World of the Court/The World of MGM

Only after his death would the degree to which Irving Thalberg had seen the studio as like the French court become apparent. Soon after he bought the rights to the Stefan Zweig biography, creative personnel began to reconstruct the structure of Versailles physically, stone by stone. Cedric Gibbons was busy on the set designs. Gilbert Adrian was importing furniture, relics and sumptuous fabric. The goal, it would seem, was to out-Versailles Versailles. The film was to be a display of Thalberg's power in which he enthroned Shearer, his devoted wife, and exercised what he believed to be his unchallenged power as head of production as well as major stockholder. One of what Thalberg called his 'prestige' motion pictures, like *Romeo and Juliet* (George Cukor, 1936), *Marie*

Antoinette was to be an exception to the budgetary constraints of lesser vehicles, the money-making pictures. But Thalberg's careful production plans never came to fruition. He was taken ill with pneumonia just after the release of *Romeo and Juliet* in 1936 and died soon after, too physically infirm to fight off the disease. The status of *Marie Antoinette* as a production as well as the participation of Norma Shearer in the film became uncertain. When Thalberg's partner, Louis B. Mayer, moved to deprive Shearer of the percentage proceeds from films produced by Thalberg, she resigned, breaking her long-term contract with MGM. Here was an aspect of the comparison between MGM and the French court that Thalberg did not necessarily anticipate. On the surface, the *mise en scène* projected by MGM was somewhat like what Zweig called the 'untroubled playworld' of Marie Antoinette (1933, p. 170). The screen face of the studio was the opulent and fun-loving world of the MGM musical. Power struggle and intrigue, however, defined the underlying structure. Like Marie Antoinette and Louis XVI, who could never trust those who had been close to them (the Duc d'Orléans, his cousin, and his own brother who wanted to replace him), Shearer could not rely upon those who professed the most sympathy at Irving's funeral. Even after she finally secured a satisfactory new contract from Mayer and head of the company, Joseph Schenk, she still was in danger, and soon Mayer found a way to snatch her victory from her. Shortly before shooting, he replaced Shearer's director, Sydney Franklin, with W. S. Van Dyke, justifying the change as a need to economise. Her favourite, Franklin, wanted to shoot the film in Technicolor and had projected a longer shooting schedule (Lambert, 1990, p. 254). The homage to the dead king, Thalberg, was thus reduced by cost-cutting measures enforced by the rival king and former partner, Mayer. It was whispered by observers at the time that in stepping into the role of Marie Antoinette, Norma Shearer was meeting the same fate as the character she was playing. At stake for her was her elevated position as Queen of the Lot. But there is another 'queen' of the lot whose reign is as important here to us, for if Norma Shearer was using the authority of the historical queen Marie Antoinette to shore up her position, Gilbert Adrian was using the authority of the historical in another way – to justify his abandonment of it. As head of the design department at MGM, it would be the last time he worked with an unfettered budget, and fidelity to the period worked to rationalise his unrestrained creativity.

History, Accuracy and Extravagance

'We have followed the gowns of Madame LeBrun's paintings to the letter,' Gilbert Adrian is reported to have said (Gutner, 2001, p. 164). Since the disingenuousness of studio publicity releases is well known, we are more interested in the contradictory practice of proclaiming authenticity while abandoning the original, a variant of the contradictory attempt to remain true to a history they were in the process of revising. While we do not doubt that Adrian studied the eight surviving paintings Madame Vigée-LeBrun did of the queen, he seems to have taken them not as his end point but as his starting point, as was his practice. As with his designs for Greta Garbo, Jean Harlow and Joan Crawford, Adrian went beyond the mere 'appropriate', pushing for 'over the top' as much as he could. Then there is the question of fidelity to fashion periodisation where the design department's abandonment of the dominant silhouette of the period and its replacement by another was a significant revision of the established historical image of the eighteenth-century French court. While the dominant silhouette of the period covered by the film, according to costume historians, is the chemise, the dominant silhouette of the film, *Marie Antoinette* is not the simple drop-waist chemise but the complex panier skirt. This is the fashion whose effect was produced by an oblong hoop extending two feet on each side of the waist with a third hoop behind, a shape that lent itself to the iconic caricature of the period that it would later become. The panier, not the dominant silhouette of the queen's 1774 to 1793 reign, was on its way out by the late 1780s, according to fashion historians (Russell, 1983, p. 296). Queen Marie Antoinette's great contribution to fashion, as recorded by these historians, was this distinctly different shape, the clinging chemise, represented in one of Madame Vigée-LeBrun's most famous portraits of her although not represented in the film. The simple chemise is neither seen on Norma Shearer nor on any other female character in the final version of the film, which instead keeps the boxy hoop in view, the one constant amid the vagaries of ornamentation. While we can easily challenge the film's representation of itself as historically accurate on several counts, the point is not finally to hold it up as inaccurate, but rather to understand the ideological purpose served by its aggrandised claim to historical authenticity.

At least two major ideological functions are performed by the emphasis on historical accuracy, taking advantage of the 'truth effect' produced by any recourse to aesthetic realism – the first having to do with sartorial excess and the second with the role of women in government. First, 'historical accuracy' works to justify extravagance, a mystification tied to the economic in the case of the Hollywood studio, a microcosm of capitalism in which capital has a mimetic relation to itself (this is seen in the necessity of spending money to make money or looking like money in order to attract money). This mimesis is something akin to what Vivian Sobchack calls mimetic imitation and cinematic or visual onomatopoeia, a representation in which the tendency is to visually reiterate, with all of the redundancy that these two, most provocative, concepts imply. Reiteration or repetition is here at the level of the way the extravagant budget is mirrored in the extravagant *mise en scène* and the way the historical event is 'imitated' through attempts at its replication (Sobchack, 1995, pp. 287, 292, 293–4). While Sobchack finds that the very repetition through the attempt at historical imitation is self-reflexive in that it 'calls attention to its existence as a representation', we find something slightly different (Ibid., p. 292). Yes, the dizzying excess of detail upon detail, too much for the eye to survey, does call attention to itself but, in the case of *Marie Antoinette,* the attempt to imitate the historical period became an attraction as the *mise en scène* that seemed to imitate went beyond realism and into the realm of the 'replication' of the fantastical, a separate problem in and of itself: the representation of a fantasy relation to what has become a fantastic history.

This flight from history may be seen where the film makes its biggest investment in historical accuracy – in the embellishment of each dress. For instance, one fashion history suggestively tells us how much ornamentation was borne by a single costume in

Norma Shearer as Marie Antoinette. Gowns designed by Gilbert Adrian. From the collection of David Chierichetti

this period: 'Hoops and panier gowns were lavishly ornamented with knots of ribbon, puffs, loops, garlands of flowers, fluted flounces, or quilting, all in one dress' (Wilcox, 1942, p. 209). But Adrian's approach to design for *Marie Antoinette* was to thoroughly rework these possibilities, historical research awarding him the licence to invent and improvise in the spirit of the absurdly ridiculous design of the late eighteenth-century French court. To give only one example, for the scene in which the Dauphine first meets her lover, the Swedish count Axel Fersen (Tyrone Power), she is represented as at the height of her frivolity, in a phase of her life dominated by pleasure-seeking and play. Her gown is a surprise concoction bearing little resemblance to the staid luxuriance of Madame Vigée-LeBrun's portraiture. Tiny stars appliquéd over a billowing silk skirt and bodice with a matching star headdress combine the connotations of stardom with those of royalty. But the effect is of a modern design superimposed on the eighteenth century. The spray of stars in her headdress is redolent of fireworks not a crown and the effect of the outfit is finally more whimsical than serious. Appearing as it does early in the film, the costume perhaps suggests the precariousness of Marie Antoinette's claim to the throne, but we will want to suggest further that it does the second kind of ideological work to which we have alluded. The question of a woman's power is not surprisingly caught up in the question of her hairdressing where the issue of the head of the 'head of state' becomes so controversial. As for the crown, Queen Marie Antoinette never did exactly wear one. In Madame Vigée-LeBrun's portraits, the crown appears to one side of her cushioned on a small table, a perfect emblem of the ambiguity of her position in France where constitutionally a woman could not ascend to the throne (Hunt, 1991, p. 109). Instead, the enormous hair and hairdressings stand in place of the crown, a towering mass of powdered curls and bows that enforces the system in which women are nothing more than ornamentation by ensuring that they are incapable of any function that requires them to do more than sit and crouch (the three-foot-high coiffure presented special difficulties when entering carriages and low doors). The attempt to emulate the tallest hairstyles, fashionable until the late 1780s, would have presented Adrian and hairdresser Sydney Guilaroff with special problems. The degree to which this towering hair became ludicrous is well known, and surely the information that the flour-paste composition of these wigs attracted infestation by vermin invites retrospective ridicule (Russell, 1983, pp. 296, 302). In late eighteenth-century France, as in 1938, the folly of woman's rule is confirmed by foibles of her hairdressing as well as the whimsy of her dress. The 'ridiculous' connotations of the style carried over into the period in which the film appeared, thus the two periods converge in their message to women: 'You can't be taken seriously.'

The contradiction between good government and fashionable trends was not lost on Marie Antoinette's mother, Empress Maria Theresa of Austria who, in a famous letter, responding to a picture she received of her daughter in a particularly elaborate costume, wrote: 'Dear Toinette: It is well to be in fashion to a reasonable extent but ... one should never be outré in one's dress. ... There is no need of such follies.' Our interest here is as much in Maria Theresa's perception as in the report that Gilbert Adrian latched onto this quote. The queen's mother, like all of the fashion detractors who thought Adrian's designing always too *outré*, in her correspondence now provides the rationale for contemporary *outré* – fidelity to history. *Outré* receives a historical justification, perhaps the closest that it could come to respectability (Gutner, 2001, p. 160). We have written before on the Adrian signature design which most classical Hollywood directors viewed as a dangerous distraction with the potential to call attention to itself at the expense of the narrative (Gaines and Herzog, 1990; Gaines, 2000). *Marie Antoinette*, based on the moment when women's dress was without a doubt more elaborate 'than in any other time in history' (Gutner, 2001, p. 164), would have been a crowning achievement for the designer after more than a decade of work at MGM, and towards the end of his career there, the last of the gargantuan-budget, historical epic films. We would conclude that *Marie Antoinette* is finally not Norma Shearer's, but Adrian's, film.[3] It is the opportunity for him to appropriate the Rococo period that attracted him – to emulate as well as to satirise – with what appeared to be no budgetary constraints whatsoever. A clue to the disjuncture between his costume fantasies and the exigencies of both history and material manufacture are his sketches, his starting point for the costumes for male as well as female characters, star actors as well as extras. This is the imaginative sketch which always appeared to have neither cognisance of the reality of the anatomy of the human body nor the labour of translation into real clothes. In this regard, neither the sketch nor the final photographic image acknowledged productive labour and both conspired in the erasure of the drudgery of the work of seamstresses, milliners, wardrobe mistresses, fabric cutters and photographic editors.[4]

We may argue that the imaginative sketch was oblivious of the labours of costume design but in the end, the pressures of profit, manifesting themselves in newly asserted principles of moderation, erased not only the labour of costuming but the labour of design. In the last instance, Adrian's imagination had to be reined in and the history that encouraged it had to be totally abandoned. To give only one example, while he might have been inspired by the accounts of eighteenth-century 'quixotic' coiffures that featured tiny ships and farms with people and animals, in the end, this wonderfully inventive tendency is watered down and represented in only a single visual scene in the film (Gutner, 2001, p. 147). As the Dauphine, Marie Antoinette is shown playing a favourite game, blind man's bluff, wearing a white powdered wig topped with a mechanical canary in a cage that chirps when she flips a switch on her head (Zweig, 1933, p. 96). If historical costume in this film is an attraction, this scene gives us not more but significantly less than the original. Motion picture costume historian Edward Maeder, for instance, refers to the birdcage hairpiece as 'absurdly small' (1987, pp. 73–4). The requirements of the commercial motion picture and classical Hollywood narrative style conspire to constrain the exigencies of historical costume in many ways. Not only was the sumptuous colour palate of this important fashion period rendered in black and white, but the actual height of the famous hair creations had to be scaled down. Consider, for instance, the astonishing height of Norma Shearer's hairdressing in one of the publicity photos. This creation never appeared in the final film, quite possibly because the horizontal frame could not accommodate its extreme verticality.

Norma Shearer as Marie Antoinette. Gowns designed by Gilbert Adrian. From the collection of David Chierichetti

Time and time again, MGM would advertise the historical accuracy of a particular costume drama and abandon authenticity to some other principle. Justification for expenditure cannot finally be spectacle since so many of the expenditures went for items that could never be seen on screen. Microscopes were used to study the embroidery in an effort to make Norma Shearer's gowns identical to those worn in the eighteenth-century court, but to what end (Gutner, 2001, p. 164)? The effect was lost because the fine stitching could not be seen with either the naked eye or the help of the focal length of the lens used. The photographic aesthetic in this film is primarily the medium long shot, adapted to ensure that the many human figures, star actors and extras, appeared on screen. Even getting the scenery on screen would have been a priority, thus the rivalry between the representation of costume and that of decor that is decided in favour of set design. For instance, the camera on the lavish wedding of the Austrian princess, Antoinette to the French Dauphin is a high-angle long shot rendering the enormity of the abbey. Although this shot is the only one that allows us to see the full length of the bridal train, its view is the antithesis of the microscopic view required to actually see the delicate needlework on the expanse of fabric that makes up the train.

There is, finally, another explanation for the extravagance that is so insistently justi-fied by 'accuracy', so circularly supported by 'historical' research. If viewers can be convinced that historical detail is accurate, the narrative may be liberated to a degree from any obligation to follow pre-existing historical accounts. Not surprisingly, MGM took licence with the events of the French Revolution. It is not just that key events of the revolutionary period, 1789 to 1793, are conflated, or that a scene between Marie Antoinette and Count Fersen just before her execution, was invented, or that Thalberg wanted her to live rather than die on the guillotine. We know, of course, that in the end one kind of 'realism' does not necessarily underwrite another. What was never tested in this case was whether the production of the visual 'history effect' was powerful enough to override an ending that reversed an event as notorious as that of the sever-ing of Marie Antoinette's head from her body on 16 October 1793. Note here the difficulty we have avoiding any recourse to the historical 'real' or to the material objects from the past as final arbiters – a difficulty one always faces in any critical discussion of the representation of historical events where we know that history is really constituted not out of documentation or documents but out of 'nothing'. Relevant is what Carolyn Steedman has called the 'double nothingness' in the analysis and the construction of history. It is, she says, 'about something that never did happen in the way it comes to be represented . . . and it is made out of materials that aren't there, in an archive or any-where else' (2002, p. 154).

The Political Economy of Extravagance

MGM in the 1930s was not an untroubled kingdom. It would be during Irving Thal-berg's reign at the studio that the Screen Actors' Guild was under formation, and unions were an anathema to him given his authoritarian style of leadership. More prob-lematic, he took the establishment of the Writers' Guild as a special personal affront since he prided himself on his excellent handling of authors in the screenwriting process

(Flamini, 1994). During these years, writers were subjected to especially bad treatment; their contributions to the screenwriting effort under the studio system often went uncredited. Rewriting the history of the French Revolution was then an attempt to cast the studio system in a favourable light during a time of social upheaval. If Marie Antoinette, the 'whore of the Revolution' could be made innocent, well meaning and misunderstood, and the French crown could be made to seem merely misguided, then the studio, that other authoritarian, hierarchical system, could be made to seem fair and even benevolent.

In this, the ideology of excess played a significant part. In the philosophy of the studio, as with the representation of the French court, the show of, the display of opulence, justifies rule. Yet who, should we ask, is this display for? To whom does this excess appeal? Strangely, the excess that shores up authority is for the very masses who underwrite the power of the king or of the studio, although we need to think the degree to which the aesthetic excess of Hollywood would be more visually available and more vicarious in the case of the idols of consumption of this century. There is also, of course, the question of social class, which does not compute perfectly across two centuries, as well as the contradictory responses of aversion and emulation. We know well the criticism of Hollywood as sexually decadent, a social criticism answered in the 1930s with the self-enforced Hays Code. To those adverse to sexual excess, MGM responded with a highly coded visual excess, answering the criticism of corruption and decadence by representing a society that was more wasteful and debauched, deflecting the criticism, but inviting it all over again in its attempt to rival the opulence of Versailles. We have stressed here the ideological functions of the 'history effect' which, as it carries its venerable connotations of truthfulness, works to justify extravagance by imitating capital, an extravagance which in turn, quite economically, justifies rule, and which, as visual excess, works to rationalise the exclusion of excessively adorned women from positions of power. Still outstanding, however, is the question of the subversive potential of the extravagant. It is tempting here to come down on the side of the extravagance as having a critical potential, especially as it challenges an older orthodoxy in which only the modernist ascetic aesthetic could perform an ideological critique of form. Welcome, then, is Vivian Sobchack's finding that the very repetitious excessiveness of historical representation (as mimetic imitation) cannot help but attract attention to itself as nothing more than representation. But however much the representational extravagance of *Marie Antoinette* asks to be seen repetitively on screen, it is always for us less rather than more, even as it leaves the realm of the document and enters the fantasy realm of the nonexistent. The story of the making of the film is important here, and we have chosen to tell it as the story of how the narrative as well as the visual opulence of the historical epic was reined in over the course of the pre-production of what would turn out to be a significantly modified epic. The troublesome excess for us is in that which could not finally be represented in the film – from the too tall wigs, to the clinging silhouette, to the decapitated body of the queen. Further, the discrepancy between the actor's body and the historical image which produces the discomfiture of 'too much' produces its own trouble in the epic based on historical biography. Here the historical realm which is thought to precede and exceed its own representation trumps all later representations. The attractions of historical accuracy in costume are nothing compared to the attractions of one cataclysmic historical event – the death of the queen of France on the scaffold at the hands of the executioner.

Coda: Star Styles

The box-office success of *Marie Antoinette* does not easily answer the question of audience aversion or emulation. The so-called democratisation of fashion based on the assumption of the mass emulation of style leaders is a kind of cruel dilution of the legacy of the French Revolution. Political rights here become nothing more than consumer rights. While Marie Antoinette's styles were copied by the court elite and circulated only within a small circle of nobility, with the rise of bourgeois culture in the ensuing centuries working-class girls were elevated through stardom to style leaders whose tastes were copied and circulated widely. The elaborate screen costumes of these leaders were mass produced in the 1930s as tie-ups and marketed as 'star styles'. But while MGM would be able to promote motion picture-inspired copies of Adrian's unusual styles for Greta Garbo in *Queen Christina* (Rouben Mamoulian, 1933), no equivalent campaign for Marie Antoinette was ever launched (see Gaines, 1989). The only evidence we have of contemporary interest in translating *Marie Antoinette* into ready-wear is a remark from Hattie Carnegie, designer for the upscale market, who thought her clientele might be interested in 'modest little hoops' (Maeder, 1987, p. 82).[5] Consider the cruel irony of the production of star styles for the 1930s' ready-wear mass market, based on the calamitous fashions of the notorious French Rococo period, worn by a queen who was beheaded for her tastes by the masses who were then the self-proclaimed enemies of fashion.

Notes

1. We are thinking of the melodramas featuring important stars in the 1930s. Sarah Berry (2000, p. 82), notes the other films in which the great stars from this era were cast as queens: Greta Garbo in *Queen Christina* (1933), Katharine Hepburn in *Mary of Scotland* (John Ford, 1936) and Marlene Dietrich in *The Scarlet Empress* (Josef von Sternberg, 1934).

2. MGM publicity used these statistics: between 1934 and 1937, 59,277 reports were made on the end of the reign, 1,538 books, 10,615 photographs and 5,000 pages of unbound manuscript were consulted. Gowns numbered 1,200, thirty-four of which were for Shearer alone (Gutner, 2001, p. 164).

3. On Adrian as a gay designer see Gaines (1992). Adrian's career at MGM spanned 1928 to 1942, during which time he designed costumes for such big budget films as *The Wizard of Oz* (Victor Fleming, 1939). For a more complete list of the films for which he designed, see Gutner (2001).

4. As many as fifty seamstresses were brought from Guadalajara, Mexico, to undertake the work of embroidering gowns and sewing on thousands of sequins (Maeder, 1987, p. 34).

5. See Herzog and Gaines (1991) and Berry (2000) on the importance of star styles.

2

Storytelling: Marlene Dietrich's Face and John Frederics' Hats

Drake Stutesman

Glamour, an old Scottish word meaning 'enchantment', is the 'supposed influence of a charm on the eye causing it to see objects under an unreal semblance' (Whitney, 1899). Screen glamour's deception is notorious, but less obvious are its many layers. The movie star is dressed in the film by the costume designer and that, as Deborah Nadoolman Landis,[1] current head of the American Costume Designers' Guild, states in her *Screencraft: Costume Design*, is a highly specialised situation:

> Fashion and costumes are not synonymous; they are antithetical. They have directly opposing and contradictory purposes. Costumes are never clothes. ... Star power is so influential, and pervasive, it becomes impossible for the public to believe that an individual was responsible for designing the costumes. Storytelling, the original function of costume, is forgotten. (2003, p. 8)

Storytelling is the purpose of costume design. As Adrian, MGM's head of costume from 1928 to 42, whose design innovations made fashion history and propelled him to become cinema's first commercially successful costume designer, so declared in 1930 when he said: 'One could line up all the gowns and tell the screen story' (Adrian).

Though couture may be an outcome of costume design, the costume is crafted at a level of minutia that leaves fashion behind. It requires an ability to go far beyond the inspired pattern and the cutting and sewing. The costume must fit the actor's personality and the plot's persona, though the two can be vastly different: the fat man has to exude sex, the bombshell seem meek, the bad boy be debonair. Added to this, the costume must conform to cinematographic demands. A yellow collar highlights the head in a dark fight scene or sequins brighten a moving body in a dim hallway. The accurately high-waisted seventeenth-century jacket is cut low because the actor looks squat in the lens. Wool is right for the weather but too matte a material for the lighting, or white suits the scene but is too sharp for the camera. The femme fatale's outfit is sensational, but would look pretty shabby on the street as it has been painted with a luminous substance. At the same time, whether contemporary, period or fantasy, the clothes must satisfy the paying public's lust for hyper-realism, mystery and style. How could a hip *Sopranos* (HBO, 1999–2004) look crowd the magazines if all we saw in the TV show were dumpy men in velour tracksuits? The costume designer, Juliet Polsca, has had to ensure that the clothing remains true to its un-styled subject while, nevertheless luring its audience (Stutesman, 2002). The costume designer has to understand and solve these oppositions. Most important, the costume must invisibly sink into the narrative yet convey potent meaning which the audience is constantly reading. Film clothes disclose who someone is (villainous, country, street), how that person feels (crazy, naive, sexual) or where s/he's going (ambitious, ruined, on-the-run) in ways that will fill out a non-expositional script. Movies like *Working Girl* (Mike Nichols, 1988), *Jungle Fever* (Spike Lee, 1991) or *Spiderman* (Sam Raimi, 2002) rely on dress explicitly to show the character's sense of self. But, just as intentional, a story can be told subliminally to force a deeper understanding of the character or to soothe fears that the narrative has brought out in the audience. The films examined here, *Shanghai Express* (Josef von Sternberg, 1932) and *Morocco* (Josef von Sternberg, 1930), which launched Marlene Dietrich onto the world stage, reveal a compelling counter-narrative to the script, as told in the clothing, and specifically, as told in Dietrich's hats made by the milliner, John Frederics.

Dietrich, by the early 1930s, was a cinematic phenomenon. Countless women imitated her low-lidded eyes, pencilled eyebrows and sexually charged remove. Her contemporaries, Joan Crawford, Norma Shearer, Jean Harlow, were superstars, but Dietrich courted a status of 'icon' beyond one of 'star'. She embodied the 'act' and the person as one as only Garbo had done before. Dietrich was ready, and able, to usurp her. She achieved this, in part, because she came to prominence internationally in the unusual 1930s' films of Vienna-born, American director, Josef von Sternberg. His movies were fantastically staged, using grids of shadow and light, hanging veils, fronds, ropes or swathes of lace, superimpositions, reflections, long dissolves or tracking sequences and images shot through lattices or across angles. Everything in the von Sternberg film counted, no detail was too petty, no role too small to engage his attention. He was, as he put it, 'a cold-eyed mechanic critical of every movement' (von Sternberg, 1965, p. 253). His unique universe was constructed to use every piece with iconic import, as Peter Wollen notes, in his germinal *Signs and Meaning in the Cinema*:

> Von Sternberg was virulently opposed to any kind of Realism. He sought, as far as possible, to disown and destroy the existential bond between the natural world and the film world. But this did not mean that he turned to the symbolic. . . . It was the iconic aspect of the sign which Von Sternberg stressed, detached from the indexical in order to conjure up a whole world, comprehensible by virtue of resemblances to the natural world, yet other than it, a kind of dream world. (1969, p. 136)

Dietrich was very much a part of this fusion and von Sternberg had her, as Wollen points out, take 'the star system to its ultimate limit' (Ibid.), where she perfectly met von Sternberg's visual and psychological goals. Despite the usual action qualities – exotic setting (China, North Africa, Germany, America), dangerous tale and headliner stars – an abstract totality pervades the von Sternberg–Dietrich vehicle because what really counts is its base drama of sexual desire, a desire that obliterates sanity. Dietrich was a smooth conveyor of these conflicts and played this repeatedly in her seven films with von Stern-berg: *The Blue Angel* (1930), *Morocco, Dishonored* (1931), *Shanghai Express, Blonde Venus* (1932), *The Scarlet Empress* (1934) and *The Devil Is a Woman* (1935). The torrid, almost eerie *Morocco*, her first film to open in the US, threw her into instant stardom, a stardom anticipated by the pre-release ad campaign, which displayed only her face on giant billboards throughout the world, promoting her as *the* image before anyone knew who she was. The advertising recognised that Dietrich's face *was* Dietrich. In dressing her for cinema, her face would have to be treated with supreme care.

Paramount, which produced these pictures, had the impressive, in-house talent of Travis Banton as head of costume. A Texan who had studied in New York, Banton was a genius with difficult material, especially the reflective lamés, silks and satins, and his inventiveness and risk-taking was legendary. He established a 'look' for Mae West, Carole Lombard and Dietrich and created many of their off-screen outfits. Dietrich recog-nised his gift as a 'real encounter' because, as she said, 'we understood that, artistically, we could get a lot out of each other' (Hanut, 1996, p. 93). But von Sternberg's metic-ulousness guaranteed his involvement; Dietrich even suggested that he 'designed all [of her] costumes' (Dietrich, 1987, p. 81). Cannily, Banton and von Sternberg introduced Dietrich to the world in *Morocco* by dressing her in what would become a Dietrich sig-nature, a man's tailed jacket and trousers (black in this film; later, in *Blonde Venus*, the suit would be white with rhinestone lapels). Extreme expertise was needed for Dietrich's hats and Banton chose, as milliner for all the von Sternberg–Dietrich pictures, John Frederics, known by the 1950s as Mr John.[2]

Born Hans Harburger in Munich in 1902,[3] and arriving in the US six years later with his family, John officially changed his name to John Frederics in the early 1920s and formed a partnership with Frederic Hirst in New York in 1928, under the hyphenated John-Frederics label. Together they established one of the century's most successful fashion businesses. By 1948, an empire had been built of men's and women's clothing, furs, accessories (cufflinks, purses, hosiery, scarves, ties etc.) and perfume. Custom salons were established in Rome, Buenos Aires, Berlin, London and throughout the US, and ready-to-wear boutiques existed in a hundred department stores. John split, acri-moniously, with Hirst in 1948 and founded his new label, Mr John, changing his name again (to avoid the association with the old John-Frederics label), to John Pico John. This label was even more successful than the previous one; *Fortune* magazine called it the 'financial phenomenon of the fashion industry' (quoted in Scott, 1979, p. 43). John was so well known that *The New Yorker* ran unnamed cartoons about him. His 1993 *New York Times* obituary recorded that John 'was as famous in the world of hats as Christ-ian Dior was in the realm of *haute couture*' (Schiro, 1993). Concurrent with his career, John worked in cinema over four decades, beginning with hats for Adrian, for whom he did many films,[4] as well as all the millinery for Adrian's seasonal, public fashion col-lections. John's work appears in at least sixty films and his hats augment some of cinema's most sensual looks. The film hat was *the* crucial accessory because it circled the libidinous face and framed that face's other-worldly close-up. It staged those facial features, revealed character, and refracted light and dark. But its most valuable function was, as John described it, 'the proper display of a woman's beauty' (John, 1951–3). The hat-and-face illusion was made from the same contradiction of all costume design: hiding in open view. The milliner, making the look, must also prevent the hat from showing off because, if the woman disappears, so will the look. As Vivien Leigh said when she met John to discuss *Gone with the Wind*'s costumes: 'All I ask is – don't let them see the hat before they see my face' (Stutesman, 1988). Garbo's jewelled, triangular helmet in *Mata Hari* (George Fitzmaurice, 1932), Leigh's wheel hat in *Gone with the Wind* (Victor Fleming, 1939), Monroe's showgirl headdress in *Gentleman Prefer Blondes* (Howard Hawks, 1953), Joanne Woodward's wild net hat in *A New Kind of Love* (Melville Shavelson, 1963), always wrongly attributed to the costume designer, were all made by John. Adrian was his primary partner but, as well as with Travis Banton, John worked with Edith Head, Irene, Howard Greer, Irene Sharaff, William Travilla, Walter Plunkett and others.

Though Dietrich and John became life-long friends and she was a frequent customer, the cinematic relationship between Marlene Dietrich and John Frederics is a fascinating one because it illustrates the indispensably powerful motif that the costume provides the film's narrative. Furthermore, the 'second' story, displayed in the hat–head dynamic, it could be argued, tells more truths than the boy-meets-girl screenplay. But why can hats carry this vital message? The hat is a cultural marker as no other article of dress. An event hidden in plain sight, the hat acts identity, combining signifier and signified as few objects do. The crown, helmet, habit, veil, yarmulke, turban reveal instant social status, exactly as each has done for thousands of years. In fashion, the hat packs the same punch. In 1979, John described why: 'A hat is the most dangerous thing in the world, because it shows what you are. . . . A dress you can overcome. But you can't overcome a hat, because that's all you have, a face' (Scott, 1979, p. 46). And Dietrich's face, as von Sternberg stated, 'promised everything' (quoted in Bach, 1992, p. 130). As such, her ability to eroticise confusion and authority as well as desire, and to express so much with motionless eyes, eyebrows and lips made the hat her perfect and necessary foil. The hat is the face's ultimate theatrical device. Dietrich was always complexly lit and she knew about lighting and lenses. Without a hat, her beauty carried itself but with a hat only her self-conscious posturing made the light illuminate her correctly. John's hats had to be part of von Sternberg's system. A system whose purpose was, as John Baxter, in his von Sternberg critique, states, to 'explore ... mood or emotional state, chart the development of an attitude, analyze the delicate evolutions of a relationship in ascendancy or decline' (1971, p. 22). To express something so ineluctable, the underlying foundation must be very sturdy.

Only two hats appear in *Shanghai Express*. The hats are in themselves remarkable, subtle and suggestive, yet a functioning component of lighting. As with Adrian's adage, the *Shanghai Express* story can be summed up in four millinery parts: Two Hats, No Hat, Return to Hat. The first hat introduces the heroine and hints at what is to come, the second hat shows conflict and the heroine's vulnerability and the third, hatlessness, shows the character in extreme danger, both mortal and romantic. The film's resolution, where the lovers rejoin, returns the heroine to the world of hats as she resumes her original demeanour. Dietrich's character, Shanghai Lily, is described as 'a woman who lives by her wits on the China coast', an obvious euphemism for her prostitution but one that focuses on her intelligence, self-reliance and daring. Her entrance must visually provoke these responses in the viewer. First seen in a crowded railway station, Lily's black dress is initially nondescript, except for her thick collar of thin plumes, a theme picked up in her eye-catching hat. She wears a rimless cloche made of black iridescent feathers which are set in swirls over her head, though the feathers are not initially obvious. Across her face, in a flat shape, is a diagonal, lined veil ending just above her lip. This effect tells all. Her cloche's shuttered, alluring veil and snug, glistening skull cap reveal sensual independence and tight-lipped, call-girl secrets. Wearing this hat she enters the train, establishes herself in her car, encounters the man who becomes her enemy and meets an old lover, a chance passenger. The hat's close veil continually alludes to self-protection but what seemed a stiff visor is later shown to be soft fabric, rippling in breezes. The tight, dark cloche reveals irregular rounds in the light-refracting feathers as Dietrich moves her head. The hat's elegant style symbolises her sophistication and her contrasting nature: she is soft and hard, in a shell and pettable, as strong as the hat's controlled structure but as full of nuances as the hat's feathery, gleaming texture. The hat's gradually exposed softnesses thus tell what is to come: that strong Lily's humanity and suffering desire will become obvious.

The second hat appears once the journey begins, literally and metaphorically. Lily wears another cloche, made of plain matte fabric, an effect virtually dividing her oval face into white and black pieces. Now having met her lover, she is at odds with her old

Symbolic feathers in *Shanghai Express* (1932)

resolutions. Her emotions are beginning to show, mirrored in opposing white sweeps of thick willowy feathers, as long as twelve inches each, at the hat's right base. These horn shapes form a V, pointing towards the face, but also represent Lily's feelings for her past lover which are spilling from her. Midway behind the hat, and upright, are white feathers, less distinct than those at the neck. Finally, and not instantly apparent, there is a veil, again diagonally crossing the face, very faint, ending below the lips, with strong black dots marking a line along its edge. Her veil appears and disappears in much the way that Lily's guard lowers and raises through her intense feelings. The hat's delineated blacks and whites contribute to von Sternberg's moiré-like patterns. The hat becomes a five-piece (cloche, veil, three sets of feathers), exceptionally co-ordinated unit of white and black, hard and soft, visible/less visible/invisible which never dominates Dietrich's exceptional beauty but is a solid frame around her features. Yet the hat is equally exceptionally beautiful, suitable for Lily to wear. Her control and strength are implicit in the hat's structure: the feathers are tightly constructed into the hat. They retain graceful softness yet never loosen even though, at her neck, they're at an awkward place of movement. The hat is steady, comfortably moving with each head turn, and retaining its specific five-piece shape. It draws the audience to Dietrich's face, is exquisite from every angle, yet acts as a light catcher or matte duller. In one scene, from long shot, in a very dark train station, surrounded by men in grey uniforms, holding upright rifles, Dietrich's white oval face is buoyed up by the V-shape at her neck, making her the more noticeable.

During the rest of the film, Lily becomes increasingly frantic for her lover's safety, overwhelmed in 'loving him madly'. Throughout, including scenes when she sacrifices herself for him, prays for him and he continues to reject her, she is vulnerable without her hat. This is especially powerful when she shakes from his touch and the camera closes on her face looking upwards into muted light. She seems on the verge of dissolution.

At the film's end, she gets off the train wearing the original cloche. Fearing her lover's loss forever (he still rejects her), the veil's lines have been intensified, as her self-protection has redoubled, all the more obvious because, having been affected again by love, she must try harder to hold herself aloof. But, ultimately, her lover humbles himself before her and, united, they kiss. She retains her hat as does he (a colonel's, which she has worn once) but significantly she denudes him of his petty props – his riding crop and gloves. Their hats are all they need. Baxter sees *Shanghai Express* as 'an elaborate excursion into sexual domination' (1971, p. 17). Certainly, Dietrich has the upper hand in many respects as an object of great desire, but the hat–hatless under-story counterpoints this 'domination' revealing her as human with wants, needs, fragilities and strengths.

Conversely, *Morocco*'s hats carry a hard and reactionary subplot. The narrative has typical romance characters: world-weary chanteuse Amy Jolly (Dietrich) who arrives in a Moroccan port to work in a nightclub, Tom Brown, (Gary Cooper) a disaffected French Foreign Legion stud who goes from woman to woman and feels no allegiance (including to the army), and aristocratic, moneyed painter, Baron La Bessière (Adolphe Menjou) who is besotted with Dietrich. But the film is really only about sex and what sexuality is allowed to do or not do. The leads are introduced in a thoroughly carnal context, both apart and together, when the film opens with three sexually specific moves: first, Cooper bargaining with a prostitute and second, in another locale, Dietrich indifferently described as 'probably a vaudeville actress', suggesting an immoral lifestyle, and third, Dietrich's languidly performed cabaret act which heats both men and women. The film ends on a sexual specific: Dietrich crazed with desire for Cooper. The plot is nothing more than their attraction to each other (over a very short period) until their 'love', unconsummated and unspoken, revolutionises their lives: Cooper falls in love for the first time and experiences honesty as demonstrated by his refusal to desert (as he had planned); Dietrich wakes from her pained ennui and, in desperation, tracks Cooper from one town to another (with lover Menjou in tow). Finally, she rejects the Baron, and barefooted, trails Cooper's legion into the desert by joining their camp-followers.

The film thoroughly blurs desire and love and, in a sense, sets up a story of, what could be called 'true desire' (versus true love); a truth through which Cooper finds himself while Dietrich loses herself. He discards his wanton ways and becomes a good soldier while she discards her career and impending marriage to wealth and comfort, to become, as implied in the film, just another fallen woman bonded to a single man. The film's end is draconian towards Dietrich, in direct contrast to the novel where Jolly, singer, active hooker and drug addict, loses both men but retains her career, such as it is, and leaves Morocco for her next engagement in Buenos Aires.[5] Why should the cinematic Jolly suffer such a humiliating punishment in the name of two star-crossed lovers being united? The hats explain why the woman must lose and the man gain, and they reveal a social substratum that confronts other interpretations of the film. Annette Tapert, in *The Power of Glamour*, feels that *Morocco* shows nothing more than 'a daring, independent woman who coolly challenged the accepted notions of womanhood and sexuality' (1998, p. 232). Gaylyn Studlar's study of masochism in von Sternberg films analyses *Morocco* through its role-reversal, particularising Cooper's feminisation and Dietrich's masculisation. However, Studlar interprets the end scene, where the two lovers salute each other farewell, as a compliment to the female power stated in Jolly's desirous stare at Brown from the stage in the film's opening. This 'gaze' is vigorous, an act usually attributed to the male and polar to the passive female-to-be-looked-at stance. This power that is 'set by her first glimpse of him' continues, according to Studlar, in Jolly's last look at Brown and 'confirms the association of the female within the active gaze' (1988, p. 64), because it results in taking action: she follows him.[6] Baxter sees Jolly as 'less character than focus' in that 'humiliation', for him, happens only to the men surrounding her (1971, p. 79). Dietrich's biographer, Steven Bach, describing *Morocco* as 'a high (or low) romantic hoot today' (1992, p. 132), even suggests Jolly is saved.

> Love ... defines and redeems Amy Jolly. She doesn't need the pearls or the French table talk of La Bessière or the sables of her past; she needs to love her man without condition, qualification, or complaint. She sacrifices the World to her heart. This is not subjugation (as more militant feminists might conclude) but loyalty to her passions. ... The consummation is her union with her romantic self. (Ibid., pp. 133–4)

These are astounding interpretations, considering that Jolly is not just falling for Cooper over Menjou or ditching a career for a new adventure but, to demonstrate her 'passions', she begins a long Saharan march without shoes, hat, or worldly ties. Why does her love constitute a death sentence (literal and psychological)? The answer is visible only in the intricate hat-play that runs through the film. The hat plot can be summed up as this: Top Hat versus Legionnaire Cap becomes Top Hat/Legionnaire Cap versus No Hat. At first, the plot centres on Dietrich as a lawless woman pitted against Cooper the irresponsible, young man, then it centres on Cooper and Menjou, the men who have returned to their rightful places in society (loyal soldier/genteel tycoon), triumphing (by stripping her identity) over Dietrich, the woman, whose rightful place in society is as abject lover and not as transgressive singer or wife-with-a-past. Amazingly, craven desire is the vehicle which has returned everyone to these selected positions. There are four Dietrich hats in the film, but the crucial ones which reveal this subtext are the opening two – her cloche and her top hat – and, of course, her hatlessness.

Dietrich is first seen at night on a ship's deck. She is in a dark, slightly shapeless outfit and wears a black, matte cloche that tightly wraps just off centre at her forehead; its veil is invisible, except for the edge, where two rows of black dots float just below her eyes. The veil is draped in two loops so that the edges cross. This effect makes Dietrich's face come lustrously forward because, framed as it is, it seems beautiful and bare. Amy Jolly is also bare. The captain marks her as 'A suicide passenger. One-way ticket. They never return' – suggesting that Jolly is down-to-the-bone. Like the double veil, she is at a crossroads and she has two choices: to live or to die; or to go with one kind of man or with the other. Nevertheless, her autonomy is underscored when she is offered help by the Baron and refuses. In this simple, striking hat, Jolly is portrayed as a strong individual who is, as the following scene reveals, tremendously in control of what little she has. She is next seen in her new club, a low-end theatre filled with wealthy Arabs, Americans, Europeans, and Legionnaires and their Moroccan girlfriends. Dietrich is in her dressing room, wearing a man's tails (the full suit). She pops out a collapsible top hat and places it at a tilt behind her head and saunters on stage singing and smoking. She handles her top hat, without removing it, throughout her act. She knocks the brim forward or taps it nonchalantly back. She works the hat with the experienced gestures of a prostitute's come-on. It shows she knows her act well, and that the act bores her and vaguely delights her at once. Her precision is like a ballet of insouciance and determination. Her gestures have a demanding quality that her slow walk and casual air don't have. By working the hat she declares, 'See me. I am. And I am in control of you'. She holds her once-jeering audience. She walks among the tables and stops to kiss a European woman on the mouth. Dietrich then, again, knocks her top hat back. She asks for the woman's flower which she eventually throws to the enthralled Cooper, who is sitting with a woman, and who answers in like gender-bending by finally putting the flower behind his ear. Thus the lovers are set up as odd equals: beautiful, desirable, sexually fearless and very experienced.

Dietrich's male attire needs some context. The top hat in particular, in the twentieth century, signified male wealth and privilege as no other.[7] By wearing hat and tails,

The top hat as power in *Morocco* (1930)

Dietrich is taking on not just men's clothing, but a class pinnacle. She upturns gender, ambition and society in one display. A woman in trousers was not unheard of; by 1926 women stars had been sporting them in public (Berry, 2000, p. 154), but a woman in a man's suit was still *outré*. This kind of cross-dressing had a European, decadent background. Von Sternberg described the late 1920s' Berlin where he made *The Blue Angel*, as 'full of females who looked and functioned like men' (von Sternberg, 1965, p. 228). He had already seen Dietrich 'wearing the full-dress regalia of a man, high hat and all' and felt this attire 'fitted her with much charm' (Ibid., 1965, p. 247). Alfred Eisenstadt photographed her in hat and tails for *Life* magazine. In Germany, Dietrich tended to wear 'trousers most the time' (Dietrich, 1987, p. 71) around her neighbourhood. Women had been wearing lounge pyjamas for some years and trousers were worn in southern California and claimed as a 'local invention' (Finch and Rosenkrantz, 1979, p. 361). Long, beach culottes and short, street ones were on the verge of being regular fashion. By 1933, women would be wearing men's suits openly, in imitation of the Dietrich trend. *Morocco*'s female-in-drag top hat and tails were not even worthy of a mention in *The New York Times* film review. Clearly, though, the scene is set up to shock because it is packed with details: Dietrich comfortably dressed in a man's tails, her expertise in using the top hat, her lesbian kiss, her sexual frankness in transferring the kiss to Cooper via the flower. Even now, the scene is remarkable because it places these events in a such a blasé atmosphere where a few gestures carry loaded cultural disturbances. Every motion is slow (the walk, the drawled song, the pauses) but the handled hat actively demonstrates who Jolly is. Who is she? This is the first sight of Dietrich by a non-German audience, as a stunning, self-contained woman dressed in a rich man's clothes who intrepidly, and almost disinterestedly, vamps both sexes. The top hat, as it identifies iconically as both maleness and money, contains all of that. The cross-dressing highlights Jolly's strength, but the film has already contextualised this strength as weak. Minutes before, in the first boat scene, it is shown to be corroded by despair. She wears her top hat because she's at the end of her rope ('a suicide passenger'). Nevertheless, whatever her motive, her thrilling infraction will meet the law: at her expense. Jolly will be reduced to a sexual compulsion that deprives her of everything, including reason.

The top hat scene is followed by her next stage act. Here Dietrich wears no hat and is dressed in what is tantamount to a bathing suit and a long feather boa and, as her clothes imply, she has become a female for sale. Now her act is to tawdrily sell apples to men in the audience, in an obviously sexualised arena. She holds her own, that is the Dietrich character, but this couldn't be more different to the top hat and tails scene. Her hatless state, as in *Shanghai Express*, is all about vulnerability. She gives Cooper her room key and, when he arrives, they square off in a hot and cold seduction. Dietrich argues their equality by telling him that she is in a 'Foreign Legion of women' because, like the Legion where 'men without a past' go, she is also a 'woman without a past'. They profess faithlessness in the opposite sex – she is burned out and he is a rover – and part. The two hats – his soldier's cap (which he wears throughout) and her top hat (still apparent in her attitude) – confront in the first part of the film. Though Dietrich is hatless, she withstands here what will become an undoing desire but her bare head augurs her vulnerability to come. However, in this scene, neither will relinquish to the other.

The storyline then turns on itself and, with no action to explain this (they are never alone again), the two lovers realise that they are soulmates. Eventually, Brown goes to see Jolly in her dressing room, where she is in her 'bathing suit'. For the first time, they kiss. Both, hatless, openly crave each other. She agrees to go with him when he deserts that night. She goes on stage. He moons around, plays with her top hat and puts it on. Now he 'has' her, he can wear the hat. But, until this moment, this hat, in all its wider cultural incarnations, has been forbidden to him. Brown is a lowly, criminally minded Legionnaire, not an acceptable, top-hattable, upper-class man.[8] Through *her*, he is allowed to breach this social protocol and is seen in the hat. But the top hat still retains tricks. It has been shown from the outset to be collapsible and, so, cheap, reminding the audience that this is a theatrical hat and thus Jolly's man act is just play. Though not a designed article, this choice of top hat would be essential to John, Banton and von Sternberg. Despite its 'theatre', in putting on *her* top hat, Brown wears something 'not right' and so also enters Jolly's world of ambiguity, where plain living is as death-defying as soldiering. Her world is broader than his and he intuits this.

But they cannot both wear the top hat. It symbolises different things: for him, as a man, it is riches and position (if he attains the right to such a hat) or the dissolution of the only authority he has – maleness; if *she* wears the hat, for her, it is an in-your-face aloofness, but won at the cost of bad loving – she has never found a true man. The message is too much for him. He writes on the mirror – 'I changed my mind. Good luck' – and leaves. But when he returns to his regiment, refusing to run away, this 'change of mind' is also a change of morals. He tells his friend why he won't desert – 'I've turned decent. I'm in love.' By wearing the top hat, a man's domain (even if not by class status), Brown begins the road to redemption as a citizen. Jolly experiences the opposite. After Brown leaves her, the Baron arrives and, for the first time, is wearing a top hat, the only person entitled to wear it. Jolly, distraught, hatless and in her 'bathing suit', agrees to his buying out her cabaret contract. She leaves the stage (and her top hat) forever to marry the Baron. Here, the hat plot switches to Top Hat/Legionnaire Cap versus No Hat, the final showdown where socially sanctioned places will resume. Desperate, once she hears that Brown may be wounded, Jolly forces the Baron to drive her to his outpost. The two lovers covertly reveal their feelings (he has carved her name in a heart; she has followed him) but pretend indifference and, in keeping with the film's sexual theme, flaunt a companion. Dietrich, hatless, watches Cooper's regiment march into the blazing sun and she leaves the Baron to join the few women straggling after them. Her fancy shoes impede her so she throws them away. The last shot is of her, barefooted, in the Saharan sand, facing death by walking after a man who does not know she is there. Her hatless *and* shoeless state starkly shows that she has lost all stature and self-possession, while the top hat has returned to its legitimate owner (Menjou) and the Legionnaire cap is being worn with pride (Cooper).

Storytelling is the purpose of costume design. The hats retell *Morocco*'s story and subliminally quell audience fears churned by its enormous demonstration of a woman's transgression, however exciting. They retell *Shanghai Express*'s story and relieve the pressure of female 'domination' by humanising the superstar. Through an intricate inter-working relationship between star and designer, the hat becomes a stage in itself where the star, so sublimely dressed, also acts out a more intense, more culturally defined drama. The Marlene Dietrich face–John Frederics hat combination, each so fully engaged in making the other work as it should, reveals the deeper level. As Mr John said, a hat is a dangerous thing, because it shows *what* you are.

Notes

1. Nadoolman Landis designed, among others, the costumes for *The Blues Brothers* (John Landis, 1980), *Raiders of the Lost Ark* (Stephen Spielberg, 1981), Michael Jackson's *Thriller* (John Landis, 1985) and *Coming to America* (John Landis, 1988).
2. As 'Mr John' is his more famous name, it is misleading to refer to him only as 'Frederics', therefore I use what is common to both, 'John', throughout.
3. John's real name, birthplace and birth date are disputed, with some five variations of each. These are the most likely.
4. Some films are *Mata Hari*, *The Painted Veil* (Richard Boleslavsky, 1934), *Queen Christina* (1933), *Blonde Bombshell* (Victor Fleming, 1933), *The Women* (George Cukor, 1939). Others are yet to be verified.
5. Recapped by Bach (1992).
6. Studlar's complex work is too lengthy to discuss in full. However, I take issue with her assertion that *Morocco* ends with female power.
7. Even in the 1960s, it still carried enormous clout. At his inauguration, John Kennedy deliberately did not wear a top hat, as many men at the ceremony did, or any hat. The first president to be sworn in hatless. Kennedy used this effect to project himself as modern and of the people.
8. The Foreign Legion, where men 'without a past' go, was a notorious hide-out for criminals.

3
Gregory Peck: Anti-Fashion Icon

Stella Bruzzi

Gregory Peck, one of Hollywood's biggest stars of the 1940s and 50s, developed through his career a consistent and specific on-screen persona, constructed around the types of roles he was most associated with playing and the way he looked. He is most readily associated with the role of Atticus Finch in *To Kill a Mockingbird* (Robert Mulligan, 1962), a part for which he won an Oscar and a character who, only a week before Peck's death in June 2003, was named the lead hero of all time in an American Film Institute poll. Atticus Finch sums up Peck's appeal – liberal, kind, honourable – so what is he doing here as the subject of a chapter on stars and fashion?

Peck is here as an icon of anti-fashionability; one of the few Hollywood stars whose potential as a sex symbol was downplayed and whose on-screen appearance was, nearly always, staid and de-eroticised. His film roles fall into several distinct categories, the most important of which are: fathers (*The Yearling* [Clarence Brown, 1946], *Gentleman's Agreement* [Elia Kazan, 1947], *The Man in the Gray Flannel Suit* [Nunnally Johnson, 1956], *Cape Fear* [J. Lee Thompson, 1962], *To Kill a Mockingbird*), lawyers (*The Paradine Case* [Alfred Hitchcock, 1947], *Cape Fear, To Kill a Mockingbird*) and soldiers/men in uniform (*Days of Glory* [Jacques Tourneur, 1944], *Twelve O'Clock High* [Henry King, 1949], *Only the Valiant* [Gordon Douglas, 1951], *Captain Horatio Hornblower* [Raoul Walsh, 1951], *The Purple Plain* [Robert Parish, 1951], *Pork Chop Hill* [Lewis Milestone, 1959], *On the Beach* [Stanley Kramer, 1959], *The Guns of Navarone* [J. Lee Thompson, 1961], *Captain Newman, M.D.* [David Miller, 1963]). Peck also made several Westerns (he was, in 1950, voted 'Cowboy star of the year')[1] and was also sometimes the romantic lead (*Spellbound* [Alfred Hitchcock, 1945], *Roman Holiday* [William Wyler, 1953], *Designing Woman* (Vincente Minnelli, 1957), *Arabesque* [Stanley Donen, 1966]). There are notable intersections between these character types, and there is a marked consistency in how Peck appeared as them. He was often serious, the leader or the protector, and his characters frequently espoused a particularly American brand of liberalism, both caring and conservative. If in love, he was often vulnerable, sometimes misguided, but he was nearly always honourable. Peck's 'tall, dark and handsome' looks alongside the curious asexuality of his characters and the way he was so often dressed in a way that echoed this asexuality, created an atypical star persona. He was a matinée idol and one of Hollywood's more bankable sex symbols (as Richard exclaims mournfully in *The Seven Year Itch* [Billy Wilder, 1955]: 'Let's face it, no pretty girl in her right mind wants me, she wants Gregory Peck') but his sexual appeal remained subdued, ambiguous in his films.

The central contradiction that defines Peck's star persona was most clearly expressed in his domestic films. It was in these that Peck – for all the glamour and attraction associated with him – became notably anti-fashionable, asexual and safe, qualities that served to problematise the notion of him as a sex symbol. Peck was sexy but always demure; despite Richard's comment in *The Seven Year Itch,* there are notably few films in which he took any of his clothes off, notwithstanding the 1950s being, as Steven Cohan has termed it, 'the age of the chest' (1997, pp. 164 ff.). Although Peck's pectorals appeared in *I Walk the Line* (John Frankenheimer, 1970), he was by then middle-aged and past his matinée idol prime. Peck's was a personalised brand of unthreatening machismo, and one cannot imagine him swapping parts with Heston in *The Greatest Story Ever Told* (George Stevens, 1965) or *The Planet of the Apes* (Franklin J. Schaffner, 1968) or *Ben-Hur* (William Wyler, 1959). Peck strayed close to Heston territory as King David in *David and Bathsheba* (Henry King, 1951), but did not look good.

British movie magazines of the 1940s offer an intriguing introduction to Peck's equivocal image. This was the era, after all, when Gregory Peck was the pin-up, and the various alluring close-ups of him accompanying the articles attest to this. Whereas *Picture Show* tended to emphasise Peck's family man credentials and only as an afterthought made reference to his looks – and then in rather coy terms ('Gregory has black hair, dark eyes and is two and a half inches over six feet in height'),[2] *Picturegoer* gives a raunchier and more thrilling account of Peck's private life – omitting the family and embellishing his pre-acting days to include a stint as a truck driver and a boat builder (the more measured accounts explain how he, as a teenager, made one boat which promptly sank upon impact with water; *Picture Show* makes no mention of the trucking experience). As one such article says – upon mentioning that Peck 'loves an outdoors life and is never happier than when spending a holiday as a cowhand on a big ranch' – 'He looks like that sort of man'.[3] These two aspects of Peck's image were broadly echoed, in the film roles of the 1940s – the worthy anti-Semite, Phil Green in *Gentleman's Agreement* as opposed to the smouldering Lewt in *Duel in the Sun* (King Vidor, 1946) – and were accentuated through the way Peck was dressed on screen. In the former, Peck is conventionally besuited; middle-aged before his time, steady and dependable; in the latter, cast as the 'bad' brother to Joseph Cotten's 'good' one, he wears a spotty cravat (reminiscent of other racy 1940s' males such as Stewart Granger in *Blanche Fury* [Marc Allégret, 1947]) and his hat at a jaunty angle, both of which contrast sharply with his brother's more sensible necktie, tied neatly under his chin, and his level hat. Although Peck became associated with the Phil Green-type roles (the safe guys) and did not often appear as menacing or eroticised, when he wore black as he does in *Duel in the Sun* or in *The Bravados* (Henry King, 1958) or when he is taking the princess for a ride in *Roman Holiday*, a certain relish replaces his otherwise staid rectitude.

Perhaps because it comes after *Spellbound*, Peck's nastiness in *Duel in the Sun* is ultimately flawed; for all the chiselled-ness of his jaw, he is just too clean cut. In Hitchcock's *Spellbound,* he plays John Ballantyne, a psychologically frail character whose impersonation of dead psychoanalyst, Anthony Edwards, is revealed to be the result of repressed childhood guilt. Through the film, Ballantyne's illness makes him passive (he swoons several times) and he is directly contrasted with Dr Constance Petersen (Ingrid Bergman) who occupies the more traditional masculine position by curing and seducing/falling in love with Ballantyne. It is *Spellbound* that for me, coming early in his career, cemented Peck's image as Hollywood's perversely asexual sex symbol – and this is achieved through the clothes. Early on, just after his arrival at the psychiatric institution, Green Manors, Constance, being rather forward, goes up to Ballantyne's bedroom late one evening in order to talk to him about the finer points of his supposed publication, *The Labyrinth of the Guilt Complex*. Her sexual intentions are implied by the shot of Bergman approaching the upstairs landing off which lies Ballantyne's room: her tentative steps, the conspicuously tufty carpet (slightly chaotic and echoing the messiness of Constance's hair upon her return from picnicking with Edwards/Ballantyne earlier that day) and the sensuous light straining to escape from the crack between door and carpeted floor. Constance, clutching Edwards' book (and her own 'guilt complex'?) tightly to her chest, knocks on the door, and, upon getting no answer, enters. Ballantyne (whom she still assumes to be Edwards) is sleeping in a chair, a book resting on his lap. In a sexually charged situation a man asleep is not a positive sign; this and Peck's crisp pyjamas and dressing gown suggest at the very least an ambivalent attitude to sex. Then follows one of Hitchcock's infamous kisses: the music sours as Peck walks towards Bergman, the angle of the camera and the direction of his gaze more than implying that he is walking towards us. He kisses Bergman but we almost kiss Peck.[4] Their kiss, to keep on the right side of the censors' scissors, is interrupted by a series of doors being flung open, symbolically emphasising the furtive innocence of their passion.

Peck's recurring passivity throughout *Spellbound* likewise interrupts the spontaneous

Peck as John Ballantyne in Hitchcock's *Spellbound* (1945), about to kiss Ingrid Bergman

passion of this night-time scene. Just as he and Bergman end their kiss, he freezes, springs back from her embrace and has one of his many psychological attacks as he stares at the lines on Bergman's dressing gown. Later, we understand that the juxtaposition of white and lines relates to two repressed memories: Edwards' murder and a childhood trauma (the source of Ballantyne's guilt complex) when Ballantyne accidentally caused the death of his brother. Ballantyne's outbursts and his fainting fits are invariably linked to his innocence and in this, they also serve to define his relationship with Constance. His sexual 'innocence' is mirrored by and articulated through Peck's appearance – his fine (in *Spellbound* fragile-seeming) features, his tousled hair – and the incredibly sensible and totally unsensuous duo of pale pyjamas and dark dressing gown. Peck's pyjamas (which return in *Cape Fear*, there one of many symbols of his character's phallic renunciation) can be likened, in their effect, to those worn by Meg Ryan in modern romantic comedies; they suggest purity and friendship rather than sex.

The Great Masculine Renunciation

Peck, oddly for such a matinée idol, was only ever uneasily or tentatively sexual. In *The Paradine Case*, for example, the obvious physical intimacy at the beginning of the film between Peck (a top London barrister) and his wife, played by Ann Todd, is incongruous. This incongruity (that a man donning a formal three-piece suit in wide, gentlemanly pinstripes could be passionate) will now be examined in relation to fashion. Peck's ambivalence as a star was exemplified by his consistent unfashionability – his sensible, functional clothes, his demureness and passivity, his penchant (even in the 1940s as John Ballantyne or Phil Green) for the signature garments not only of the professional man but of the dull man's leisure wardrobe – cardigans, slacks and comfortable shoes.

The man's suit is in itself an equivocal sartorial symbol. There are suits and there are suits, and Peck's suits in *The Paradine Case* or later in *The Man in the Gray Flannel Suit* lack the brashness, sensuality and elegance of Cary Grant's sleek grey ones in *North by Northwest* (Alfred Hitchcock, 1959) or *To Catch a Thief* (Alfred Hitchcock, 1955). In 'His Story of Fashion' (a lighthearted saunter through fashionable male archetypes), fashion and cultural historian Tim Edwards proposes as the important 1940s' model (there is no 1950s' model) Cary Grant,

> ... wearing a new, smooth lounge suit cut with a wide silhouette that heightens his stature, whilst the low 'V' cut of his jacket displays a crisp white shirt and a most decorative silk tie. His shoes are highly polished and his hair is kept short, whilst he views the countryside from his new motor car. (1997, p. 3)

Tim Edwards also claims that the anonymous suit itself can be sexual, arguing that,

> The main example of the utility of menswear, namely the suit, is as much a symbol of masculine sexuality in terms of broadening shoulders and chest and connecting larynx to crotch through collar and tie, as it is a practical (if historically uncomfortable) uniform of respectability. (Ibid.)

There is one film in particular in which Peck cuts a dash in a suit. In *Roman Holiday*, Peck plays the slightly seedy (but by the end reformed) journalist, Joe Bradley and complements Audrey Hepburn's fresh elegance with his light suits and his Vespa, the foreigner living *la dolce vita* in Rome. Near the beginning of the film (Peck having taken Hepburn, an escaped princess, home with him in a stupefied state) there is a pyjama moment that contrasts neatly with the parallel scene in *Spellbound*. Peck offers Hepburn his own stripy brushed cotton pyjamas to sleep in (and at the end, lends her his silk dressing gown). This is a similar dull regulation ensemble to the one worn by John Ballantyne – until Hepburn puts it on, at which point it serves to accentuate and eroticise her gamine androgyny.

Even in *Roman Holiday* though, there reside unresolved tensions to do with sex as the romance between Bradley and Princess Ann remains chaste, Bradley's desire to exploit his friendship with the runaway princess being thwarted (ironically) by his falling in love with her. As in *Spellbound*, Peck's appearance in *Roman Holiday* thus expresses a residual emotional, psychological fragility. In his more traditional, domestic roles – as he became increasingly synonymous with paternalism, authority and a strong but asexual masculinity – Peck's appearance increasingly emphasised these intimations of celibacy, intellectualism and detachment from eroticism and desire.

The clothes his characters wear (the anonymous grey flannel suit, slacks and homely pyjamas) come to connote (to borrow J. C. Flügel's term) a second 'great masculine renunciation'. Flügel (a psychologist who in 1930 published *The Psychology of Clothes*) dated to the end of the eighteenth century the 'sudden reduction of male sartorial decorativeness' that, he argued, has characterised men's fashion since (1930, p. 110). With the French Revolution and the subsequent rise of the professional middle classes, men's fashions became more uniform and democratic, as 'Man abandoned his claim to be considered beautiful' (Ibid., p. 111). As with Peck's typical grey flannel suit, male fashions became more inhibited, more moral, more functional and less expressive, Flügel ultimately arguing that,

> ... modern man's clothing abounds in features which symbolise his devotion to the principles of duty, of renunciation and of self-control. The whole relatively 'fixed' system of his clothing is, in fact, an outward and visible sign of the strictness of his adherence to the social code. (Ibid., p. 113)

Notions of repression and functionality have been attached to men's fashions ever since. Jennifer Craik suggests that it was in the 1960s that men started, once more, to be fashionable and body-conscious (Craik, 1994, p. 178); the 1950s and early 60s thus represent the last gasp of traditionalism before London *et al.* began to swing.

Tom Rath, Peck's character in the film adaptation of the bestseller, *The Man in the Gray Flannel Suit*, was the archetypal 1950s' man: a breadwinner father who commutes from Connecticut to New York to provide for his wife Betsy (Jennifer Jones) and their three children. Rath is the post-French Revolutionary Flügelian male; he has renounced his desirability and submerged his attractiveness into his anonymous suit, his routine job and his fatherly duties. In wearing the uniform of the 1950s' middle-class American male Peck outwardly epitomises Anne Hollander's conception of non-fashion. While fashion, Hollander argues, 'abhors fixity, of form or meaning, of knowledge or feeling, of the past itself', non-fashion 'creates its visual projections primarily to illustrate the confirmation of established custom, and to embody the desire for stable meaning even if custom changes – it is normative' (1994, p. 17). Like Edwards, however, Hollander seeks to affirm that even non-fashion possesses (perhaps unconsciously) 'great beauty and originality of form, great subtlety of color and pattern' (Ibid., p. 18).

The contradictions inherent within 'non-fashion' are commensurate with those epitomised by Gregory Peck's repeated portrayal of the non-fashionable man. Of *The Man in the Gray Flannel Suit,* Steve Cohan remarks that, 'if you take away the suit, you will have trouble finding the man' (1997, p. 78). This is a witty but an over-simplifying conclusion, for the anonymous grey flannel suit, as worn by Peck, signals repression more than emptiness, the breadwinner father here having become a figure of trauma and conflict. Unsurprisingly, this repression is the result of sexual renunciation. During World War II, Tom Rath served in the American infantry, and so, as Cohan identifies, conforms to the 'standard biography of hegemonic masculinity' in 1950s' America (Ibid., p. 36). While in Italy, however, he had an affair with an Italian woman, Maria (Marisa Pavan), and later learns she bore their son.[5] This is not an archetypal component of the 1950s' hegemonic male's biography; the tension created by this repressed past – Tom finally tells Betsy about Maria and his son – almost wrecks his marriage. Not only is Tom very different in the flashbacks (above all he is emotional – he sings, he is passionate, he is deeply traumatised after accidentally having caused the death in battle of his best friend) but also he looks very different in his infantry officer's garb. As Tim Edwards again remarks, a strong sense of glamour and eroticism was associated with 'American GIs dressed in their crispest uniforms' (1997, p. 16).

In stark contrast to how he looks in Italy, Peck as the steady, unexciting breadwinner after the war is a tense, sad figure whose performance and appearance signal loss and the strain of maintaining the breadwinner masquerade. Sexual, dynamic masculinity in the mid-1950s was exemplified not by Peck but by Marlon Brando or James Dean; as men's fashion historian, Farid Chenoune articulates, the youthful male in 'jeans, T-shirt and leather jacket' set himself up in opposition to the respectable, suited male, a differentiation opening up from this moment between 'upper and lower classes, between center and fringe, between establishment and nonconformists' (1993, p. 236). Peck's suits are about responsibility and maturity.

The symbolic value of the breadwinner's appearance is exemplified by a scene in *The Man in the Gray Flannel Suit* in which Tom and Betsy argue over Tom's lack of ambition. Betsy vents her frustration at Tom's unspectacular $7,000 salary and declares their comfortable, suburban home to be a 'graveyard' that 'smells of defeat'. It is manifestly Tom whom she thinks 'smells of defeat', as she continues: 'ever since the war ... you've lost your guts and all of a sudden I'm ashamed of you'. Tom counters Betsy's rejection by assuring her that his job is 'an absolutely safe spot' and that 'the war is over, forgotten'. To be 'safe' within this context is to be emasculated, and the couple's argument takes place in a flawlessly dull, suburban kitchen – fridge, linoleum, checked tablecloth – with Tom, in his grey tank top, the embodiment of Betsy's fears. Tom's de-eroticisation is emphasised by his leisurewear – of cardigans, slacks and comfortable shoes. These items, along with affiliated garments such as the tank top, comprised the casual uniform of the middle-class, mid-twentieth-century male, the uniform that declared his traditionalism, his relative affluence, his social status. These clothes also signify the breadwinner's sexual renunciation, for, while they denote his hegemonic (and by association phallic) security, they also notably connote the repression of desire and the loss of desirability. Just as there is a notable difference between the suave and the anonymous grey suit, so there is an important distinction to be drawn between the bold sporting sweaters made popular by the Duke of Windsor in the 1920s and 30s and the inconspicuous tank woollens worn by Tom Rath and many another on-screen dad of the 40s, 50s and early 1960s, for example Tom Corbett (Glenn Ford) in Vincente Minnelli's *The Courtship of Eddie's Father* (1963).

Peck's image was further solidified by two key films made in 1962, J. Lee Thompson's *Cape Fear* and Robert Mulligan's *To Kill a Mockingbird*. In both, Peck played a lawyer whose family is under threat from 'bad' men. In *Cape Fear*, Sam Bowden (Peck) is confident in his role as protector of his wife Betty and daughter Nancy until the arrival in town of Max Cady (Robert Mitchum), a rapist recently released from jail who, blaming Bowden for having provided the evidence that convicted him, stalks him and his family with the intention of violating Nancy and destroying that wholesome unit. Bowden is the traditional patriarch and Cady his repressed and violent Other, an opposition established from the outset. *Cape Fear* opens with Cady, in an ostentatious white suit and Panama hat, strutting nonchalantly towards the courthouse where Bowden works, swaggering to the menacing strains of Bernard Herrmann's score. In the subsequent scene, before he has seen Cady, Bowden is in court, confident, suave and oozing the unctuous superiority of a man who feels in control; he jokes easily with the judge and, after an overnight adjournment, walks to his car. Cady catches Bowden unawares and whips his car keys from the safety of their lock; his belligerent violation of Bowden's personal space instantly alerts the classic patriarch to the force of Cady's threat. Cady's threat is uncontainable; he can slip through the cordon of power and legitimacy Bowden assumes protects and shrouds him in the same way that he, as father, protects and shrouds his family.

With any binary opposition, power rests with one element at the expense of the other. Cady's power against the legitimised father figure is exemplified by his difference from Bowden. Bowden's social role is encapsulated in his appearance: at work he wears a classic, single-breasted, dark suit over a stiff-collared white shirt and tie, while at home he dons a series of clichés from within the narrow confines of the middle-class gentleman's 'smart casuals' wardrobe: white deck shoes – too pristine to have ever been seriously used, cardigans, peg-top trousers and pyjamas buttoned up to his throat. Conversely, Cady dresses extravagantly in pale colours, striped T-shirts and his signature Panama; his clothes are unstructured, suggestive of freedom or carelessness, complementing Mitchum's swaggering sexuality, an overall image rounded off by the succulent cigars that rest between his lips. The respective wardrobes also imply very different relationships to the characters' bodies. Whereas the grey flannel-suited anonymity represses Bowden's sexuality and very definitely hides his body, Cady's more carefree, open-necked style draws attention to his body and his masculinity. More conspicuously than in the earlier films, Peck's appearance in *Cape Fear* comes to signal phallic lack.

In an early scene, in which Bowden still thinks it will be possible for the police to stop Cady within the parameters of the law, Cady is strip-searched. Rather than disempowering Cady as no doubt it is intended to do, getting him to take off everything down to his boxer shorts (and Panama hat) has the effect of emphasising what the sombre-suited father figure has conspicuously forfeited. Cady is happy to be strip-searched, ultimately because it enables him to flaunt his possession of the phallus and thus to question Bowden's impregnability. In several films, Mitchum's swelled, muscular chest comes to connote virility and untamed masculinity (*Home from the Hill* [Vincente Minnelli, 1960], for example) and in *Cape Fear*, Thompson's framing in the strip-search sequence takes to an extreme the notion that the tough body is the phallic body. Mitchum stands, often in the foreground, with his waist sucked in and his pectoral muscles puffed up; his image is cropped at the waist to prioritise a chest whose fullness and smooth contours throw into sharp relief the comparative emptiness under Bowden's respectable checked suit. Having renounced aggressive masculinity, Bowden belatedly discovers that he has also renounced the means to combat it. In this stand-off with Cady, it is not difficult to ascertain who has the phallus.

Through *Cape Fear*, Cady's transgressive presence precipitates the disintegration of the good father and the destabilisation of his family. It is notable that Bowden swiftly recognises that, if Cady is to be effectively challenged, he must become more like Cady and give up his trust in morality, the law and goodness. As Severs, the private detective Bowden hires, comments after advising the upstanding lawyer to think about paying some men to rough Cady up: 'a type like that is an animal, so you've got to fight him like an animal'. Bowden is outraged, but instead does something just as dubious, which is to offer Cady money to stay away, before eventually hiring men to beat him up, but unsuccessfully. Cady had rejected Bowden's offer of money, saying he preferred to inflict on Bowden death by a thousand cuts. Bowden assumes Cady means to attack his family before coming for him, to which Cady replies 'Now that's your train of thought, counsellor, not mine.' In a sense it is Bowden's train of thought that has brought him to this conclusion, but, as the end of *Cape Fear* attests, it is also Cady's intention to attack Nancy. As the film progresses and Bowden loses some of his moral certainty, so his conventional appearance comes to seem ever more an uncomfortable masquerade.

Cape Fear culminates in a watery duel between Cady and Bowden that, against the odds, Bowden wins. Although, after having been left for dead under water, Bowden resurfaces – in much the same way, ironically, as the monster from the deep is prone to do (there is maybe a link to be made with the 'monstrousness' Peck's appearance keeps under wraps). He clubs Cady on the head, incapacitates him and finally holds him at gunpoint; his decision not to shoot Cady but to have him given life imprisonment (a reciprocal death by a thousand cuts) leaves the threat, however, of his return open. This menace is re-evoked by the image of the Bowden family leaving 'Cape Fear' in a motor-boat immediately after the fight, a family superficially safe and secure but now profoundly undermined, their fractured-ness being conveyed by the destabilising effect of having the three of them together but not looking at each other. Sam Bowden's stern, defiant stare out from the boat may indicate his desire to resume his role as the family's great protector, but the look is also one of haunted resignation. Bowden's clothes by this stage are less definite, less self-assuredly dominant; in fact, Bowden, just as he has started to think like and so resemble Cady, so he has started to look a little more like him. As he fights and finally traps Cady, Bowden is wearing a checked shirt and, as he and his family sail away from Cape Fear, Sam has added a dark windcheater, both items that recall costumes Cady has worn, albeit neater and less showy versions of them. The troubles of the patriarch have been transmuted onto a more uncertain appearance.

The contradictions embodied by the peculiar intersection of Peck's beauty and his asexuality are exemplified by his role in John Frankenheimer's *I Walk the Line* as middle-aged Sheriff Henry Tawes who falls hopelessly in love with a much younger woman, Alma McCain (Tuesday Weld). As Tawes is married and Alma is still living with her family, their sex scenes are hardly prolonged and fulsome; instead their *amour fou* is expressed via a series of snatched, fraught encounters, either in McCain's house when her family are out or in Tawes' now derelict family home. One of these, however, has a certain frisson about it because it grants us a rare glimpse of Peck's chest. Because, as a young star, he had been neither fashionable nor overtly sexual, the sight of him bare-chested as a middle-aged man – with his beauty subsided and his eroticism subdued – is difficult to interpret. The formality of Peck's appearance was so much part of how Hollywood used him as an object of disavowal, denying us a glimpse of his body while trading on his obvious physical attractiveness. Now, in *I Walk the Line*, the dialogue between audience and star has suddenly and surprisingly altered.

Peck is in bed with Weld, naked from the chest up. We see him only barely, first through the bars of their bed and then lying behind Weld, whose body is much more on display. This scene is in part sleazy (what is this married man doing with a girl young enough to be his daughter?), in part melancholy (the relationship cannot last) and in part highly erotic – because it offers us finally, after all these years, what *Roman Holiday et al.* lacked: Peck's flesh. This is a charged, complex cinematic moment. It is inappropriate for a family man and sheriff to be doing this, it is also an inappropriate encounter for Peck. Encapsulated in this moment of lust (as the tag line on the commercial video reads: 'a sheriff walks the line between law and lust!') is the impossibility of Hollywood's most chaste male star being able to shed his safe asexuality. *I Walk the Line* comes pretty close to giving Peck the opportunity, although, being a tale of mad love, it all ends catastrophically, with the death of one of Peck's deputies and messy fisticuffs between Peck and Alma's father which ends with Alma intervening and wounding Sheriff Tawes in the shoulder with a gruesome meat hook.

For the first time, as the film races to its inevitable conclusion, maintaining the Peck persona seems impossible. As Sheriff Tawes, he is pent up and virtually monosyllabic at home, as if responding to his wife – even when she has guessed he is having an affair and wants to leave – would be enough to puncture his flimsy masquerade. There is one domestic scene that illustrates this: after the sheriff has spent the night with Alma, his wife has tried to embark upon a dialogue about why her husband is having an affair (to her suggestion that he is suffering some kind of midlife crisis, he just repeats 'That ain't it'). Peck, getting ready for work, emerges from the bathroom in a white T-shirt, soon to be covered by his khaki sheriff's shirt. The white T-shirt has been the quintessential Hollywood garment for eroticising the male torso when gladiatorial combat is not a possibility; from *The Wild One* (Laslo Benedek, 1953) or *Rebel Without a Cause* (Nicholas Ray, 1955) in the 1950s, to *Speed* (Jan De Bont, 1994) in the 1990s, the white T-shirt telegraphs the male star's eroticism and his availability as an object of desire. After decades of chastity, it is unsurprising that Peck swiftly covers up this sexual signifier with his uniform. As Sheriff Tawes, most of his energy has gone into bottling up his desires.

Peck has been vulnerable in love before, most notably in *The Paradine Case*, in which he falls for Alida Valli, but also in *The Man in the Gray Flannel Suit*. In both cases, Peck's character is saved by a more than commonly accommodating and understanding wife. Passion is an aberration for Peck – hence the staid suited persona he adopted so easily – but in *I Walk the Line* it is all but ruinous. In the past, Peck would have let a woman such as Alma McCain go, but as Sheriff Tawes he does not. Having just assisted in the disposal of his deputy's body (one thing that makes *I Walk the Line* doubly poignant is that the sheriff fails to realise the extent to which the McCains are using him) and upon realising that Alma has left town, he is indeed on the brink of turning back, but, to the strains of Johnny Cash's 'Flesh and Blood' ('Flesh and blood needs flesh and blood and you're the one I need'), he whips his sheriff's car around, turns on his siren and police lights and goes after the object of his lust. This is a wonderful sequence, and one that conveys the sheer physicality of Peck's quest, the urgency of it. He skids round bends, roars through puddles and his tyres throw up clouds of dust. His face glistening with sweat, he finally catches up with the McCains and pulls them over. Alma's father confronts him with a rifle and Alma tells him she can't go with him. The sheriff and McCain fight, the former shoots the latter in the arm and, in defence of her father, Alma sinks the meat hook into her lover's shoulder. The expression on Peck's face as the McCain truck chunters off is one of confusion, grief and desolation; as the close-up on his anguish very slowly cross-fades into a shot of the hills around, Peck's teary eyes widen, as if he is going insane with grief. Cash's 'I Walk the Line' starts up again. Peck always walked the line and stayed on the safe side of eroticisation. Having seen him finally, late in his career, be the sexual object, I wish he hadn't.

Notes

1. Peck, in interview, is a little unsure of the date of this award (see Shay, 1969).
2. *Picture Show* 50, 1278, p. 15; December 1945, p. 11. A virtually identical description of Peck is given in a later *Picture Show* (57, 1490, 20 October 1951, p. 12).
3. *Picturegoer* 16, 684, p. 24; May 1947, p. 3.
4. A very similar almost-kiss between star (looking directly to camera) and apparatus is to be found in *Rear Window* (Alfred Hitchcock, 1954) as Grace Kelly bends down to kiss and wake James Stewart. Here it is, far more conventionally, the female star who is the object of our collective desires.
5. In the original novel, Tom knows Maria is pregnant before he leaves Italy.

4

Pillow Talk's Repackaging of Doris Day: 'Under all those dirndls . . .'

Tamar Jeffers

Doris Day attained a top box-office position in the US during two separate periods in the mid-20th century.[1] These two periods can be seen to correspond to two different Doris Days being marketed and bought by consumers.[2] The first Doris is the archetypal girl-next-door character, a star persona based on roles in such films as *On Moonlight Bay* (Roy Del Ruth, 1951), *By the light of the silvery moon* (David Butler,1953) and *Calamity Jane* (David Butler, 1953), in which Day plays an innocent, energetic tomboy, made more of a lady through an awakening love, retaining her perkiness despite swapping dungarees or buckskins for skirts in the last reel.

The other Day persona, established post-1959, which attained even greater dominance at the box office, could not be more different: sophisticated, mature, well dressed and urban, she is like the older, city-dwelling sister of the earlier Day incarnation. The film which achieved this persona transformation was *Pillow Talk* (Michael Gordon, 1959); its makers consciously intended to repackage the star. Day's 'autobiography', part-written by A. E. Hotchner, quotes *Pillow Talk*'s producer, Ross Hunter:

> Doris hadn't a clue to her potential as a sex image and no one realized that under all those dirndls lurked one of the wildest asses in Hollywood. I felt that it was essential for Doris to change her image if she was going to survive as a top star. (1976, p. 230)

Hunter's efforts to rebrand the star were noted as innovatory – 'the new Doris goes sexy'[3] – but despite the film's high returns at the box office and the numerous awards the film and star were either nominated for or actually won,[4] it has to be asked whether the repackaging inaugurated an alteration of Day's star persona which actually succeeded in helping her 'survive as a top star'.

Film theorists who have looked in detail at costume have noted that a character's clothes are often responsible for conveying information about her, frequently suggesting traits or motivations that are not overtly given anywhere else; such writers as Turim (1984), Gaines (1990), Harper (1987), Cook (1996) and Bruzzi (1997) have outlined how a woman's clothes in film – especially a woman's clothes – can play a part in either carrying or disrupting a film narrative. The costumes in *Pillow Talk* conform to these notions, in that while the clothes worn by the Day character, Jan Morrow, do carry information about her which bears out what the performance, the script and the narrative are telling us, they also provide further information which is not conveyed elsewhere.

One major lacuna in most film-costume theory is the intention to embed the costume moment within a larger context of the featured star's persona. This chapter will attempt to show how vital awareness of Day's previously established connotations is to the understanding of the costumes in *Pillow Talk*. The white evening dress, analysed at length below, establishes her desirability and thus sets the masquerade plot of the film in motion, since Brad cannot woo her as himself and invents an alias, the Texan millionaire, 'Rex Stetson'. The outfit both absorbs and imposes meaning within the narrative and extra-diegetically, featuring in the advertising used to demonstrate the newly sexualised star. The importance of this white dress is supreme to both the intended revamping of Day's persona and the actual outcome of the costume strategy, which I feel to be the inauguration of the 'mature virgin' cliché which bedevilled Day for the rest of her active career, and beyond.

This chapter attempts to draw links between this mature virgin characterisation of Day and the *Pillow Talk* costumes, first examining the clothes within the film, with closest emphasis placed on the white dress the Day character, Jan, is wearing on her first meeting with 'Rex Stetson'. Second, the focus shifts to exploration of how the costumes, and especially this white dress, were intended to glamorise the star, examining how the star's established persona was augmented or contradicted by the costume connotations. In conclusion, the chapter will indicate how *Pillow Talk*'s sophisticated costume formula led eventually to trouble for Day because of the particular strategy taken by the film to modernise and sexualise the star.

The Costumes in Context

Day's remarketing around the time of *Pillow Talk* was explicitly referred to as a radical change in wardrobe for her. Her filmic outfits from this point onwards also became a major part of her star appeal to audiences: as many of Jackie Stacey's respondents revealed, they went to see Day films because they could rely on each new movie to show the star in a collection of glamorous fashions (Stacey, 1994, pp. 195, 198).

During the period under examination there were, broadly, two predominant outlines for the female costume: the New Look-inspired swing-skirted silhouette, with tight waist and multiple, full stiff petticoats supporting circular skirts, versus more tailored, figure-hugging sheaths. Generally it seems that the former is used as cinematic shorthand for virgins and significantly, also for wives, while the latter symbolised more overtly sexually accessible women and career girls – emphasising that they were in the office to attract men rather than taking their careers seriously.

According to the Sears catalogue at this time real-life fashions had no such rigid divide: while the woman in her twenties could choose to adopt either outline for any outfit, even younger girls were being offered both the bouffant skirts and the sheath look too,[5] which might prompt one to ask why, if their ingénue counterparts in the audience could actually buy them, screen virgins were not being seen in figure-hugging clothes? The movies can be seen enforcing the symbolism that real life lacked: while it was difficult to render the possession or lack of in/experience on screen, films of the period did attempt to do so, the characters' clothes being one way to give outward expression to an internal quality.

The linking by costume of female roles (sweethearts and wives) across what was often perceived as the ultimate divide, coitus, seems initially curious but is sustained by examination of the costumes in films from this period. Putting both virgins and married women in the full-skirted outline was perhaps motivated by the fact that their sexuality is safely contained – the former as yet dormant, the latter licensed by marriage, while *iconographically* the sheer bulk of the circular skirts and stiff petticoats could be seen to be effective in keeping men at a distance. By contrast, the sheath shape both clung to the body, revealing its curves to the viewer, and simultaneously permitted approach thanks to its more parsimonious occupation of space. By employing these two outlines in a symbolic way, film-makers maintained the 'storytelling wardrobe' tradition, providing information about the characters not overtly spoken.

Two other films of 1959, the year of *Pillow Talk*'s release, clearly establish a costume discourse that carries information about the sexual status of the characters, aligning the wives and virgins on one side of a sartorial divide, and post-virgins on the other. In *Some Came Running* (Vincente Minnelli, 1959) clear-cut distinctions are established between virginal Gwen (Martha Hyer) and party girl, Ginny (Shirley MacLaine) not only through the narrative and performances, but also by opposing the 'touch me not' silhouette employed by the one with the looser, *déshabillé* style of the other. Other female characters in the film are similarly taxonomised through sartorial style: 'Bama's sexy girlfriend and Edith, Frank's secretary who has an affair with him, both wear the post-virginal sheath outline; Frank's chaste daughter, however, wears the full-skirted dresses of the ingénue, as does her mother who, significantly, is seen rejecting her husband's sexual advances. Similarly, in *The Best of Everything* (Jean Negulesco, 1959) attention to the clothes codes that the film sets up makes obvious one character's post-virginal status, which is presented as a plot revelation: whereas the true innocent wears the full-skirted outline even in her office suits. Caroline (Hope Lange) is seen throughout the film in the more figure-hugging form that may permit more movement in the office, but also has sexual connotations due to its tightness and the way it displays the body.

Hollywood thus attempted to represent the unrepresentable: at a time when Production Code and societal mores forbade on-screen representation of sex, dress codes and allusiveness were made to serve the function of dichotomising women as virgins/post-virgins. Significantly, following the general filmic rule that sexually experienced women showed off their bodies in the tight silhouette, the fact that the costumes designed by Jean Louis for Day in *Pillow Talk* are tight and figure-hugging is clearly meant to relay information about her sexual status. By maintaining the emphasis on slim-line clothes that hug and display the body, a look which Turim has identified with the 'sexual warrior' (1984, p. 9), Jean Louis's clothes for Jan align her with cinematic gold-diggers and career girls, rather than sweethearts and wives.

'All those colours and fabrics . . .'[6]

Besides being sexualised via her status as a career woman, there are other signifiers in *Pillow Talk* which help convey the idea that the character played by Day is to be understood as a modern, sophisticated woman about town, i.e. not necessarily a virgin. First, there is her name: 'Jan Morrow' is obviously a play on the name of the French star, Jeanne Moreau, rendered clipped and brisk in American English but still retaining the European connotations of mature adult sexuality. Since the usual films of the two women were not in similar genres, it seems as if the *Pillow Talk* character's name is more a joke specific to the film than to the woman playing her, and intended to signal to the audience that she is an experienced woman.

There are also direct script references about the character's previous experiences, when Jan talks to herself in soliloquy. While her remark, in contemplating 'Rex' with delight, 'You've gone out with a lot of men in your time, but this, this is the jackpot!' does not necessarily confirm that she has had sex with any of the earlier men, it initiates a context in which Jan's familiarity with male company is established. This is supported by the fact that the suggestion that they go away for the weekend together comes from *her* and not from him; her response, when Rex pretends to be shocked at her frankness, that 'we're both over twenty-one', further works to underline her mature and active sexuality: coupling her age with her agency, Jan seems to be telling Rex that she is as post-virginal as a woman of her maturity has a right to be. Finally, the film presents a sung soliloquy, in which Jan incites Rex both to 'make love to me', implying her active desire for him, and to 'kiss me right', establishing the notion of some experiential basis to her demands.

Most noticeable of all, however, is the costume strategy of the film which works to establish Jan's sexual maturity at the same time as remaking Day as an overtly sexualised star. In their design, colours, fabric, numbers and symbolism, the clothes for Jan work hard to showcase the woman's erotic allure. Confirming Jan's position as career woman, for daytime she wears the sheath outline in dress and coat suits, with the dress tight, cut to emphasise the shape of her bust, hips and bottom, and the coat trapezoid, drawing attention to her long legs. The sheath outline is also maintained in her evening outfits; here there is greater emphasis on surplus amount of fabric, as the tight skirt of the evening dress is often built up and supplemented with a skirt-length train and worn with a large sumptuous coat (as in the dazzling emerald green dress and coat outfit worn for the first date with 'Rex').

Throughout the film Jan's clothes are marked by their expensive appearance, rich and vibrant colours, and lack of distracting details. Her suits and accessories are usually vividly colourful, twinning electric blue with black, white with red, pairing two shades of green; this accent on rich colour is maintained in Jan's evening wear – emerald, ruby, dazzling white – with soft fabrics – shiny silk, velvet, soft wool – to contrast with her pale skin and wrap her in tactile cloth. The vivid colours Jan wears for the outside world do not often modulate even when she is alone at home. Her bedroom and lounging wear includes bright turquoise silk Chinese-style pyjamas and a vivid sunshine yellow robe. Within the film, these rich colours speak to her straightforward character, not unfeminine but not fluffy or frilly. They also speak to her pride in and commitment to her work: Jan's position as an interior decorator means that she has to project the image of someone who is daring with colours, fabrics, textures, since through her outfits she is promoting the idea of her professional self. The surprising colour combinations in outfits are therefore there intra-diegetically to confirm her designing proficiency. Steven Cohan has noted that Jan's job gives her access to rich people and it may be that the fabrics' tightness on her body are to sell Jan herself alongside the idea of her professional skill (1997, p. 281). With the spectacular display of different furs, numerous coats, suits, dresses, shoes, handbags, jewels, Jan's outfits are also an investment for herself as well as an advert for her proficiency as an interior designer.

The continuation of the bright-colour motif into her after-work clothes shows that Jan feels no split between her working and off-duty personae: her active, go-ahead, straightforward self finds expression in the clean lines and colours she enjoys at play and at work. However, on a few occasions Jan is seen in nightwear which employs softer shades to suggest she has a gentle side also; besides their softer colourings, pale pink, yellow and blue (neatly matching the blue pyjamas we see Brad in and thus suggesting their eventual couple-dom) the design of the nightwear is noticeable in being frilly, rather out of keeping with the modern, clean lines of Jan's more public outfits. It is possible to see a split in Jan, evident between those costumes she expects to be seen in and these that she clearly does not, these latter outfits presenting a more traditionally feminine side of the character. For example, Jan, when moving around her home when her maid is there, wears bold turquoise silk pyjamas in the then-modish mandarin style (see Shih, 1997, p. 85). When on her own, however, tucked up in bed after first meeting Rex, talking intimately with him on the phone but not seen by anyone, she is in a frilly pink nightie both tied and buttoned up at the neck.

While the day and evening costumes posit a Jan who is modern, straightforward, go-getting, the clothes worn for these more private moments suggest a side of her much more in keeping with other, earlier 'sweetheart' roles played by the star and thus set up a tension in the characterisation which, as shall be examined later, had serious implications for this repackaging of Day.

The White Dress

Symbolically, the film uses Jan's clothes to contrast her with the other characters, especially Brad's other women; the most sustained focus is on Marie, a showgirl who is the willing recipient of Brad's attentions. While the narrative sets them up in similar situations, cutting between the two women in scenes of potential seduction (Marie's invited, Jan's unwilling), the costume strategy goes to some length to demonstrate Jan's superiority, her right to usurp Marie as the appropriate partner for Brad. As the narrative exigencies build to bring the two romantic leads together, with both couples converging on the Copa del Rio, the dresses of the two women are contrasted in a clear schematic: opposing 'artificial' and 'natural'. Marie's obviously dyed dress and hair and coloured beads contrast with the more natural white dress, blonde hair and clear stones of Jan''s outfit. Marie is further connoted as 'display' against Jan's 'restraint' in her showing of her bust and bare arms through their diaphanous tulle coverings. The obvious expensiveness of Jan's real diamonds and pure white fur coat is posited against the man-made blue beads and badly contrasting brown fur Marie carries. The white fabric flower worn at Marie's waist, which has no link thematically with any of the rest of her outfit, hints at an incoherence in dress brought on by lack of taste, in sharp contrast to the unity of Jan's ensemble, again speaking to her role as a decorator who understands the rules of style. Jan's sensuousness is brought out by the soft, yielding nature of the wool dress and this contrasts with the scratchy tulle Marie wears, signalling Jan's commitment to her own erotic pleasure, not just the man's.

Within *Pillow Talk*, the white evening dress also performs functions besides the contrast with Marie: it carries further levels of meaning in speaking to aspects of Jan's character. Outside the film, also, it significantly featured prominently in the studio publicity for the film, thus impacting on the public perception of the refashioning of the Day persona. Crucial within the film's narrative for what it says about the character, and extra-diegetically for what it connotes about the star, this dress merits close scrutiny and analysis. It proclaims its own presence within the scene, as well as being a departure, in its overt sexiness, for Day herself on screen.

The white dress is important for what it says about Jan, the dichotomy in its structure signalling a playful eroticism. Made in pristine bridal white, with the associated colour

The white dress: clad in pristine white, Jan (Doris Day) ignores Brad (Rock Hudson) in *Pillow Talk* (1959)

connotations of purity, the dress seems from the front very prim, as it is ankle length, with no splits which might permit a view of legs, and with a high slash neckline cut close to the throat ruling out the possibility of cleavage. The back view of the dress, however, confounds this primness. The material clings very tightly to Jan's bottom – prompting Brad's pun to himself in seeing 'the other end of your party line' – but above the jiggling derrière the dress is virtually backless. From the front the dress appears to cover her entirely, from top to toe, aided by the fact that Jan wears long white gloves to her elbow; but from behind the material is cut to show lots of her back, and square cut too, like the neckline, not softly rounded or draped, but clean cut. The refusal of drapings or softening in the design pulls the back into coherence with the front of the gown, despite their radical differences in display of flesh, the effect of the severe edges of cloth against the bare skin suggesting a combination of the puritan and the sexy.

The dichotomy within the dress design acknowledges a teasing sensuality in Jan, an awareness of the pleasures of display and concealment; while it speaks to a playfulness in manipulating assumptions, the emphasis on sensuous detail which pleasures *her* (the softness of wool and fur, the frisson of air on the nude back) also signals a mature engagement with sexuality very much at odds with the lasting image of Day as over-ripe virgin.

Side-on to the camera, Jan gives the audience a glimpse of 'the other end' of Brad's party line, as Tony (Nick Adams) looks on (*Pillow Talk*)

The dress is a masterpiece of symbolism, a garment which goes beyond the narrative to embody a multitude of unspoken details about the heroine and the star playing her.

Speaking to different elements within Jan herself, costume within *Pillow Talk* can be seen backing up the script's notion of her as a chic, experienced woman. But it is possible to read the tension in this garment between front and back, concealment and revelation, as an indication of the character's own riven nature, caught between the impulses towards overt sexualisation indicated in her day and evening wear, which put her body clearly on display for the viewer, and her private bed attire in which she seems to revert to a maidenly modesty which acknowledges that no one will see her in bed before marriage.

Despite the glamorous array of outfits that Jan wears throughout the film, she ends it in pyjamas. It is significant that a woman who has been defined by her extensive range of outfits and perfectly matching accessories is seen in the culmination of the film's narrative wearing none of them. Gone are her array of hats, her significant jewellery, her vivid suits and high-heeled shoes: in bare feet, with tousled hair and 'no' (i.e. minimal) make-up, she is carried out of her modish apartment by Brad, wrapped in a blanket. Her positioning in the pyjamas marks the end of her glamorous, exciting life on the town as a career girl: in this climactic scene her vivid suits are missing to confirm that she will not need these clothes again. They have achieved their end: to catch her a mate. The wardrobe of *Pillow Talk* is a study in excess, since the clothes are more exciting than the life she is going to, but that speaks at once to their beauty and flaw: they succeed too well in their job, thus rendering themselves obsolete. It is possible to think about the simultaneous success and failure of the costumes and especially the white dress in the same way, within the wider context of Day's star persona.

'The New Doris Goes Sexy'

Pillow Talk begins its repackaging of Day as Hunter's 'sex image' from the first shot after the opening credits: a close-up on her long leg clad in a nude-coloured stocking, which Day smooths into place idly humming the tune from the title song. This *coup de cinéma* – Doris Day's thigh! – rivets the attention and acts as a proclamation of the birth of the new Doris. The fashionableness and the frequency of costume changes underlines the new investment in the star as an object of glamour, as do the rich fabrics used to dress the character.

The clothes designed for Day by Jean Louis were not the first film outfits worn by the star that were supposed to be modern or alluring; but they were perhaps unique in being both at once. Previous Day roles set in 'the present' had included ones where she was a housewife (*Storm Warning*, Stuart Heisler, 1951) or factory worker (*The Pajama Game*, George Abbott, 1957): here she wore functional outfits which were attractive but did not exhibit the intentional ravishing glamour of the *Pillow Talk* outfits. She had worn an evening dress somewhat like the white dress showcased in *Pillow Talk* in *Teacher's Pet* (George Seaton, 1958) but this black-and-white film does not dwell on the dress or its wearer in the same sensuous way. Finally, she had appeared in intentionally sexy clothes before, but in the period musical biopic, *Love Me Or Leave Me* (Charles Vidor, 1955), where she portrayed Ruth Etting. *Pillow Talk* therefore marked the first moment when modishness, glamour, colour and overt sexual allure all combined. Here was Doris at last being sexy as 'herself': a modern urban woman.

The costume brief from producer Ross Hunter was that the star should wear modish outfits, as the film's script called for Jan to be a chic businesswoman with an 'in' wardrobe (Hotchner, 1976, p. 222). With the clothes for Jan in *Pillow Talk*, Jean Louis did not attempt to create new styles or shapes, but to reproduce high-class and expensive renderings of what was then contemporary fashion: outfits similar to the ones sported by Day can be found in the Sears catalogues from the same period.[7]

Jean Louis's previous celebrated screen designs included the famous dress Rita Hayworth wore for her sultry striptease in *Gilda* (Charles Vidor, 1947), and in all, he designed the outfits for nine of Hayworth's films. The designer was also associated with costuming Marilyn Monroe and Marlene Dietrich, being responsible for the 'nude', sequin-covered dress Monroe wore when singing 'Happy Birthday' to John F. Kennedy, and Dietrich's many concert outfits which gave the implication of the star baring her flesh when in actuality everything was both covered and even held together by the clever layering of tulle. These outfits promote the notion of Jean Louis creating designs which set out to tease and tantalise the viewer with the outline of the female form on display and by the exposure and eroticising of flesh. In *Gilda*, Hayworth's upper arms and bust area become the primary eroticised zone, the rest of her covered in slippery black satin; *Pillow Talk*'s white wool dress, by fetishising Day's 'wild ass' puts the emphasis literally on the reverse of that of a standard evening gown.

Tasked with the project of revamping Day's star persona, the white dress carries out Hunter's determination to reveal the ass 'under all those dirndls'. The rest of the spectacular costumes Jean Louis designed for *Pillow Talk* also plainly sexualise the star in a new way, but with a noticeable trend: while the 'wild ass' may not always be as obviously on show as in the white evening dress, the star's breasts are never afforded the attention that one would associate with a 1950s' film, coming from the decade Marjorie Rosen accused of revealing America's 'mammary madness' (1973, p. 267). While Jean Louis's costumes do show the outline of Day's bust, with the breasts' torpedo-like shape popular at the time, not one costume creates the opportunity for the display of cleavage.

Several reasons for this could be imagined: perhaps Jean Louis was more comfortable designing clothes without the necessity for cleavage display, or perhaps cleavage was not fashionable in 1959. Other 1959 films with costumes designed by him, however, reveal that he was capable of designing costumes that did foreground the female star's chest: several of the costumes made for Lana Turner in *Imitation of Life* (Douglas Sirk, 1959) and Kim Novak in *Middle of the Night* (Delbert Mann, 1959) highlight the breast area. While uncredited on the film itself, Jean Louis was also, according to some sources, the designer responsible for Elizabeth Taylor's costumes in *Suddenly, Last Summer* (Joseph L. Mankiewicz, 1959), in which the well-endowed star is displayed in a variety of dresses which create a showcase for her ample bust.

The existence of other 1959 designs by Jean Louis which do foreground the contemporary obsession with breasts indicates the necessity for reading costume choices in the context of particular stars. Looking at the other female stars mentioned, one finds their sexual allure resting largely on their prominently displayed chests, with Lana the original 'Sweater Girl', Kim a glamour puss and Liz known for cinematic exposure of her (covered) breasts. With Doris, however, there is not that pre-existing association of the star either with overt sexualisation or with chest exposure. In *Pillow Talk* itself, the star at times seems almost flat-chested in some of the scenes; looking at her other films there is no cleavage either, with the possible exception of *Love Me Or Leave Me*. Here the costumes do go out of their way to display chest-area flesh, despite being set in the 1920s when clothes actually downplayed the breast entirely. Perhaps within this film the storytelling wardrobe impetus was observable: while the narrative works very hard to maintain the chastity of the character (she is not to be understood as selling herself to men to get ahead in her music career), the clothes in their overt display of sexualised flesh could be attempting to imply a different and more cynical story.

Molly Haskell interviewed Doris Day for *Ms* magazine in the 1970s, when the star was already beginning to wane. Describing the star, Haskell presents her astonishment on one specific factor in an aside to the reader:

> She has thin, well-proportioned legs, a small waist, and an enormous bust – the biggest shock, because who ever knew she had it? She usually wore the kind of gear – lumberjack shirts, suits or shirtwaist dresses – designed to conceal it . . . (If I had known, in my anxious adolescent years, that Calamity Jane not only had a secret love but also a secret bosom the size of Marilyn Monroe's, I think I would have turned away in misery. She was a tomboy and therefore on one side – my side – of the chasm that separated the 'women' from the 'girls' in the most sexually schizophrenic of decades). (1997, p. 32)

This anecdote suggests that the film's commitment to costumes which do not put Day's cleavage on view, even when she is wearing a low neckline, can thus possibly be attributed to the star herself. Examination of outfits worn by the star in other films and for off-screen public events such as movie premieres and parties also seems to bear out her preference for clothes that do not reveal breast-area flesh. Even dressed for Oscars night in a tightly clinging gown, while the outline of Day's bust is emphasised, the star's flesh remains hidden. A personal sense of modesty, perhaps accompanied by that inability to perceive herself as 'a sex image' which Hunter noted, might therefore feed into Jean Louis's witty back-emphasis gown and the other *Pillow Talk* costumes. Evidently, regardless of who was responsible for them, the costume choices impact both the character and the star playing her. Intra-diegetically, the fact that Jan's body is simultaneously on display (its outline) and hidden (its flesh) hints at tensions within the character herself over sexuality, between restraint and enjoyment. Outside the world of the film, the costumes' privileging of restraint over display could be – and was – read as an obsessive modesty, prudery, 'terminal virginity' (Dowdy, 1973, p. 183).

Conclusion

By the time Day came to play Jan, the connotations evoked by her were firmly in place. *Pillow Talk* attempted to modulate these connotations, while working within the parameters of her established persona. Due to the specific strategy adopted to sexualise and modernise the star which the film's costumes promote, however, it can be seen that insufficient distance was established between the old Doris and the new one: she may have been perceived by some critics to have 'gone sexy' but to others and to the subsequent dominant memory of her, the change was unconvincing.

Day's name beside a character in a cast list always signalled to the audience that the woman she played would be: independent, feisty, energetic, hard-working. These elements were present from her first role, as Georgia Garrett, a perky, wisecracking, gum-chewing chanteuse, in *It's Magic/Romance on the High Seas* (Michael Curtiz, 1948). Examination of Day's performance in this film shows a persona not yet settled: outside of referencing Day's established celebrity as a big-band singer, there is a marked confusion of elements, with the character's easygoing raunchiness sitting uneasily besides her occasional naiveté. Day's perkiness and energy in this performance were inherited by other characters she played while other qualities, such as Georgia's cynicism, coarseness and upfront sexiness, were quickly phased out. Examining one of the many Warner Bros musicals Day starred in during the 1950s, *Tea for Two* (David Butler, 1950), for example, one sees Day's image refined into an archetype of the good girl-next-door. While again there is the enthusiastic performance of songs, the vocal mastery, the persona is softer than when playing Georgia, more innocent, romantic rather than sexual. Despite also playing mothers and wives in other films, these ingénue qualities seemed to be a fixture of the Day persona in the first half of her career. *Pillow Talk* consciously attempted to leave behind the rural girl-next-door, repackaging the star as a modern urban woman. This new accent on the glamour and sexiness of character and star, however, was laid on top of a foundation of the earlier connotations, the independence and feistiness, the hard-working determination to get ahead, seen in *Pillow Talk* through the comfortable lifestyle Jan's business success has earned.

Significantly, the other element which acts as a link to previous portrayals and is still discernible in Day's characterisation of Jan is a suggestion of prudishness; this can be gleaned from her old-maid night attire and from a reading of the film's narrative which privileges effects (Jan departs from the weekend cottage without sleeping with Brad) rather than their causes (Jan has discovered 'Rex's true identity). Coupling her flight with Jan's earlier attempts to fend off Tony's passes, it is possible to see the character as trying to avoid sex, even though the narrative indicates her motives are romantic rather than neurotic. This sex evasion connects to the innocence not out of place in the teenage girls Day had previously played, but which seemed more pathological in a hip, urban sophisticate like Jan.

There is a conflict evident in *Pillow Talk*, in that the film is trying to present a new Doris but also to link her with the old one so that she is a believable incarnation. The costumes of the film are an obvious attempt to refashion the star, but even in their glamour, modishness and overt sexiness simultaneously serve as part of the connection back to the old Doris through their lack of bust emphasis, as the white dress demonstrates. The character's links with the old Day associations confound the attempts of the narrative to promote Jan as a woman with a mature and active sexuality. It is paradoxical that the film moment which launched Day as a sexualised star also, because of its specific strategy of sexualisation, its emphasis on revealing the 'wild ass' rather than the 'secret bosom', resulted in the birth of the mature virgin persona which crystallised as the dominant memory and meaning of the star's persona.

Notes

1. 1951–2 and 1959–63. See 'Women at the Box Office' (Basinger, 1994, pp. 509–10).
2. I am leaving aside for the purposes of clarity at this point the darker films Day starred in which showcased her skills in different ways, for example, *Storm Warning*, *Julie* (Andrew L. Stone, 1956), *The Man Who Knew Too Much* (Alfred Hitchcock, 1956), and *Midnight Lace* (David Miller, 1960). While very obviously having the potential to establish aspects of her persona that would be different from the easygoing girl-next-door, these films were (and perhaps still are) perceived as problematic by fans and critics, in some sense threatening to the idea of the 'real' Day.
3. Anonymous reviewer, *The Hollywood Reporter*, 16 September 1959.
4. The film was number one at the box office for many weeks, and garnered five Academy Award nominations, including one each for Day and the glossy art direction. Day and co-star Rock Hudson both received the Theatre Owners of America Exhibitor's laurel award as the top stars of 1959 for their performances (see Young, 1977, p. 41).
5. 'Two-way chemise dresses . . . Sheath and Bouffant styles . . . Fall/Winter, 1958' (Shih, 1997, p. 115).
6. Brad as 'Rex' attempts to worry Jan about his masculinity by showing an interest in her job.
7. Compare, for example, Jan's white belted wool dress, which she is wearing when Jonathan kisses her, with two items from Sears: '100% Acrilon Jersey Pullover Dress, Relaxed easy fit you shape with the belt' (Fall/Winter, 1957) and 'Rich Wool Flannel Jacketed Dress, Jacket banded all round, bowed in front. Fully lined sheath' (Fall/Winter, 1959) (Shih, 1997, pp. 26, 45).

5

Brad Pitt and George Clooney, the Rough and the Smooth: Male Costuming in Contemporary Hollywood

Pamela Church Gibson

On the cover of *Vanity Fair* for April 2003 is a group portrait of some of the most popular male actors in present-day Hollywood. This image – given the differences of costuming and stance – resembles a recording for posterity of the male members of some extended family, posed carefully at a casual but important gathering – a birthday, an anniversary, whatever. The photograph, taken by Annie Liebowitz, is artfully staged. The central figure in her carefully arranged grouping is Jack Nicholson, wearing dark glasses, a well-cut jacket and open-necked white shirt; looking raffishly elegant, he leans forward, grinning broadly into the lens. He is the Bad Father and Errant Husband of classic Hollywood cinema – a cinematic version of Black Jack Bouvier. Leaning on his shoulder affectionately, and smiling gently at the photographer, is Brad Pitt, here presented as the favourite son, a gentle, artistic boy; his hair falls softly over his shoulders and he has a wispy goatee beard, while he wears a rumpled T-shirt beneath a mismatched velvet jacket. On the other side of Nicholson is Tom Cruise, beaming and athletic in black, short-sleeved shirt and jeans. He could be Pitt's protective, outgoing older brother – good at sports, popular with everybody, putative prom king. Behind Nicholson stands Harrison Ford, grey of hair and correctly dressed – Good Father, Responsible Younger Brother and Reliable Uncle of the older generation within this imagined 'family'. The figure sitting on the floor at the front could be his very own son – Tom Hanks as corporate lawyer off duty, casual but smart in neat shirt and tank top. I describe this picture in such detail because it seems to have, as a subtext, Hollywood's continuing fascination with the father and son problematic, with masculine identity and types of role models, and also to display overtly the diversity and yet congruence of the male star personae that dominate contemporary cinema.

This portrait is not the end of the cover story; it forms the first panel of a fold-out, landscape-format image containing more male stars, again seemingly divergent and yet with certain perceptible similarities, coyly tagged 'It's Reigning Men'. Jude Law, studiedly elegant despite his jeans, in pristine white shirt and beautifully cut navy blue blazer, could have stepped out of a fashion spread – Abby Field, in the story of the shoot, describes Law as 'an exception to the rule that a young male movie star must always dress like a mechanic from San Bernadino' (Tabach-Bank and Field, 2003, p. 128).

Sprawled across the front of the panels is a languid Hugh Grant; he exemplifies the classic Wayward Bachelor, the smooth Ladies' Man. Clooney, the other archetypal

Lounge Lizard of contemporary Hollywood, is, strangely, absent from this particular line-up, this roll-call of polarised archetypes – heroes and attractive villains, fathers and sons, the smoothly suave and the down-home, blue-collar guys who dominate contemporary Hollywood and, arguably, are part of a complex trajectory within its history. So confused are contemporary ideals and ideas around and concerning masculinity that these hybrid yet interrelated personae are both necessary and familiar. Cinematic icons, on and off screen, reflect current bewilderment and the need for reassurance together with a wish for fashion leaders whose style makes some clear statement about the particular form of masculinity they embody.

Certainly the dress codes found within this picture encapsulate current trends; this declared aim of the typical younger movie star 'to look like a mechanic', a style often consciously deployed within the diegeses of contemporary Hollywood, has found its way into the vocabulary of current street fashion. In clubs, pubs and bars, it is possible to see just how many young white men have adopted this particular look. But the uniformity of their dress does not necessarily indicate any uniformity of attitude – unless it be con-fusion about their social role and the behaviour now expected of them. And of course, there is their new worry about their own looks, their faces and bodies; men are finding that a set of standards and norms, similar to those by which they have judged women for so long, are now applicable to them. It is equally harsh, youth-dominated and nar-row in its focus. As Tim Edwards observes,

> The positive or valorized images of masculinity remain, despite variations, primarily young and white, slim and trim ... a hierarchy of masculinities is emerging, according to image and appearance, where young white men with pumped-up pecs, strong jaw-lines and flat stomachs rule over the rest with a phallocentric intensity. (1997, p. 130)

This description of the dominant ideal of male desirability perfectly describes Brad Pitt, one of the two contemporary icons considered here. This particular male image was reinforced, if not created, within the world of advertising, in the so-called 'menswear revolution' of the 1980s (Mort, 1996; Nixon, 1998; Simpson, 1996).

The other star examined here is George Clooney, Pitt's antithesis and co-star in *Ocean's Eleven* (Steven Soderbergh, 2001), a seminal text and perfect model of current codes of costuming in contemporary Hollywood. Clooney's omission from the line-up of 'reigning men' is odd, given the power he currently wields within Hollywood and his considerable popularity. He represents the primary contrasting type or 'variation'; he is, perhaps, no longer 'young', but he fits in perfectly with the debonair Lotharios who also hold sway within current cinematic narratives, the 'smooth' men who are not, necess-arily, the cloth from which an ideal father can be cut, but who are presented as possessing undeniable appeal for women.

(Overleaf) The rough and the smooth personified, or two ways with a suit and shades (*Ocean's Eleven*, 2001)

Clooney is invariably seen on screen fully clothed; he is the suited hero, the antithesis of the rugged, bare-chested man so ready for action. The suited hero, of course, harks back to an earlier era in the history of Hollywood. He may indeed possess the 'pumped-up pecs' needed to meet today's exacting standards of male beauty – but his body is in the main outlined by his clothes, sheathed rather than stripped. Unlike the body of Pitt, that of Clooney is not presented to us as fetishistic spectacle. It is, rather, hinted at – tantalising glimpses may be provided and the contours be clear at moments, but the effect of conventional 'smart' menswear – sports jacket and slacks as well as the suit – is to shroud and to sheath. Interestingly, when his body was first, briefly, revealed on screen, as he prepared to seduce Jennifer Lopez in *Out of Sight* (Steven Soderbergh, 1998), he was wearing pristine white boxer shorts, which he did not remove. Neither did the matinée idols of classic Hollywood – and, like them, Clooney is Eternal Bachelor, whereas Pitt is often cast as husband material, his off-screen lifestyle reinforcing this notion.

Masculinity and Its New Configurations: From *Fight Club* to *Ocean's Eleven*

Debates around masculinity are currently centre stage – within cinema studies, the arguments that Steve Neale initiated (1983) now figure prominently, with anthologies appearing apace. Many of them, sadly, ignore dress codes – just as literature within cultural studies too often neglects the influence of film. Meanwhile, cinematic texts themselves seek to show us increasingly complex narratives of masculinity – while at the same time trying to offer up solutions or models. *Fight Club* (David Fincher, 1999) features Ed Norton as corporate man – white-collar educated, besuited and bored, who is forced to dream up a 'rough trade' alter ego to be what he wants to be, do what he wants to do. Significantly Pitt, that same alter ego, explains his creation by Norton as the man who can 'fight the way you want to fight, fuck the way you want to fuck'. This is no slur on 'smooth' man's sexual prowess; Norton is near-nerd, not 'smooth' man at all. Announcing early on in the film that 'We're a generation of men raised without fathers', Pitt devotes his energy to providing a way for such men to reconfigure their destabilised male identities.

In so many Hollywood films today the central relationship of the film is that between two male protagonists – buddies or enemies, mismatched workmates or genuine siblings, surrogate father and longed-for son – and invariably, the bonds between them form the emotional epicentre of the film. The relationship between Pitt's character, Rusty, in *Ocean's Eleven* and his friend and co-conspirator, the suave Danny Ocean (Clooney) is just as significant as that between Danny and his ex-wife, Tess (Julia Roberts). 'We ought to find Rusty a girlfriend,' Tess tells Danny when they are finally reunited in the closing moments of the film. Rusty's reply 'There's a women's prison right down the road,' is good-humoured but disingenuous – Rusty will remain with Danny (and Tess) whatever relationships with women he may or may not initiate.

Both men are splendidly costumed – often besuited – throughout, but significantly they wear their suits with a difference, marking clearly their 'rough' and 'smooth' personae. Pitt's hair is contemporary in cut, spiky and gelled; he munches on junk food throughout, undercutting and democratising the glamour of his outfits. But Clooney, even when stripped down to vest and jeans for the heist that forms the plotline, is still effortlessly elegant in black co-ordinates. And when released from prison in the opening scenes, he is wearing the dinner jacket in which he was arrested – with the untied bow tie slung around his neck like a scarf. The jacket itself is a very dark navy blue, with a satin lapel; this particular sartorial style was initiated by the Duke of Windsor, fashion leader of the 1920s. In the scene around the poker table, where he is reunited with Rusty after three years in prison, he wears a black polo sweater under matching sports jacket, further confining and hiding his body from view, while Pitt, although he is wearing a co-ordinating tie with his silky beige shirt, soon discards it and runs a hand up through his hair, rendering himself rumpled, vulnerable.

Ocean's Eleven is particularly interesting in terms of contemporary costuming and of the argument advanced within this essay, for we have here, at the forefront of the film, these two central archetypes of cinema today, as sketched out within this essay – the sophisticated man and the man seemingly without artifice. Furthermore, they are located within an all-male group, the members of whom are brought together by Danny and Rusty to carry out the heist, and who form a kind of shambolic family, a group of ill-assorted, squabbling, racially mixed siblings who have an elderly 'uncle' in the retired conman, Saul (Carl Reiner) and a surrogate grandfather, Reuben, the casino owner (Elliott Gould). Andy Garcia, who plays the villain, Terry Benedict – the owner of the three largest casinos in Las Vegas, who has bought Reuben's own former casino in order to raze it to the ground, and who is now living with Tess – has extremely stylish clothes. In fact, they are too perfect, too artfully arranged – always a sign of danger. Stella Bruzzi has written the definitive account of gangster style and its inherent 'instabilities' (1997,

Different strokes for different folks – contrasting models of masculinity (*Ocean's Eleven*)

pp. 67–95). From the moment we see Garcia, with his slicked-back hair, expressionless face, black suit, high-buttoned waistcoat and tie, his watch-chain and the slim black case he carries, we are convinced of the truth of Reuben's warning words 'He'll kill you – and then he'll go to work on you.' For where Clooney is debonair, Garcia is terrifyingly dapper – there is something insouciant in Clooney's self-presentation, whereas Garcia is so immaculate it is chilling. Later outfits reinforce his status as arch-villain who has purchased Tess, just as surely as the Bracque painting he has bought for his gallery at her instigation, and who has chosen many of her clothes: the Nehru-collared linen jackets both wear as they inspect the canvas, the matching cream outfits with long coats donned for the public demolition of Reuben's former much-loved casino, and Garcia's own brocade waistcoats and heavily patterned silk ties, plus a wing-collared shirt and white tie that he wears to watch a prizefight. We are, therefore, unsurprised when he agrees to the suggestion that he release Tess from their relationship in exchange for the return of his stolen millions. Here is a man whose suits and formal attire conceal a real, psychotic menace – not, as with Clooney, the pleasures and promise of his hidden physicality.

This film is not only a template for the current state of Hollywood costuming; it was very popular at the box office, and, as with so many films intended primarily to reach the main target audience – young (eighteen to twenty-four) and male – it was picked up by the fashion and style magazines targeted at the young male consumer. This is perhaps the moment for some reflection on the socio-cultural implications of men's fashions past and present – together with a consideration of the precise meanings of the suit and the recent growth of oppositional styles around and in relation to it.

Suits, Sexuality and the New Oppositional Chic

The suit – analysed carefully and constantly by those working on the cultural significance of fashion – both sheaths and conceals. But above all, surely, it renders the male body totally inaccessible, something no-one has yet mentioned. Zippered in, buttoned up, it is thus presented to the world as a monolithic, even phallic, block. The tie is another phallic hint, but again the phallus is inaccessible, controlled, regulated, just as the tie is carefully knotted. Conversely, significantly, since the 60s, women's clothes have made their bodies increasingly visible objects of desire – and more than ever accessible. The disappearance of protective undergarments, the exposure of so many erogenous zones simultaneously, the proffering of so much flesh; women are constantly visible, available.

However, since the 80s, when the lucrative power of the young male consumer was identified and targeted as never before, we have become accustomed to the visibility of the male body – which, interestingly, coincided with the suit becoming a fashionable outfit, desired by the young, rather than connoting the stuffy, bureaucratic adult world. The 'buff' male torso first appeared in Calvin Klein advertisements and in fashion spreads, tucked away within the pages of magazines, but it moved swiftly onto billboards and television screens. It is now a familiar sight, used to advertise everything from Nike sportswear to soft drinks. It has become just as much an object of commodification as the female body before it – and one of emulation, with a tranche of glossy magazines now available – to show the man whose body is far from perfect ways in which he might seek to remedy the situation.

The 'rough' image, personified by Pitt and currently so fashionable – for the bodies of the Calvin Klein models are now offset by designer stubble and tousled hair – renders the male body available, as opposed to the protection provided by the concealing, sheathing suit. Jeans hug the buttocks, T-shirts reveal the biceps and pectoral muscles, the chest may be bared or visible through an unbuttoned shirt, and tousled hair hints at body hair beneath. The 'rough' star constantly disrobes – while the suited man, personified by Clooney, is usually kept from view, the hints of his physical strength shown through shots of arms, hands and the occasional topless moment, always an integral part of the plot and invariably fleeting. Lastly, of course, the 'rough' look suggests not only the man of action but more importantly the blue-collar worker and proletarian roots.

The suit indicated, historically, that its wearer was either a man of leisure and wealth, or a member of the rapidly expanding professional middle classes. Since its revival it has had 'aspirational' associations; in the Thatcherite economic boom, the young man of working-class origins with a City job could purchase the high-street suits swiftly made available. Chenoune suggests that the suit was revived in a very particular way; with the spread of sportswear across class and generation, front-pleated, fluid trousers became popular for business wear, as did looser jackets – a move that started on the streets and was quickly assimilated by designers, culminating in Armani's enormously influential unstructured jackets. 'The goal of unstructured garments was to make suits and jackets lighter and more comfortable, putting an end to the sartorial schizophrenia of white-collar professionals' (Chenoune, 1993, p. 292).

These changes did not mean that the split between work and leisure disappeared – nor that class differences in dress are no longer significant. Diane Crane, the only fashion scholar to have chronicled carefully the relationship between dress and social class, sees the changes of the 1980s differently:

> Despite recent changes in executive dress codes, two very different clothing cultures remain in effect, one representing the world of work and the other ... the world of leisure. Clothes in the workplace mark social hierarchies very precisely. Leisure clothing, by contrast, tends to blur social class differences. Rich and poor participate in the same stylistic world, which is dominated by images from popular culture and the entertainment media. (2001, p. 178)

It is against these changing patterns that we should place contemporary Hollywood costuming, which as I have argued has a 'sartorial schizophrenia' of its own, with a different cultural agenda. The two contrasting modes of self-presentation found in contemporary cinema, located within a dual trajectory of male typology, have their roots in the 1950s. During this decade, the classic Hollywood hero was joined on screen by a new type of male star. The 'oppositional' look, first seen on these stars – Marlon Brando, James Dean, Montgomery Clift – has since been widely adopted and is no longer associated with youthful rebellion. Brando claimed to be the first to have adopted garments intended for agricultural labour, heavy industry and military service as ordinary day wear; he accused Dean of having stolen his trademark 'slob' look and used it for his on-screen costumes.

The Naked and the Dressed

The most significant tenet in the literature on menswear has been discussed by Stella Bruzzi in her chapter in this collection. It is Flügel's notion of 'the Great Masculine Renunciation' (1930, p. 110), the assertion that at the end of the eighteenth century men rejected fashionable dress, which became thereafter exclusively feminine. Others have refined Flügel's idea and taken it in different directions, tying it in more specifically with the rise of industrial capitalism, the increasing power and influence of the professional middle classes and the triumph of the Protestant work ethic, or even refuted it (Craik, 1994; Wilson, 2001).

However, sumptuous garments and other aspects of ostentatious self-presentation did become gender-specific in the late eighteenth century, while fashionable men adopted the three-piece suit, a static and utilitarian form of dress which has remained remarkably similar for over two hundred years.

Anne Hollander, however, suggests that the notion of the 'renunciation' is 'far too easy' (1994, p. 22), for men were embracing a style which was to embody modernism, to remain highly desirable – and which would be emulated by women. She argues that the suit is not only stylish, but, in its controlled way, sexy – an argument which I have here taken much further. Hollander sees the suit as hinting at the body beneath, emphasising its contours – since clothes may 'unconsciously imitate and mock bodily forms' (Ibid., p. 36), so she sees the suit as the '3D casing of the body of the antique male hero'. Tailors, she argues, set out to create 'an abstract statue of the naked hero' of classical antiquity (Ibid., p. 86) – the suit as body cast. She emphasises the 'nude suggestion' (Ibid., p. 112) but it is that of the body; I would argue, however, that the 'cast' of the torso is, rather, a 'cast' of the phallus itself; today, when the unsheathed torso is everywhere, surely the suit is robust condom rather than cast, the torso/phallus inaccessible rather than available.

Class and Change

The rise of 'youth cultures' and the young stars of the cinema initiated changes in menswear, and the 1960s, that decade of social mobility, saw more widespread changes. Now, the anti-heroes of the 1950s were superseded by a new form of hero.

Dean was always outsider and misfit, complex and problematic, moody and difficult, but as today's journalistic cliché has it, he was in touch with his feminine side. The first scene in Rebel Without a Cause shows him wrapping his coat around the shivering Plato (Sal Mineo), and there are the flowers in the milk bottle with which he attempts to liven up his shanty-dwelling when Elizabeth Taylor comes to tea in Giant (George Stevens, 1956). However, no-one could accuse Brando of being in touch with his feminine side – and while Stanley Kowalski may be blue-collar sexuality personified, he is most emphatically not a hero. Heroes of the 1960s were more macho and cool than Dean, less sulky and antagonistic than Brando – and often authentically blue-collar in their own right. The contact with their feminine side would come with their successors, after the changes wrought by feminism and the moves by advertising executives to identify and target the 'New Man'.

Steve McQueen, real-life 'garage mechanic', who continued to service his own vehicles, was arguably the first of this new type of hero, the first to dress and behave in a qualitatively different way. The trends he set continue to the present day, on and off screen. He is currently the face of Tag Heuer watches, expensive toys demanded by today's would-be men of action. He had acted in various films before *The Magnificent Seven* (John Sturges, 1960). Supposedly Yul Brynner's sidekick here, it was his appearance to which the audience responded and which made him a star. In *The Great Escape* (John Sturges, 1963) McQueen plays Hilts, a laconic American loner who spends most of his time in solitary confinement. When the mass breakout takes place, he participates in the necessary teamwork – and then takes off, commandeering a motorbike on which he reaches the Swiss border. Having vaulted the lower level of barbed wire, he tries to jump the motorbike over the final barrier that forms the last obstacle to freedom. Here as throughout the film, his clothes were of the moment – indeed dateless. Everybody else is correctly dressed in uniform – only he wears, anachronistically, blue T-shirt and chinos. But what gave him his extra edge was the fact that he performed most of his stunts himself. It was known that he was a real-life Action Man, who spent his time fixing and racing cars and motorbikes. In other words, unlike his predecessors Brando and Dean, who adopted a blue-collar image to reflect their oppositional stance, McQueen was possessed of authentic proletarian origins. In *The Thomas Crown Affair* (Norman Jewison, 1968), he escapes from the boredom of his wealthy existence not only through masterminding the heist around which the film is built, but by exchanging his elegant business suits (and his ironic comment on the dress of corporate post-Renunciation Man, the fob watch which he wears) for sports clothes. He is seen gliding, racing a dune buggy and playing polo. Both work outfits and the nature of his preferred activities make an interesting comparison with Pierce Brosnan in the 1996 remake of the film. Brosnan – 'smooth man' – is impeccably tailored, as in his Bond roles. As the 'reconstructed' Thomas Crown, Brosnan doesn't feel any need to swap his work clothes for play clothes – when he is seen off-duty he plays golf in elegant slacks and sweater. The one rogue action – when he deliberately overturns an expensive catamaran during a yachting race – is done while wearing the traditional yachting clothes of American WASPS.

The change in the ending is also worthy of comment. McQueen's Crown demanded that the heroine choose – either love or money – and decamped, leaving her sobbing. But in 1996, Brosnan's hero pretends to do the same – then appears in the seat behind her when she is sadly and dutifully flying home. It seems that our stories, like our heroes, must be without McQueen's harshness.

While filming *The Getaway* (Sam Peckinpah, 1972), McQueen began an off-screen affair with his co-star, Ali McGraw. Within the text, there is a memorable scene in which, discovering her infidelity, he slaps her hard across the face, not once but several times.

It was rumoured that the filming of this scene formed a prelude to the physical con-summation of their relationship – McGraw, the middle-class girl, was thrilled by the discovery that the 'rough' exterior concealed a truly rough temperament and was excited by his seemingly genuine violence. Later it would form a central part of her divorce plea.

If McQueen, however, was the 'real thing', today's rough-looking heroes must con-ceal beneath an unruly exterior a soft heart, a very different persona. Their exterior must figure forth their robust physicality, their ability to carry out dangerous tasks and to fight if necessary to defend their women or children – but within the butch clothing, now become designer dishevelment, they must be new men, reconstructed men, able to express and articulate their feelings. Ideal husband material, in fact – and in the era of celebrity culture, of endless magazine stories and tabloid headlines, there is a conflation of the star's on-screen persona with their well-documented off-screen personal lives. Celebrity-led journalism means the dissemination of much extra-diegetic material, which the stars bring with them as baggage to their films. Here the prominence of Pitt as the 'rough' and Clooney as the suave heartbreaker is easily explained.

'Beautiful Brad' versus 'Gorgeous George' – Divergent Siblings?

Pitt is a much softer McQueen for the new millennium – and his personal life is exem-plary. Through his marriage to Jennifer Aniston, Pitt forms part of that new unit, the 'celebrity couple'. He seems to be genuinely uxorious and will talk happily to interview-ers of his desire for children, his love of stability. *Vanity Fair* (1998) put him on their cover in jeans and white T-shirt – then included an editorial which praised Pitt for his real-life physical strength and bravery. During the drive back from location shooting, the weather changed dramatically – and Pitt took over the wheel of the hired jeep, driving the terri-fied magazine staff to safety.

Like McQueen, he had played several roles before one film captured the public imagination. In *Thelma and Louise* (Ridley Scott, 1991) he is only on screen for ten min-utes or so. However, wearing a cowboy outfit with a Stetson pulled low over his forehead, he seems to be paying sartorial homage to both James Dean and to McQueen himself. But it was the sex scene with Geena Davis that was most memorable. He appears on her doorstep, dripping wet, and within minutes she has had the first vagi-nal orgasm of her life. The scene is notable for the way in which the two bodies are presented to the spectator. In an inversion of Hollywood norms, we see far more of his body than we do of hers. His perfectly proportioned, honed, toned torso fills the screen – the camera lingers lovingly upon it. It is both erotic object and offered to us for aes-thetic appreciation – for it is posed and lit to resemble, at moments, a Greek statue on display in a well-appointed museum. It is there as fetishised object in every way – for sexual pleasure or more demure appreciation. Cinema has perhaps finally incorporated the 'homospectorial gaze' (Nixon, 1998, p. 83).

A River Runs through It (Robert Redford, 1992) is set in Montana in 1910 – given fashion's inability to escape from its involvement with 'retro' and its endless recycling of the past, Pitt looks as if he would fit perfectly into a Ralph Lauren fashion shoot. In *Legends of the Fall* (Edward Zwick, 1994) he is back in Montana in 1913, as Tristan, wild sibling with rugged exterior and good heart. He falls in love with his younger brother's fiancée – she admires him, as do we, while he wrestles with bears, rides horses, shoots perfectly. Again he is dressed in authentic period costume that is curiously of the moment – the long gabardine coat he wears resembles the Drizabone mackintosh, imported from Australia in the early 1990s. With the outbreak of World War I, the action shifts to France, where the younger brother dies. But Tristan does nothing as ignoble as to return and claim his brother's wife for himself. He avenges his brother, takes his heart back to Montana for burial – and disappears into the wilds.

In *Se7en* (David Fincher, 1995) he is loving young husband and rookie detective, tie askew and hair spiked-up, paired with the much older Morgan Freeman, tidily dressed, well educated and ultimately paternalistic. *Fight Club* is interesting in terms of both consumption and spectacle. 'Tyler Durden' is supposedly unfashionable and has declared war on consumerism. Yet Pitt is, paradoxically, the epitome of thrift-shop chic – and once again the torso is proffered up that we may gaze upon it. There is a deliberate, gradual mutilation of face and body as if to prove that this spectacle can withstand anything – blood streams from his nose, his eyes are blackened, his nose broken, his teeth chipped. In *Snatch* (Guy Ritchie, 2000), his body is decorated with an elaborate pattern of Celtic tattoos. So often stripped, so frequently venerated – no wonder he was chosen to play Achilles in *Troy* (Wolfgang Petersen, 2004). Only for his wedding did Pitt don designer clothes – and he has refused advertising contracts; Clooney has, however, accepted one – he became the face of Police sunglasses. His clothed body replaced the naked torso of David Beckham on posters and hoardings. Perhaps, in the circling of rough and smooth, the latter is temporarily in the ascendant.

Clooney had languished in televisual doldrums, or made forgettable films such as *Return of the Killer Tomatoes* (John de Bello, 1988) until cast as Dr Ross in the television show *ER* (1994–). The character he played encapsulated the 'smooth' persona – Ross was lady killer incarnate. In the film *One Fine Day* (Michael Hoffman, 1996), he played a feckless divorced father – smooth-talking, well dressed and irresistible to women. He can look extraordinarily dapper in army uniform – as in *The Peacemaker* (Mimi Leder, 1997) *The Thin Red Line* (Terrence Malick, 1998) and *Three Kings* (David O. Russell, 1999). In *Out of Sight* he is a debonair bank robber; in *O Brother, Where Art Thou?* (Joel Coen, 2000) he shows the ability to send up this same persona. On the run from a chain gang, he seeks out the correct pomade needed to keep up smooth appearances, one trademarked 'Dapper Dan', and sleeps with his hair in a net. The same self-mocking strain is present in *Intolerable Cruelty* (Joel Coen, 2003), which begins with a close-up of his perfect white teeth as they undergo cosmetic dentistry. He does try, occasionally, to do blue-collar roles – as in *The Perfect Storm* (Wolfgang Petersen, 2000) and *Welcome to Collinwood* (Anthony Russo, 2002), but he looks here rather as if he were in fancy dress – he seems less dressed up, paradoxically, when in his usual smart turnout. Off screen, Clooney's persona matches his most effective roles – there have been many girlfriends, but there is no wife and no ties. The frequent magazine profiles emphasise his understated chic, his ability to look well dressed even in shorts and T-shirt and his 'old-fashioned' charm and sexuality.

Suave man and rugged man circle each other, in cinema, in magazines, in advertising campaigns. With the Oscar ceremonies the world's foremost catwalk show, fashion and film are inextricably intertwined. In the mind of the fashion designer and the stylist, 'rough' and 'smooth' are there to rotate on a seasonal basis. It is for film scholarship to decide exactly what the co-existence and continued popularity of these two archetypes might mean and to predict their survival within the currency of popular culture.

6

Samuel L. Jackson:
Beyond the Post-Soul Male

Russell White

Over the course of a career spanning thirty years, Samuel L. Jackson has established himself as one of the best-known and most popular actors currently working in Hollywood
cinema. The recent Channel 4 television poll to find the '100 Greatest Actors of All Time',
for example, placed Jackson at number 11 ahead of Morgan Freeman (at 27), Denzel
Washington (28), Will Smith (51), Sidney Poitier (52), Eddie Murphy (67) and Wesley
Snipes (96). While such polls are notoriously fickle in the way in which they privilege the
present day and, as such, need to be approached with caution, his presence as the highest placed African-American in the list is testimony to his popularity and reputation as
a character actor and star. However, while Jackson can clearly be bracketed with the
likes of Washington, Freeman, Snipes and Fishburne (if not Smith who is the first genuine African American star of the 'hip-hop generation'), he does embody a different
model of black masculinity to these other stars. More specifically, I want to contend here
that the on-screen and off-screen personae presented by Jackson represent a heavily
ironic and performative move beyond the so-called 'soul' and 'post-soul' constructions
of black maleness identified by African-American scholars in particular.

The term 'post-soul' was coined by Nelson George to describe a shift in the 'tenor of
African-American culture' away from 'the "we-shall-overcome" tradition of noble struggle' to a 'time of goin-for-mine materialism' (1992, p. 1). The emergence of this
'post-soul' sensibility is, in many ways, concomitant with what Cornel West has identified as the rise of an increasingly nihilistic take on the black condition and the black
experience within working-class black urban communities and young working-class
males especially. In his influential essay, 'Nihilism in Black America', published in his 1993
book *Race Matters*, West defines this outlook as 'the lived experience of coping with
a life of horrifying meaninglessness, hopelessness and (most important) loveless-ness'
(p. 14). For West and George, the experiences of desegregation and de-industrialisation,
together with continued political and economic disenfranchisement, have led many
young working-class African-Americans to abandon any hope of 'a better tomorrow'.
One of the ways in which this shift from 'soul' to 'post-soul' can be traced is through
changing modes and representations of black masculinity in black-identified popular culture. Where the 'soul' male was politically engaged, responsible and disciplined, the
'post-soul' male is politically disengaged, retributive and, as West would have it,

fundamentally loveless. This perspective has been used to explain the often explicit violence, misogyny and homophobia that underpin certain types of rap music (most obviously gangsta rap) and the so-called 'gangsploitation' films produced by the new wave of African-American film-makers that emerged at the end of the 1980s and early 1990s.

Jackson's history and background are consistent with cultural perceptions of the soul-identified male. Born in 1948, Jackson grew up in Tennessee during the Civil Rights era. In the 1960s, Jackson attended Morehouse University in Atlanta where he became active in student politics. He was suspended from Morehouse in 1969 for his part in a student sit-in that involved taking hostage several members of the Board of Trustees. That he lived through and played an active part in one of the most tumultuous periods in America's recent history lends him kudos among politically motivated sections of the black community. Indeed, in this regard, he shares similarities with some of rap music's elder statesmen such as Public Enemy's Chuck D. The respect afforded Jackson is to some extent contingent on discourses of authenticity as they have been conceived and conceptualised in relation to black-identified popular culture. As Stuart Hall points out in his often cited 1992 essay 'What Is This "Black" in Black Popular Culture?', authenticity in black popular culture is based on lived experience. The experience of living through the era of Civil Rights and Black Power ensures that Jackson's standing is powerfully anchored for the contemporary audience.

Adding to this authority is Jackson's background in drama and, particularly, the Black Arts movement that articulated and expressed many of the principles of Black Power. In 1977, Jackson moved to New York, where he joined the Negro Ensemble Company and the New York Shakespeare Company. That he was apprenticed in the theatre before embarking on a career in films again lends him credibility. It is also worth noting here that stardom has come to Jackson relatively late in his career. The notion of 'paying one's dues' or 'coming up', as the vernacular would have it, is a powerful one in black culture. It also helps to explain his well-documented criticisms of those rap stars who have attempted to make a too quick transition from music to film with often mixed results. Jackson's general reluctance to appear in films with rap stars is based on a suspicion that, for them, acting is a 'whim'.[1] As interviews with Jackson make clear, he considers acting to be a 'craft' that needs to be worked on and honed. Interestingly, the fact that in the early 1990s Jackson changed the way he was billed from Sam Jackson to the much more formal Samuel L. Jackson, seems to indicate a desire to be seen by the audience as a serious actor.

However, all this stands in apparent opposition to the fact that Jackson's late career popularity has evidently been founded on two ultra-stylised representations of black male-ness: the bible-quoting hitman, Jules Winnfield in *Pulp Fiction* (Quentin Tarantino, 1994) and gun-runner, Ordell Robbie in *Jackie Brown* (Quentin Tarantino, 1997). It was certainly these roles which ensured and cemented Jackson's shift from a well-respected character actor to an established star and style icon. Moreover, it is in the stylisations of Jules and Ordell that Jackson explores and performs constructions of 'post-soul' masculinity, something vitally represented in how he looks, walks, and talks as a black man.

As such, I will focus on these films and then on John Singleton's remake of the 1970s' 'blaxploitation' classic, *Shaft* (2000), a movie in which Jackson's newly minted 'post-soul persona' totally inhabits the title role.

Blaxploitation Cinema and Post-Soul Black Popular Culture

Just as post-soul derives from soul, so the depiction of black maleness apparently epit-omised by Jackson cannot be understood without reference to the so-called 'blaxploitation' cinema of the early to mid-1970s.[2] Blaxploitation presented the first popular redefinition of the types of roles open to African-Americans (especially male) in American cinema and broke the mould of earlier, more supine black characterisations such as those offered by Sidney Poitier and Harry Belafonte. Films such as *Sweet Sweet-back's Baadasssss Song* (Melvin Van Peebles, 1971), *Shaft* (Gordon Parks Snr, 1971) and *Superfly* (Gordon Parks Jnr, 1972) – in many ways the 'Holy Trinity' of blaxploitation movies – featured strong black protagonists 'getting one over' the white man. It is unsur-prising, then, that such characters as John Shaft, Youngblood Priest, Cleopatra Jones and Foxy Brown, along with the actors who played them, (former *Ebony* model Richard Roundtree, Ron O'Neal, Tamara Dobson and Pam Grier) became such role and style models for African-American youth during the 1970s. That said, blaxploitation is often criticised for its crude portrayal of the ghetto as a crime-ridden hell and for effectively replacing one set of black stereotypes (servants, slaves) with another (pimps, pushers, studs, hot mamas). While such accounts often ignore blaxploitation's use of parody, sub-version and humour, these films do provide an early example of the nihilistic sensibility which characterises what cultural critic Mark Anthony Neal (2002), drawing on Nelson George, has termed the 'post-soul aesthetic'.

Such aesthetics can clearly be seen at work in the movies of the new wave of young African-American film-makers which emerged at the end of the 1980s and beginning of the 1990s. Following on the success of Spike Lee, many clearly took their cue from the blaxploitation movies of their own youth. Indeed, films like *Menace II Society* (Allen Hughes, 1993) and *Juice* (Ernest Dickerson, 1992) were quickly labelled 'gangsploita-tion' films by some, in recognition of the way in which they depicted graphic violence and dealt in crude stereotypes that saw black men as 'gang bangers' and black women as 'welfare queens'. Perhaps the best example of blaxploitation's legacy, however, lies not in cinema but in hip-hop. West Coast gangsta artists like Snoop Dogg, Too $hort and Dru Down have looked to blaxploitation films for inspiration, incorporating samples from films like *The Mack* (Michael Campus, 1973) and *Superfly* into their recordings. Moreover, these artists have adopted the identity and personae of the pimp and the mack seen in these films.[3] The video for Snoop Dogg's 'Doggy Dogg World', which sees Snoop resplendent in fedora and fur-lined trench coat – an exaggerated version of the literary and cinematic pimp's costume – and which features cameos from, among others, Pam Grier, Fred Williamson and Antonio Fargas is wonderfully indicative in this regard.

It is not just black artists that have been inspired by blaxploitation however. Both *Pulp Fiction* and *Jackie Brown* have been described as nouveau blaxploitation films (even though *Jackie Brown* is based on Elmore Leonard's *Rum Punch*). The link between

Tarantino's oeuvre and classic blaxploitation cinema is acknowledged by Manohla Dargis, who suggests that *Pulp Fiction*, in particular, 'repopularised a vision of black male-ness not seen since 1970s Blaxploitation' (1996, p. 7). Tarantino's engagement with and utilisation of the tropes associated with blaxploitation is part of a wider project of recuperation. Cultural magpie and pop culture aficionado that he is, Tarantino's recuperative projects take the form of investing value in cultural forms that have comparatively little cultural capital and, as such, can be considered as prime examples of kitsch.[4]

Though clearly fluent in the cultural codes of black culture, Tarantino's embrace of blaxploitation tropes has been widely criticised – not least by Spike Lee, who objected most of all to the liberal use of the culturally taboo term 'nigger' by a white film-maker. Lee's criticisms tap into widely documented histories of black representation within American popular cinema, which have seen white film-makers present black people in ways that are clearly derogatory and two-dimensional. While gangsta rappers have attempted to rehabilitate the word, stripping it of its historical usage as a racial epithet and re-coding it as a term of respect, this remains a deeply problematic term for whites to use. Gangsta rappers' recoding of 'nigga' (signalled linguistically through the replacing of 'er' at the end of the word with 'a') represents an attempt to reverse the negative connotations attached to the post-soul male and thus an attempt to recuperate postsoul masculinity.

Whatever the intentions of gangsta rappers, however, many black commentators believe that white artists should steer clear of deploying the term at all, something acknowledged by linguist, Geneva Smitherman, who suggests that 'widespread controversy rages about . . . whether or not whites can have license to the [the term]' (1977, p. 168). Smitherman and Lee's objections are based on an essentialist understanding of blackness, which suggests that only black people truly understand the nuances and tropes of black culture. To be fair to Tarantino, however, he is much more careful in the way in which he deploys the term 'nigga' than Lee suggests or acknowledges.

In *Jackie Brown*, for example, it is noticeable that the term is only ever used by Jackson or by blaxploitation icon Pam Grier and never by the characters played by Robert De Niro, Bridget Fonda, Michael Keaton or Robert Forster. Clearly, then, Tarantino is, at the very least, aware of these debates. In his performance of post-soul masculinity, Jackson shows that blackness is a culturally constructed item, capable of amendment and evolution and even mature enough to be spoofed, not least by a black actor in a white script.

It is also noticeable that Lee's criticisms ignore the fact that the stereotypes seen in blaxploitation cinema and after had ironic roots themselves. The pimps, pushers and hustlers who inhabit the ghetto have much in common with the white-generated stereotype of the black buck identified by Donald Bogle (1989). Indeed, the figure of the pimp and that of the mack can be traced back even further to those late nineteenth-century 'toasts' that featured the character of Stagolee (sometimes referred to as Stackalee). Smitherman describes Stagolee as the 'omnipotent black hustler' and sums up his character as 'fearless, defiant, openly rebellious and full of braggadocio about his masculinity, sexuality, fighting ability and general badness' (1977, p. 157). Like Stagolee,

the pimp celebrates a lifestyle that is rooted in drug use, violence and the sexual exploita-
tion of women through prostitution. As Kelly notes, the pimp boasts about 'his ability
to sexually please women, the number of women he sleeps with, and the money he is
making in the process' (1996, p. 141).

Post-Soul Style Politics and Constructions of Masculinity in *Pulp Fiction*, *Jackie Brown* and *Shaft*

While the 'impenitent trigger men' (Dargis, 1996, p. 7) played by Jackson in *Pulp Fiction*, *Jackie Brown* and *Shaft* exhibit traits similar to those of figures featured in classic
blaxploitation cinema, they offer a different model of masculinity – the post-soul hero
– but with a further ironic twist. The most obvious ways in which Jackson's portrayal is
encoded are through his dress and his hairstyle. The significance of dress and hairstyle
in the construction of identity is discussed by Kobena Mercer in his essay 'Black Hair/Style
Politics'. As Mercer writes, 'issues of style are as highly charged as issues about our very
identity' (1994, p. 100). Style politics are as central to nouveau blaxploitation films as
they were to classic blaxploitation cinema. The latter provides a catalogue of soul-identified fashions and hairstyles, many of which seem very flamboyant and somewhat
excessive by today's tastes. Interestingly, these styles have been introduced to contemporary audiences as much through black-identified, 1970s' music cultures like disco and
soul as through blaxploitation. While such fashions are now seen as something to spoof
(witness the penchant of white British clubbers attending 1970s' nights to dress up in
flares and Afro wigs), in the 1970s, these styles tapped into and articulated the notion
that 'Black is beautiful'.

Pulp Fiction sees Jackson dressed in black suit, black tie and white shirt. Tarantino
seems to favour this particular style configuration as the uniform of the hitman or the
bank robber and it is noticeable that the characters in his debut feature, *Reservoir Dogs*
(Quentin Tarantino, 1992) are dressed in exactly the same way. Interestingly, in contemporary black culture, the black suit is perhaps most closely identified with members
of the Nation of Islam. For members of the Nation, the suit represents discipline and

'Let's go to work': Jackson as professional hitman, Jules Winnfield (*Pulp Fiction*, 1994)

professionalism and is a part of an attempt to legitimise the organisation's somewhat leftfield belief system. The notion that the suit connotes professionalism is also a central aspect of Tarantino's usage. In both films it is clear that these are career criminals, whose *business* is crime (I am reminded here of the tag line 'Let's go to work' which adorned posters for *Reservoir Dogs*).

That the black suit, black tie and white shirt ensemble is a work uniform is highlighted in the scenes which follow the accidental shooting of Marvin in the back of Jules' car. The aftermath sees Jules and Vincent seeking refuge at Jules' highly strung friend Jimmy's house. Faced with the wrath of Jimmy's wife Bonnie, due home in an hour, Jules' and Vincent's boss, Marcellus Wallace sends professional 'cleaner' Winston Wolf (who is even more dressed up, wearing a black dinner jacket, white shirt and black bow tie) to clean up the mess. After cleaning the car, Jules and Vincent are forced to remove their blood-stained suits and, after being hosed down, are forced to change into T-shirts and baggy shorts. This becomes the source of several gags in the film – Winston asks Jimmy, 'What do they look like Jimmy?' Jimmy replies, 'Dorks. They look like dorks.' Later at Monster Joe's breaker's yard, Winston's girlfriend Raquel asks, 'What's with the outfits? You guys going to a volleyball game or something?' Because they have behaved unprofessionally (through accidentally shooting Marvin in the head), the professional, disciplined veneer provided by the suits (and linked in black culture to Black Nationalism) is taken away from them.

This leaves the jherri-curl or curly perm hairstyle (which is actually a wig) as the only surviving element of Jules' post-soul style persona. As Mercer has suggested, the jherri-curl was one of the post-liberated, post-soul hairstyles that displaced the Afro during the 1970s and 1980s (Ibid., p. 99). During the 1980s and early 1990s, in particular, the jherri-curl perm had been adopted by a large number of African-American rap artists (NWA for example). Interestingly, many of the fan websites that sprang up in the wake of *Pulp Fiction* suggest that Tarantino intended Jackson to wear an Afro wig. However, because an Afro wig was unavailable, Jackson was forced to turn to the jherri-curl. Moreover, the fact that Jackson sports a wig is further evidence of the fact that this is a performance of post-soul maleness.

Jackson's character of Ordell Robbie in *Jackie Brown*, in particular, stands as the embodiment of the New Jack/post-soul gangsta criminal which NWA depicted. He is a gun-runner who sells various high-powered automatic weapons to the highest bidder. As such, he embodies fears expressed by black academics, Republican and Democrat politicians, black political organisations such as the NAACP and nationalist-orientated rap artists about the proliferation of guns and drugs in working-class black communities, the spread of gun culture into every major conurbation in the United States and black on black crime. As with the character of John Shaft, there are elements of the pimp to his character as well – particularly in the way in which he looks to exert control and power over women. As he tells Lewis (Robert De Niro) at the Cockatoo Inn, 'I got Mel over Hermosa Beach and I rent this place in Compton for Simone over in Compton where you're staying and about four blocks away I got this young nineteen-year-old country girl called Shironda.' He is no 'stud' however.

We never see him indulging in sex with any of the female characters in the film. Instead, the women in the film fear him. While watching *Women Who Love Guns* on TV, the phone rings. Ordell says to Melanie, 'Grab that for me would you baby?' Melanie replies, 'You know it's for you,' to which Ordell, staring at her, says 'Girl, don't make me put my foot in your ass.' The camera then cuts between close-ups of Melanie and Ordell as the tension mounts. Realising that Ordell is not joking, Melanie relents and answers the phone. That she picks up the phone says 'hello' but then without waiting to see who the caller is says 'It's for you' is indicative of the way in which Melanie tries to undermine him throughout the film. Indeed, in terms of the control he exerts over women, Ordell Robbie is in some ways less successful than Shaft. And, of course, it is not just Melanie who undermines his power, but Jackie Brown (played by Pam Grier) as well. In that sense, *Jackie Brown* is part of a long tradition of blaxploitation gangster films like *Foxy Brown* (Jack Hill, 1974), *Coffy* (Jack Hill, 1973) and *Cleopatra Jones* (Jack Starrett, 1973) that feature black women figures getting the better of men.

In terms of his attire, Ordell is the most mack-like of the characters that I want to look at. Throughout the film, he appears wearing a variety of garish clothing together with a long ponytail and plaited goatee beard. Indeed, it is apparent that in most scenes in which he appears Ordell wears something different. Perhaps the most noticeable element of his attire, however, is the array of Kangol berets (red, black, white with two black stripes and powder blue) which he wears at different times in the film. This provides an interesting example of the way in which Jackson's on- and off-screen personae begin to blur. Off screen, Jackson is rarely seen without his Kangol beret. He is one of a number of African-American performers who have adopted the Kangol brand (rap artist LL Cool J is another example). Since Kangol is based in the United Kingdom and was originally associated with the sort of clothing used in outdoor pursuits, this is a clear

Ordell Robbie: the embodiment of the post-soul gangsta criminal (*Jackie Brown*, 1997)

example of reverse appropriation. That said, the fact that the beret is usually worn back-to-front so that the Kangol logo is at the front represents a distinctive black stylistic inflection. Interestingly, this particular inflection has now in turn become the preferred way for white style icons such as Justin Timberlake and David Beckham to wear the Kangol beret. Given that Timberlake and Beckham have immersed themselves in black-identified cultural forms (for example Timberlake's well-documented fascination with *Off the Wall*-era Michael Jackson and Beckham's interest in rap music) and are fluent in black-identified cultural and stylistic codes (for example Beckham's recent corn row braids) this is unsurprising.

Perhaps the most iconic (and so also now the most ironic) 1970s-identified 'look', is that associated with the Black Panther Party. The 'guerrilla chic' style adopted by figures such as Bobby Seale and Huey P. Newton, comprising the black beret, black turtleneck, black leather jacket and dark glasses 'encoded', according to Mercer, 'a uniform of protest and militancy' (1994, p. 107). Clearly, the Kangol beret can be interpreted as the post-soul version of the berets that were adopted by the Panthers. That said, the relationship between them is quite complex. The black berets worn by the Panthers were a sartorial and political statement, indicating membership in a political faction. In contrast, the Kangol beret would, at first glance, seem to be a depoliticised item. Wearing one does not signal membership in a Black Nationalist-orientated organisation and rather like the various T-shirts, hats and other items of clothing that bore the 'X' logo and which were released in the wake of Spike Lee's biopic of *Malcolm X* (Spike Lee, 1992), the specific political significance of the garment or the symbol has been lost. Quite simply, these garments and symbols have become little more than style statements, which are all about surface appearance and have very little substance. However, an alternative and much more sympathetic reading of the beret and indeed T-shirts and hats bearing an 'X' would be to suggest that these garments echo and recognise history without being imprisoned by it.

The fact that the Panthers' clothes were all black lent the organisation 'the romantic aura of dangerousness' (Ibid.). This explains why '1960s-inspired' hip-hop nationalists such as Public Enemy have chosen to incorporate Panther iconography into their respective sampling strategies.[5] The link between black(ness), dangerousness and notions of 'cool' was represented in Gordon Parks' 1971 movie in which the myth of black male sexual performance was personified in the eponymous hero – a black man called, quite simply, John Shaft (penis penis?). This identification is both attenuated and ironised in the remake of *Shaft*, in which Jackson is rarely seen out of black clothing. The poster for the film, for example, features Jackson in black turtleneck, black leather trench coat and black leather trousers. Leather of course connotes virility and sexual potency and is entirely in keeping with the character's persona. Like his Uncle (played by Richard Roundtree, star of the original film), Jackson's Shaft is very much a 'stud'. The character's sexual power is shown in the opening line to Isaac Hayes' Oscar-winning theme tune (so familiar and reprised in the remake): 'Who's the private dick that's a sex machine to all the chicks – Shaft!' And, there are numerous instances in the film itself where Shaft's virility and appeal to women is shown. When invited home by the bar waitress after a party thrown in his honour, Shaft accepts, telling her, 'It's my duty to please that booty.'

However, there is a vital difference: in the remake Shaft isn't a private dick, he's a police officer, albeit a maverick. This is another example of the way in which some actors and directors have attempted to recuperate post-soul masculinity, turning it from a model of maleness with wholly negative connotations, to one which is, potentially at least, much more positive. In this regard, Jackson's Shaft is linked to other recent African-American policemen including Alonzo Harris, played by Denzel Washington in *Training Day* (Antoine Fuqua, 2001) and Scotty Appleton, played by Ice-T in *New Jack City* (Mario Van Peebles, 1991). All three are, to borrow a phrase from *New Jack City*, 'New Jack cops' whose role is to catch 'New Jack gangstas' and who blur the line between policing and vigilantism (especially Harris who succumbs to corruption). That these detectives are very much at home in the 'hood is also signalled through their use of black slang and African-American vernacular English, and through the ease with which they move round their environment and their easy fraternisation with shady, criminal elements. Shaft doesn't just dress in a manner reminiscent of the Black Panthers; he also shares the Panthers' belief in communal, self-reliant responsibility. Although he adopts unorthodox methods and is often is in conflict with his superiors (who fail to appreciate his rather distinctive approach to community policing, especially drug dealing), he remains a policeman, however stylised his plain clothes may be.

Conclusion

Samuel L. Jackson's screen persona is not just iconic of post-soul black masculinity. If it were, then Jackson's appeal would be little more than a reprise of classic blaxploitation, perhaps reconfigured for the hip-hop generation. However, Jackson also provides an ironic take on contemporary black masculinity for the audience – black and white. In the very obvious stylisation of his signature characters, and in the fact that this is a performance, by an actor in his mid-fifties, one balding but frequently bewigged, hatted, or shaven headed, Jackson has crossed over the bridge between soul and post-soul constructions of black male-ness. This is perhaps most evident in a recent series of commercials for British TV, in which 'Samuel L. Jackson' is realised on screen in a persona clearly made up of the amalgamated characteristics, dress and style of Winnfield, Robbie and Shaft, all put together for a set of impressive ninety-second rants to camera. That this is problematic is not to be doubted, but the ironisation of these otherwise potentially nihilistic and self-destructive characteristics that this provides is to be cherished. These adverts reveal that identity is performative, not essentialist and that black people can take elements from their past and re-use them, even to the point of parody. That the commercials are for Barclays Bank, a major multinational corporation, only makes the irony stronger. Ultimately Jackson performs this 'beyond the post-soul male' act and it is an act that is rich in meaning.

Notes

1. I say general reluctance because one of Jackson's co-stars in *Shaft* (John Singleton, 2000) is the rap artist, Busta Rhymes.

2. Although blaxploitation is often thought of as an action genre, it is actually much more diverse than this. Blaxploitation encompassed detective films, kung fu, slapstick comedy and even horror movies.

3. Moreover, gangsta rap is often cited as the quintessential expression of this emergent nihilistic sensibility. It is certainly true that gangsta rap and its musical cousin g-funk (or gangsta funk) has moved away from any desire to address the problems facing young African-Americans in post-industrial America and has been reduced to a series of clichés. By presenting narratives that celebrate drive-bys, pimping and the consumption of drugs, gangsta rappers venerate criminality and criminal behaviour. And, of course, it has been widely criticised on this basis. Gangsta rap is often portrayed as a cancer eating away at the moral fibre of African-American and white youth. However, while gangsta artists are often accused of producing music that is at odds with the values of mainstream America, gangsta rap, like blaxploitation, embodies and reinforces certain American myths about individualism.

4. There are other examples of this in the Tarantino canon. The Tarantino-scripted *True Romance* (Tony Scott, 1993) represents a particularly good example of the way in which Tarantino has embraced cultural forms that are kitsch. The same is true of *Kill Bill* (Quentin Tarantino, 2003), which takes its cue from so-called 'chop-socky' films (as well as Spaghetti Westerns and Japanese Yakuza films). Nor is Tarantino alone in this. The Wachowski Brothers have clearly borrowed heavily from Hong-Kong-made kung fu films and from Japanese manga and anime in *The Matrix* series (1999, 2001, 2003), while rap group, Wu-Tang Clan litter their albums and recordings with samples from the lunatic fringe of kung fu cinema.

5   Public Enemy, especially, provide numerous examples in this context. The group's target logo, for instance, features the silhouette of a Black Panther member caught in the cross hairs of a rifle sight. Elsewhere, songs like 'Power to the People' and 'Revolutionary Generation' are based on Panther slogans, while members of Public Enemy's pseudo-paramilitary cadre, the Security of the First World (S1Ws), wear Panther-style attire and have titles ('Minister of Information', 'Czar of Education' etc.) reminiscent of those adopted by Panther members.

PART TWO

Asia, Latin America and Europe

7

Sulochana: Clothes, Stardom and Gender in Early Indian Cinema

Kaushik Bhaumik

In a 1920's newspaper article entitled 'Indian Films, Vamps at Work', a contemporary journalist describing film production at the Sharda studios in Bombay observed that 'The heroine had sacrificed her girlish modesty and dressed up in trousers and a moustache in an endeavour to save the bemused juvenile.'[1] Such a scene could have been epigrammatic of the bulk of film production in Bombay in this decade. After all, the article purported to speak for a general state of affairs in 'Indian Films'. However, the picture of Indian cinema peopled by heroines in trousers and moustaches sits uneasily with the general historiographic view of early Indian cinema that has sought to align silent cinema with the agendas of Indian nationalism of this period. Current writing on early Indian cinema has almost exclusively focused on D. G. Phalke and his oeuvre of mythological films, to construct a view that silent Indian cinema sought to project an 'Indian' way of showing and narrating that was distinct from representational styles imported from the West. Much has been made of traditional themes of righteous kingship and godly behaviour utilised by early film-makers to convey an Indian agenda for nationalist awakening. Opposition to colonial culture required a re-articulation of tradition in order to provide Indians with a plausible blueprint for reform and political awakening that could be understood in 'Indian' terms. A subtext of this historiography is that nationalist leaders or cultural producers had to connect with the deep structures of 'Indian' culture, its emotive realities, in order to be comprehensible to ordinary Indians. In the case of cinema, a direct emotional cinematic style emphasising the traditional was necessary, it seems, for the requirements of mass nationalism based on mobilising Indians towards its political and cultural aims (Rajadhyaksha, 1987).

When scholars have cast outside the 'devotional' corpus of films, they have unerringly focused on an 'Indian' notion of spatial dynamics that delimits the righteous and traditional 'inner' world of the patriarch from the modern 'outer' world of politics and temporal activities (Rajadhyaksha, 1994). According to Partha Chatterjee, this delimitation of the 'traditional' sphere of the home from the 'modern' world was necessitated by the Indian bourgeoisie's drive to construct an autonomous sphere of 'Indian-ness' now under threat from the challenges of modernity imported by the minions of colonialism. In this world, women were repositories of traditional 'Indian' values: chaste, deferential to men and elders and helpful to their husbands (Chatterjee, 1993)

Chatterjee's formulation and variations on the theme of 'home' and 'world' have been widely used by scholars of Indian cinema (Rajadhyaksha, 1994). Although almost nothing has been written about feminine imagery in early Indian films, it would not be unreasonable to surmise that, given the exclusive focus on mythological films, submissive women and the cultural agendas of Indian nationalists would have been the favourite tropes chosen by historians and film scholars to discuss the ideological charge of early Indian cinema.

Problems arise when historians seek to analyse a limited corpus of films and extend the argument to the entirety of a film culture or, the other way around, fall back upon cultural constructs like the 'Indian' way of viewing to explain film styles. In the former analytical grid, the history of Indian cinema gets essentialised to certain 'characteristic' features and in the latter, the entirety of Indian culture is reduced to 'a way of seeing'. Either way, the historical conditions of cultural production are wished away in favour of static 'views' of cultural action. In what follows I hope to provide a brief overview of images of femininity in early Indian cinema and the cultural context for the production of such images, especially as evinced from the sartorial codes employed in mainstream Bombay films of the 1920s. Even a cursory glance at this imagery shows that films of this period generated a heterogeneous mass of images of femininity, few of which had anything to do with traditional feminine values. Indeed, how then is one to fit the journalist's view of Indian films characterised by heroines in trousers and moustaches with what historians have written about the subject? If there is some truth to the historian's story, then which women and which India are they talking about? How representative were such women of 'India' in the 1920s? Or were the women in trousers fictions, mere figments of an overheated imagination?

Despite the lack of actual films, there is a wealth of material consisting of film reviews, stills, film booklets and the evidence presented by industry personnel, journalists and public officials at the Indian Cinematograph Committee (ICC) proceedings of 1926–7 that problematise the conventional historiography on early Indian cinema, modern Indian women and nationalism. Indeed, it may be argued that the 1920s were a decade of experimentation with multiple models of Indian culture, and by extension of Indian femininity, and if popular film-watching habits are anything to go by, the image of the traditional Indian woman had limited takers. Undoubtedly, the traditional Indian woman was one of the models in circulation in the public sphere but it was not until the 1930s that such a model began to assume hegemonic value in Indian society and cinematic production. Filmic, industrial and critical discourses on sartorial codes formed a prominent part of the strategies employed to marginalise visions of femininity that had been generated in the 1920s. Until the 1930s, the sari-clad, traditional Hindu woman was just one image of Indian femininity that co-existed with many others. However, through the decade, Hindu girlish modesty clad in a sari became the flavour of the 'Indian' public sphere, riding on the approbation of a numerically limited but politically powerful elite. A mass popular medium like cinema could hardly remain untouched by such discursive currents. What will be seen in this chapter is how a model of femininity limited by its class, religious and, to some extent, regional appeal could assume a place of prestige in

Indian culture and cinema through economic and political manipulations backed by the rhetorical power of the upper-class, upper-caste Hindu elite. So powerful was the popularity of alternative images of Indian femininity that critics had to employ a vitriolic and derogatory critical counter-discourse that went against the very modesty of women that they were trying to establish. It is with these alternative images that the story begins.

The Star and Fashion in Early Bombay Films: The Case of Sulochana

By the early 1920s' film production in Bombay was beginning to become regularised around the output of a few film companies run by Gujarati entrepreneurs. Films in this period mainly dealt with traditional stories culled from the Gujarati regional versions of the epic traditions, especially the *Mahabharata*, and the *puranas*. Film companies could profit from the double benefits of a corpus of narratives that were recognised both at the all-India level as well as in the regional cultural traditions. Thus films like *Rukmini Haran/Triumph of Love* (Kanjibhai Rathod, 1921), *Markandeya Avatar/Devotion's Reward* (S. N. Patankar, 1922) or *Yadav Vinas/Doom of the Yadavas* (1923), although featuring characters familiar to audiences all over India nevertheless had a particularly strong following in western India, especially in the Gujarat region.[2] Indeed, what made these films 'Gujarati' was the use of the Gujarati style of dressing – the sari worn by women in the films closely mimicking the sartorial practices of women of the Gujarati merchant classes. Additionally, films like *Kacha Devyani* (S. N. Patankar, 1919) featured distinctive genres of cultural performance like the *garba* dance that coded the film as belonging to the Gujarati cultural ecumene. Such a strategy was useful in a period when film companies had to depend primarily on audiences in western India, especially those in Bombay, for their profits. A maximum of two to three prints were produced, limiting a film's wide-scale dissemination. Films would first be shown in Bombay, dominated by the Gujarati film-watching public, and then sent on an all-Indian tour that sometimes took almost a year to complete. If film production had to be organised on an industrial scale, it had to be on the basis of faster profit generation in the local markets in western India rather than on the sluggish all-India receipts. Dress played a crucial role in ensuring the success of these films among the first mass audiences for Bombay films that were dominated by Gujaratis.[3]

By the mid-1920s, the picture was to alter considerably as the studios hit upon a formula that was to integrate film markets and lay the foundations for a full-scale film industry. Central to this formula was the re-definition of the image of the female film star. Indeed, it may be argued that it was in this period that the concept of the modern Indian film star first took shape. From around this period, Bombay film production in the main turned towards adventure-romance films, popularly referred to as stunt films, and films dealing with issues of social reform and social change, popularly referred to as the social. Folkloric, mythological and historical films continued to be made but formed a small proportion of overall film production. Another genre, less produced but extremely popular, was the Arabian Nights genre of cinema which dealt with exotic tales of mystery and romance.[4]

Around 1925, Kohinoor, the then largest studio in Bombay, produced a number of

social films featuring their new-found star Ruby Myers, more popularly known as
Sulochana. An erstwhile employee at the Grant Road telephone exchange in Bombay,
she was discovered by Mohan Bhavnani, a young director at Kohinoor, and went on to
become the first superstar of the Bombay film industry. In the early part of her career,
Sulochana specialised in playing the modern Indian working woman in social films like
Cinema-ni Rani/Cinema Queen (Mohan Bhavnani, 1925), *Telephone-ni Taruni/Telephone
Girl* (Homi Master, 1926) and *Typist Girl* (Chandulal Shah/Gajanan Devare, 1926) with
Kohinoor. Aiding Sulochana's ascendance to stardom was her status as a young and
attractive educated woman (emphasised by her real-life role as telephone operator) at
ease with the modern public sphere. But it also seems that the star's worth had to be
doubly emphasised through the kind of roles she was playing on screen. She had to be
established as a good actress and this could only be done through the 'serious' genre
of the social film.

More importantly, the studios promoted Sulochana as a modern cosmopolitan star
through advertising and the kinds of roles she essayed in her films. *Telephone-ni Taruni*
was touted as a 'long awaited cosmopolitan picture' (*Bombay Chronicle*, 10 July 1926).
In *Typist Girl,* Sulochana played a Christian office secretary at odds with the conservative patriarchs of society while in *Cinema-ni Rani* she played a glamorous film actress to
extend her repertoire of modern cosmopolitan roles. The films were set in modern Bombay and the social spaces documented were the modern workplace rather than the
traditional home. Sulochana's superstardom was reinforced during her stint with the
Imperial Film Company where her reputation was consolidated through a number of
Orientalist adventure-romance films. These included historical or semi-historical films like
Anarkali/Monument of Tears (R. S. Choudhury, 1928) and *Madhuri* (R. S. Choudhury,
1928) which established her reputation as an actress capable of playing serious roles.
Her performance in *Anarkali* was widely acclaimed and was emulated by subsequent
female stars. But her mass popularity was based on her persona as a romantic adventure queen in films like *Mewad-nu Moti/The Jewel of Rajputana* (Bhagwati Prasad
Mishra, 1928), *Khwab-e-Hasti/Magic Flute* (Mohan Bhavnani, 1929), *Noor-e-
Alam/Queen of Love* (Nanubhai Vakil, 1931) and *Khuda ki Shaan/Wrath* (R. S.
Choudhury, 1931), among others, which fused the personae of the heroines of the
imported serial films like Pearl White with that of the Oriental femme fatale of the Arabian Nights genre of films. Usually paired with Dinshaw Bilimoria, Sulochana played roles
that involved slipping in and out of multiple personae – from demure middle-class girl,
to heroic horse-riding adventuress, to sultry Oriental seductress.[5]

The crucial factor promoting the cosmopolitan superstar was fashion. Stills from her
early films depict her with stylish coiffure, hair sleeked back, in sleeveless blouse and
heavily made up. She wore her sari lightly across her shoulders exposing her neck and
upper bust, giving the sari an altogether modern touch. In films like *Daku ki Ladki/The
Dacoit's Daughter* (Moti B. Gidwani, 1933), Sulochana was seen sporting cowboy-style
trousers and shirt with a headdress that probably emulated Valentino's Sheik. In *Indira
B.A.* (R. S. Choudhury, 1929) she played a fashionable, Westernised Indian woman who
lived a glamorous independent lifestyle. In other films, she wore ornate variants of the

The many faces of Sulochana: the love of a Mughal prince in *Anarkali* (1928)

The modern Eve contemplating romance (with Raja Sandow) in *Indira M.A.* (1934)

skirt and bodice with a light wrap around her shoulders associated with Indo-Persian courtly fashions and painterly and narrative traditions of glamorous heroines and daring adventuresses. The tight cut of the blouse and new skirt designs gave the clothes a modern feel. More importantly, it was the cinematic context of fashion – the romantic situations, moments of adventure and the dancing that mixed both Western and Indian dance styles – that gave Sulochana's clothes a new modern meaning. Stills from films of this period show her in passionate clinches with Bilimoria and most of her films involved long mouth-to-mouth kisses with her co-stars (for example, *Hamarun Hindustan/Father India* [1930]). A dance featuring the superstar was obligatory in most of the films she appeared in. She was praised for her 'amazing originality coupled with Western acting style' (*Varieties Weekly*, 13 May 1933, pp. 5–6). Sulochana was thus pushing the envelope of the cosmopolitanism espoused by the industry that had begun with her career with Kohinoor. Her films tended to project an overall atmosphere of glamour and an aura of the fashionable, both of which conveyed a sense of the daring and of the experimental. Dress and on-screen lifestyle fed off each other to underscore the persona of a modern working woman fully in charge of her life and at ease in the public sphere and this could be as attractive for men as it was for women.

The cosmopolitanism of the modern star was not restricted to the screen. Sulochana was famed for her beauty and her glamorous lifestyle. Her slimness, offset by new fashions, gave her persona a new glamorous edge, a new kind of public persona that was unprecedented in the Indian public sphere. Homi Wadia, eminent film-maker of the 1930s, recalled that her on-screen fashion styles were widely emulated by middle-class women.[6] Gohar, another female star at Kohinoor who specialised in traditional roles and was Sulochana's contemporary recalled that, 'We played exactly opposite kinds of roles. She was a beautiful woman. Very glamorous – I was quite plain' (Karnad, 1980). The line between on- and off-screen personae seems to have been obliterated. Undoubtedly the studio promoted Sulochana's glamorous cosmopolitan persona as a public craze about her swept across the subcontinent. At the height of her popularity, a film clip featuring a hugely popular dance from *Madhuri* with fully synchronised sound effects was shown alongside a short film depicting Mahatma Gandhi opening a Khadi exhibition <www.upperstall.com/people/sulochana.html>. Her public appearances became regular occasions for large adulatory crowds to gather. She was the highest-paid star in the industry and owned the only other Mercedes in the city after the governor. In 1926, A. Narayanan, a film renter in Madras, had predicted at the ICC sessions that stars like Sulochana and the kinds of films they appeared in were the future of the industry:

> Our industry is now advancing on the star system. Just as when they have stars like Norma Talmadge or Eddie Polo, people go in large numbers, so also when Miss Sulochana and stars of that type appear people go in large numbers. (Evidence of the Indian Cinematograph Committee, vol. III, p. 296. Henceforth ICCE)

Subsequent developments proved him right.

The rise of Sulochana's fortunes needs to be contextualised against the backdop of a decade that saw momentous changes in the social landscape of Indian cities. Evidence presented at the ICC indicates that the bulk of the audience at a Sulochana film consisted of young students. Not only this, they were watching films at a time when the younger generation in India was ushering in new modes of public behaviour in unprecedented ways. The entry of middle-class women into the public sphere was probably the most significant of these transformations. This was especially so in a society where, until the 1900s, the public visibility of women from educated or middle-class backgrounds was minimal. Through the 1920s, women became public figures in politics and ran for municipal office. They entered secretarial jobs, became schoolteachers and nurses, even doctors and lawyers. They became consumers of fashion and, with the mass sale of ready-made clothes hitting an all-time high in the 1920s, women's access to fashion improved and proliferated. This was accompanied by a dramatic transformation in the lifestyles of women from the educated classes. 'Even Indians are dancing now,' observed the chairman of the ICC (*ICCE*, vol. I, p. 149). Satires about women's consumption and leisure habits mushroomed in print and on celluloid. The economic, political and social changes rocking society considerably increased interaction between the sexes in public spaces. Co-education in colleges and women entering the public services meant that they came in contact with men more than ever before. With the unprecedented debate on the changing roles of women, changing intersexual behaviour came in for close social scrutiny. There was a 'greater tendency to discuss sex questions now than there was a few years ago' (Ibid., p. 115). A. Soares, the principal of a Catholic school in Byculla, Bombay, attributed the 'demoralisation' arising from sexual freedom to 'post-war anarchy of thought' (Ibid., p. 390). Intercaste and interreligious marriage were idealistically discussed and even practised. Young people increasingly saw companionate marriage as the ideal relationship. What Soares missed was that it was the context of nationalism that made reform of marriage, modernisation and romance into a political ideal and it was not surprising that Sulochana, hailed as the 'Queen of Romance', was the top star in this period. No wonder her glamorous dance was considered the ideal companion piece for Gandhi's message for national awakening.

Young Indians lived on the cusp of the 'traditional' and the 'modern'. When Sulochana essayed eight roles in *Mumbai-ni Biladi/Wildcat of Bombay* (Mohan Bhavnani, 1927) including a European blonde, a pickpocket, a banana seller and an Oriental gentleman, she was pointing to times of tremendous social flux when social identities were being re-defined across a wide range of choices available in unforeseen ways. This was in keeping with the ease with which in her other films she moved through various socio-scapes – some 'traditional' and some 'modern'. It may be argued that this mobility of screen personae across socio-scapes was a symptom of times when modern Indian society was becoming increasingly mobile and interactive, throwing people together in a variety of social and cultural scenarios, a situation that demanded a variety of self-presentational skills from the individual. Moreover, at such moments of large-scale social change, identities were negotiated through choices that displayed a melange of features culled from different cultural registers rather than easily falling into one category or another. The face that the new presence of women in Indian public spheres was to wear had to be 'invented' almost from scratch. Indeed, most of Sulochana's on-screen fashion reflects the dominant tendency in Indian society in this period to adapt the past to the present and vice-versa. A cowboy-style costume would be combined with an Arab-style headdress, the sari would be worn in a 'modern' way, or the dress of an Oriental hero-ine would begin to take on contemporary lines. Thus the discursive framework for women's fashion in 1920s' India stressed neither 'traditional' nor 'modern' but experi-mentation with a variety of options, all of which signalled a momentous shift in social mores but not necessarily a visibly radical break with the past.

The very ease with which Sulochana passed from one persona to another made her accessible to different segments of an audience and contributed to her superstardom. But above all it was the alterity of her persona that reached out to spectators in a society that was for the first time coming to consist of large modern middle or proto-middle classes with urban lifestyles shot through with radical heterogeneity, almost unnotice-able due to the subtle ways in which things were mixed and matched, that normalised the changes. Large sections of society were differentiated yet conjoined by overlapping links of subtly differentiated lifestyles. Thus audiences were on the whole united in their horizons of expectations regarding modernisation and social mobility, a unity made all the more palpable by a sense of belonging to a common urban ecumene as well as by the dialogues facilitated by discourses of reform and nationalism. By the 1930s, a var-iety of fashion styles were being experimented with by various sections of Indian society. Upper-class women could be seen wearing trousers and shirts, aristocratic circles were modulating clothing styles deemed more suitable for the public sphere in the twentieth century, middle-class women were taking up secretarial jobs that entailed wearing skirts while others were adapting 'traditional' wear to modern requirements. More import-antly, these films reflect the cultural tenor of a period in the history of India's modernisation when no single model of public clothing was favoured over others and a number of options were open to members of society entering the public sphere. In a sense, therefore, the films reflected both reality and Utopia. Since whatever fashions were depicted in these films *were* worn by some section of Indian society or the other, these films were reflecting reality. The Utopia was the dream that women could adapt a single type of clothes to multiple cultural registers or wear different kinds of clothes for different cultural scenarios.

If the fond nostalgic memories of writer Pran Nevile, resident of Lahore in the 1940s, are to be taken on board, then going to the movies in their best clothing and watching a Sulochana flick was integral to this process – the clothes, the films and the star com-bined to give a sense of participating in the excitement of modernisation.[7] Even if people could not afford to be decked up as film stars they could partake of the sense of free-dom to experiment with one's public persona that on-screen glamour brought in its wake.

Fashion and the Reform of Indian Cinema in the 1930s
With the arrival of the talkies, the cultural landscape of Bombay films underwent a sig-nificant shift. The early talkie years were the site of a remarkable struggle for control of

the industry between the cinema of the 1920s and a new generation of film-makers mainly belonging to the Hindu upper-class, upper-caste elite. With the arrival of sound, song and dance became the lynchpin of a successful film and this meant that more than ever before glamorous women became pivotal to financial success in the industry. Thus the years between 1931 and 1936 saw a slew of films that highlighted the dancing and singing skills of countless female film performers. Countering this development was the large-scale entry of film personnel from the upper classes who became interested in the talkies precisely because sound allowed them to translate experiments in bourgeois theatrical and literary circles on to the screen. Yet the overwhelming popularity of song-and-dance films meant that their access to screens was limited. Over time, they solved the problem by melding songs with social realist melodramas that achieved huge public success in the early talkie years. The simultaneous success of all kinds of films in this period points to the remarkable expansion in the audience base in the wake of the arrival of sound. This opened up new markets and new audience niches, allowing more variation in the production repertoire of the industry.[8] However, the new generation were not content with mere financial success, they proceeded to re-define the cultural landscape of Indian cinema by rooting out or re-moulding all that they felt was detrimental to their cause. In this period, dance and the female performer, in particular, attracted the ire of the new generation of upper-class, upper-caste film personnel.

New film companies of the 1930s like New Theatres in Calcutta, Bombay Talkies in Bombay and Prabhat in Poona increasingly came to depend on social realist melodramas based on literary or theatrical styles for establishing their reputation as 'respectable' film companies. In a scheme of things where 'respectable' narratives dealt exclusively with issues of social reform, dance and the sexy presence of female stars were anathema. Thus film criticism of the period in English, mostly under the control of upper-class, upper-caste critics, is replete with derogatory remarks about the female star and her performative style. A realist film like *Devdas* (Pramathesh Chandra Barva, 1935) was praised for depicting 'the daily tragedies and tedium of any Indian'. It was 'coherent, compact and quick moving' with 'not one incident, not a bit of dialogue, not a movement' wasted (*The Times of India*, 19 October 1935). There was 'no pandering to the baser instincts with dances and display that have hitherto been regarded as indispensable requisites from the box-office point of view' (*The Times of India*, 5 October 1935). For the bourgeois critic, the use of female dancing as a vital selling point of the early talkies was the surest sign of the popular cinema's frivolity. By 1935, one critic declared: 'Barring dance sequels, Indian films possess no such "Evil".' The 'Evil' being disavowed was on-screen violence and sexuality targeted by social activism in America since the very inception of motion pictures (Editorial, *Moving Pictures Monthly*, Annual Issue, 1935, in Bandyopadhyay 1993, p. 28). The critique of on-screen dance was used to construct contemporary female performers in popular cinema as mere dancers, not worthy of being considered artistic 'actresses'.

Not only this, the actress who danced on the screen was consistently likened to the Indo-Persian courtesan to convey to the readers the disreputable nature of on-screen dance. A review of *Joydev* (Jyotish Bannerjee, 1933) lamented the presence of a '*baijee* type' heroine in the film characterised by her coquetry and 'V-shaped blouse' (*Filmland*, 1 July 1933, p. 15). The *baijee*, or the courtesan from the Indo-Persian tradition, was famed for her flamboyant style of dressing as well as for her glamorous sexuality. Critics slammed any actress dancing in this tradition with the opprobrium of being nothing short of the prostitute-courtesan. Thus Zubeida, a top star of the silent and early talkie era, reminded a critic through her dress and gestures of Tara, a popular stage dancer in Calcutta and connected with the courtesan class (*Filmland*, New Year Issue, 1933, p. 49). Equally, actresses were criticised for wearing 'modern' clothing and romancing men in 'Western' ways in films that belonged to the Indian cultural ecumene. Zubeida's performance in *Zarina* (Ezra Mir, 1932) raised a public controversy because of her daring dances in revealing clothes and the eighty-six mouth-to-mouth kisses that contributed to the film's legendary status. It was found lewd and vulgar, displaying too much nudity and was 'repulsive to Indian ideals' (*Varieties Weekly*, 15 July 1933, p. 5). For one critic a 'Western atmosphere had replaced an Indian one' (*Filmland*, New Year Issue, 1933, p. 49). Another critic cautioned film-makers that, 'Directors lose sight of the fact that India would be stumbling into degeneration if all the toilet-room and ballroom fashions and formalities are introduced in our pictures' (Mohamed, 1933, p. 12). And yet the fact remained that the film was set in the Indo-Persian pastoralist cultural milieu of northwestern India which allowed director Ezra Mir to test out the sexual ambiguities projected by an Oriental heroine who could also perform 'Western' gypsy dances, a slippage entirely understood by audiences in tune with such performative genres. Thus the style of female stardom established by Sulochana which could slip between modern and Indo-Persian cultural registers was increasingly criticised by upper-class, upper-caste writers. Its fashions and the concomitant sexuality and morality jarred with the cultural agenda of film-makers and producers who sought to promote the demure housewife clad in a sari in the 'Hindu' manner as the symbol of modern India. By doing so, the new generation of film personnel were trying to connect up with the dominant strand of cultural nationalism which sought to provide a model for social regeneration through a return to traditional Hindu values. Modulating public femininity to fall into line with tradition was a major component of the neo-Hindu revival of the 1930s.[9] Over time, the sari-clad 'traditional' Hindu housewife would become the dominant image of femininity for socially mobile classes to emulate.

The control of the public face of femininity was vital at a time when middle-class women were entering the world of public performance in large numbers. Cultural reformers like Rukmini Arundale campaigned to de-eroticise Indian dance so that reinvented 'classical' dances could be safely taught to middle-class girls. By the 1920s, art reformers like V. N. Bhatkhande and V. D. Paluskar, in alliance with middle-class performers, had sought to textualise Indian musical traditions and separate music from dance (Sundar, 1996). Vidya Rao notes that this process of textualisation was at the expense of 'light classical' musical forms like the *thumri* and the *kajri*, precisely the forms connected to the *tawaif* (courtesan) (1996, p. 301). Bhatkhande blamed the illiterate Muslim singers and their ignorance of Sanskrit traditions for the lewdness of light classical musical forms. Indeed, he refused to meet the *tawaifs* who 'would not help in the systematization of music, his primary aim in life' (Chinchore, 1990, p. 22). Nita Kumar also notes a similar marginalisation of the *kajri* from the repertoire of classical performers in Banaras. Her description of the city's popular culture makes the ubiquitous public presence of the *tawaif* in north Indian towns very clear. Until the 1920s, she was an essential component of religious fairs. Going by Kumar's description of this culture, the numbers of courtesans performing publicly for ordinary people seems to have been very large indeed (1988, pp. 127–9).

A 1934 review of the film industry announced the rise of a new kind of star. Grudgingly acknowledging that the older stars of the silent era like Sulochana and Gohar still dominated the star market, it enthusiastically highlighted the rise of the new stars, products of the new studio orders of Prabhat and New Theatres: '1934 saw two players attaining full-fledged stardom with but one picture to their name – Shanta Apte and Umasashi.' Older stars such as Zubeida and Gulab were merely 'giving some convincing portrayals' (Editorial, *Moving Pictures Monthly*, Annual Issue, 1935 in Bandyopadhyay 1993, p. 26). Apte and Umasashi had excelled at portraying the shy and demure Hindu woman in films like *Amritmanthan/The Churning of the Oceans* (V. Shantaram, 1934) and *Chandidas* (Debaki Bose, 1932). Critics clearly sided with the new generation of actresses groomed by the studios to play dutiful Hindu women. By the late 1930s, Sulochana and Zubeida had faded away but so had an entire generation of female performers who had made their debut in the 1930s and had emulated them, muscled out of the industry by the upper-class, upper-caste personnel and by the rise of the 'respectable' middle classes as a separate audience niche.[10] With them passed away the film industry and Indian culture's ability to 'groom' the public face of Indian femininity to adapt to the exciting possibilities of the modern world in unconventional ways. Models of social behaviour and fashions that stressed alterity and experimentation were binned in favour of repression and cultural homogeneity.

Notes

1. See *Flashback, The Times of India Sesquicentennial* (1990, p. 67).
2. All films referred to in this chapter were produced in India.
3. For a fuller description of film-making in Bombay in the 1920s, see Bhaumik (2002).
4. For more details, see Ibid.
5. This is in contrast with Kathryn Hansen's argument about the construction of Sulochana's persona as traditional Hindu girl. See Hansen (1999).
6. Personal interview with Homi Wadia, 1997.
7. Personal interview with Pran Nevile, 2002.
8. For a detailed analysis of the arrival of talkies in India, see Bhaumik (2002).
9. For a historical description of the construction of Hindu femininity by Indian cultural nationalists, see Sarkar (2001).
10. For a detailed analysis of the reorganisation of the Bombay industry in the 1930s, see Bhaumik (2002).

8

The Hollywood Movie Star and the Mexican *Chica Moderna*

Joanne Hershfield

According to Elizabeth Wilson, the cinema was one of the most influential elements of mass culture 'in creating new ways for men and women to move, dance, dress, make love, be' (1985, p. 169). And it was Hollywood movie stars who demonstrated these modes of being. By 1925, Hollywood movie stars had emerged as profitable commodities or 'sites of productivity' (de Cordova, 1990, p. 19). Stars were used to differentiate a studio's product from the products of other studios and to differentiate one motion picture from another. Stars also served as markers of standardisation in that a film could be promoted as a 'Mary Pickford' film or a film starring Clark Gable or Douglas Fairbanks. And around the world, Hollywood movie stars were setting the fashion for style and beauty through the marketing of the stars themselves and through product tie-ins. French designers and ready-to-wear manufacturers employed stars such Norma Shearer, Bette Davis, Greta Garbo and Joan Crawford, to model the newest fashions. While stars were engaged in the business of advertising fashion, they were also promoting various ideologies of modernity and the modern woman to American and international audiences. And finally, Gilles Lipovetsky suggests that for audiences in the 1930s Hollywood movie stars were brought:

> closer to the standards of reality and everyday life. . . . Despite their exceptional beauty and seductive power movie stars also had private lives which were put on display as part of Hollywood's marketing ploy, depicted off the screen as 'real people' with marriages, divorces, houses, kitchens. They had beauty problems and secrets. (1994, p. 184)

Just as modernity has generally been perceived as a Western phenomenon, the idea of the new woman has been represented as European or North American, embodied in the figure of the American flapper, the German prostitute, or the British urban, lower middle-class working woman. If we look at the images of the modern Mexican woman of the 1930s in fashion magazines, newspapers and other popular forms of visual culture, we see that she very much resembles her European and North American counterparts. The middle-class and well-to-do modern Mexican woman, living in Mexico City, Guadalajara or Merida, wore slim dresses with wide shoulders and a smart cloche hat over her short bob. She smoked Monte Carlos in public and occasionally had the nerve to wear trousers. This resemblance can be linked to the transnational distribution of the ideologies and commodities of style and fashion, disbursed through the mass media and through the Hollywood films that dominated Mexican screens.[1] However, Mexican modernity was specifically Mexican. It was first and foremost wrought by the socio-political drive for national unity, characterised by an abrupt and massive political and cultural transformation. While Western-influenced industrialisation and urbanisation marked its course, it was also shaped by what Jesus Martín Barbero describes as 'the countertempo of profound differences and cultural discontinuities' (Martín Barbero, 1993, p. 151).

The transformation from the second Porfirian regime (1898–1910) to the post-revolutionary cannot be characterised as a movement from tradition to modernity. It was, instead, a transformation from one kind of modernising project to another, an accelerated moment of modernisation in the service of nationalism (and vice versa). The post-revolutionary Mexican state, with the aid of Mexican intellectuals and artists, was actively promoting a campaign aimed at producing a specific form of nationalism. This campaign was concerned with moulding a national identity that came to be known as *mexicanidad*. *Mexicanidad* was formed through a set of discourses, stereotypes, myths and histories represented through numerous official cultural projects that included the painting of huge murals in public places, the building of monuments to revolutionary heroes and the ideology of *indigenismo*, a network of intellectual, political and artistic ideas advocating that while the modern Mexican was *mestizo* (of mixed race), the roots of Mexican national identity lay in Mexico's Indian cultures.[2]

However, as Mary Kay Vaughan points out, despite their intentions, the states are 'limited in their implementation of policy' by a number of social and economic factors. As Vaughan puts it in regard to the Mexican case, there was 'a big gap between policy formulation and implementation' (2000, p. 195). According to Alan Knight, post-revolutionary 'cultural transformation and homogenization' emanated from the market rather than the state and was 'basically socioeconomic, not political' (1980, p. 230). In other words, even if the state projected its campaign as a 'national' project, it 'drew from a transnational discourse' about reform and modernisation, a discourse that was, for the most part, made available to the Mexican public through popular culture (Ibid., p. 202). In response to the tension between nationalism and transnationalism, 'it was the emergent mass culture, rather than the radical message of *Cardenismo*, which pointed the way forward' towards modernity (Ibid., p. 261).[3] While on one hand, the state commissioned and distributed short films, posters, radio programmes and pamphlets in order to 'educate' the populace about national identity, on the other hand, radio programmes, recorded music, magazines, comic books and the Mexican cinema blanketed the nation with images of a modern Mexico which were not always in agreement with the state's vision but, instead, promoted a vision of modernity which was more and more transnational.

Mexican Women and Modernity

As in other historical contexts, modernity in Mexico in the 1930s was marked by debate and anxiety concerning the rapidly changing role of women in the home and in social and economic spaces.[4] The new social order required new kinds of subjects and new social relationships. The fashioning of *la chica moderna*, or the modern Mexican woman (as well as a modern Mexican man) was therefore one of the projects of the post-revolutionary state. Sexual politics were inexorably intertwined with cultural and economic politics in the modernising project. There were new models for being a woman in the post-revolutionary Mexican nation that were formed from economic, cultural and individual needs and experiences.[5] However, the debate around new roles for women in Mexico was also inflected by the transnational discourse of modernity and new forms of femininity that were circulated through advertising and popular culture. One of the transnational discourses that shaped *la chica moderna* was that of fashion.[6] While the state promoted images of their version of Mexican women in state-sponsored projects such as public murals, tourism promotions, state-funded motion pictures, educational pamphlets and illustrated books and magazines, Mexican women eagerly perused newspapers and magazines for other information on how to be a modern woman. Articles and advertisements in the popular press advised women on what to wear for particular occasions, how to apply their make-up, how to keep their figure trim and healthy, and how to decorate the modern home. If the state's version of the Mexican woman emphasised 'national' images in the form of traditional dress and national archetypes, popular culture promoted a transnational modernity: a Chevrolet advertisement pictured a modern Mexican woman at the wheel of the new 1939 model (*Hoy*, 20 May 1939); a full-page advertisement for Monte Carlo cigarettes in the weekly magazine *Todo* told its readers that 'charming, interesting women naturally smoke Monte Carlo' (19 March 1935) – the ad featured two dark-haired women, wearing hats cocked jauntily over their bobbed cuts, holding cigarettes in their hands as if smoking was the most natural thing in the world.

But, it was Mexico's film culture that most forcefully promoted transnational femininity. Pierre Sorlin defines a national film culture as a 'context in which spectators see and enjoy' all types of films, foreign and domestically produced' as well as 'the local practices of movie-going and the ways in which movie-going fits into the socio-economic context of audiences' everyday life' (1996, pp. 8–9). Despite a thriving Mexican film industry, in the 1930s Mexican film culture was dominated by Hollywood. The Mexican film historian, Aurelio de los Reyes, has noted that the international nature of cinema made it a powerful instrument of modernity in Mexico 'diffusing other customs, other ways of life, other inclinations' (1996, p. 17). If Mexican-made films offered Mexicans the opportunity to see their own lives displayed on the screen, to view, in cinematic form, their histories, their customs, their everyday lives and their familial and romantic relations, Hollywood films and Hollywood movie stars exposed Mexican audiences to different worlds and new ways of being.[7]

However, the context of film culture encompasses more than just films and film viewing. A national film culture includes the written and visual material of film promotion that is presented to the public: newspaper advertisements, film posters, public appearances by directors and movie stars, as well as public gossip and discussions about films and stars. In his study of Italian film culture during the 1920s, Sorlin finds that Italian actresses and actors 'played a crucial role in helping the Italians to construct "a repertory of images" likely to be read as "we are like that" or "this is how others see us"' (1996, p. 170). Similarly, in Mexico actors such as Sara García, Jorge Negrete and Pedro Infante provided a visual link to the cinematic nation that was portrayed on neighbourhood screens around the country. There is no doubt that Mexican stars such as Esperanza Iris, Esther Fernández and Andrea Palma influenced Mexican women's notions of what it meant to be a Mexican woman in the 1930s. However, ultimately it was Hollywood movie stars who modelled how to be *la chica moderna*, a modern woman.

A glance through popular weekly magazines reveals that, although there were regular columns devoted to 'Cinematográficas nacionales', 'Nuestra cinema', or 'El cine Mexicano', Hollywood films and Hollywood movie stars dominated film culture in Mexico. And it was Hollywood movie stars who were featured in the advertising and promotion of new fashions and ideologies of beauty. In a promotion for the film *Marie Antoinette* (W. S. Van Dyke, 1938), for example, Diana Cook models a hairstyle described as 'exquisitely modernized for the 20th century . . . not complicated like those of the 18th century [but] admirably adapted for the style of our modern women' (*Hoy*, 23 July 1938, p. 42). In contrast, Mexican stars, if they appeared at all, were pictured wearing 'costumes'. For example, in an article on Mexican actors in Hollywood, Margarita Bolado, who had a small role in the 1935 film *Rumba* (Marion Grering), starring George Raft, is photographed wearing a 'tango' dress (*Todo*, 26 February 1935). Interestingly, the only female Mexican movie star who appears in any of the 1938 issues of a popular weekly magazine, *Hoy*, is Esther Fernández in an advertisement promoting the Mexican film, *La Adelita* (G. Hernández, 1938) (9 April, p. 52). In three stills, Fernández wears the traditional costume and hairstyle of *la china poblana*, a national 'character' who wore a style of folkloric dress from the city Puebla, south of Mexico City.

By the 1930s, fashion was democratic thanks to the twin processes of mass production and mass marketing. The introduction and marketing of dress patterns, the accessibility of less expensive synthetic materials, the appearance of department stores in large and small urban centres, and the increased representation of fashion in women's magazines and in the cinema, put Paris and New York fashion styles in the hands of modern, middle-class women all over the world. In London, Paris, Des Moines and Mexico City,

> wide shoulders and slender hips seemed to be every woman's ideal, exemplified in the figure of Greta Garbo. Dresses were slim and straight being sometimes wider at the shoulders than at the hips. Tall girls were admired, and all the tricks of the couturier were employed to give the impression of increased height . . . The hair was dressed rather close, with a small curl at the back of the neck. On top was a gay little hat perched over one eye. Day dresses usually came to about ten inches above the ground, while evening dresses reached to the toes. The bolero was extremely fashionable.
> (Laver, 1983, pp. 244–5)

Weekly articles in popular Mexican magazines published in Mexico City addressed to women, such as *Hoy* and *Todo*, featured popular young starlets from Warner Bros., Paramount and 20th Century-Fox promoting hairstyles, the latest Paris and New York fashion, make-up and the modern woman's lifestyle. *Hoy*, for example, carried a regular column on hairstyles, called 'Peinados' (Hairstyles) featuring Hollywood stars modelling the latest in hair fashions. In the 2 July issue, Anita Louise, star of the film *Marie Antoinette* exhibits a 'modern adaptation' of the styles of the Versailles Palace (2 July 1938, p. 71). Another issue presents Hollywood movie stars, Bette Davis, Shirley Deane, Dolores Casey and Shirley Ross offering their fans a number of different hairstyles so that 'the modern woman will be able to choose among them the appropriate hairstyle for different social activities' such as dancing, attending gala dinners, afternoon teas or special formal occasions (16 July 1938, p. 40).

While Mexico City was the political, economic and cultural centre of the modern nation, women in the provincial cities of Guadalajara and Merida were also aspiring to modernity and Hollywood stars served in the same capacity as they did in the capital. A 13 February 1938 article in the Sunday supplement of *El Diario del Sureste*, the major daily newspaper in the Yucatán city of Merida, suggested that women 'that pursue glamour, are at times able to succeed in their quest by copying the individual details of the fashion of some movie stars, such as the hairstyle of Carole Lombard, for example'. The 17 February 1938 *El Diario del Sureste* featured articles on the 'Latest dictates of fashion: the Panama sombrero' (itself an example of the transnational circulation of style and commodities) and included photos of the American star, Joan Bennett, wearing a wide-brimmed Panama adorned with a green sash.

However, it wasn't merely new fashion styles that were being promoted by Bette Davis, Joan Crawford and Carole Lombard. Hollywood movie stars also portrayed new ways to be female and new distinctions between *kinds* of femininity. Wearing black-and-white, fur-trimmed lounging pyjamas and a head of short curls, 'the beautiful wife of Douglas Fairbanks Jnr characterises the perfect modern flapper' (*Illustrada*, 2 May 1929, p. 33). Another article in the daily newspaper *Excelsior* demonstrates the 'difference' between 'the elegant woman and the extravagant woman' (30 January 1930). According to the article, this difference was marked by a choice of fashion – the 'elegant' woman was pictured wearing a calf-length coat, gloves, a cloche hat and high heels while the extravagant woman wore a tight-fitting long black gown with a plunging neckline. However, the difference was also emphasised by the choice of models: an attractive, middle-aged Mexican woman served as the model for elegance while the Hollywood actress, Mae West, personified extravagance. While one might read this as suggesting that Mexican women strived for elegance while American women were merely extravagant, it is important to note that even in the US, Mae West was considered extravagant. In her reading of reviews and articles about West in US newspapers and periodicals in the 1930s, Ramona Curry notes that West's appearance was generally read as a 'gaudy display rather than glamour or elegance' as well as an indication of a woman who was 'sexually available' (1996, p. 8).[8] According to the *Excelsior* article, it seems that archetypes of elegance and extravagance crossed national geographic borders along with fashion styles.

Of course, fashion was not the only thing on women's agendas in Mexico during the 1930s. Women entered the workforce in markedly increased numbers; they agitated for the right to vote, and they worked in the area of social reforms for women and children. Stories and photographs of women involved in social, educational and cultural spheres were featured daily in the newspapers. Articles on such topics as 'Women and International Peace', 'Feminism, Long Live the Small Differences', 'The Mexican Woman Who Murders', 'The Mother as Educational Factor' and 'Women Who Work and Men Who Don't Work' were interspersed among national, international and local stories.[9] The major newspaper in the city of Merida in the Yucatán, *El Diario del Sureste*, had a regular Sunday feature called 'Pagina para las damas' that addressed two full pages to the paper's female readership. The 22 November 1930 issue included two poems written by women and a number of 'serious' articles including 'Breve psicologia del amor moderna' and 'Musa femenina', as well as articles devoted to fashion and homemaking. And a column address to the female readership in weekly magazine *Hoy*, entitled 'Charla entre mujeres' (Chatter among Women) featured conversations between women on such subjects as contemporary political leaders (6 May 1939, p. 71) and petroleum expropriation (8 April 1939, p. 49).

But fashion was important to women. It is a mistake to dismiss fashion and women's concern with fashion as merely a product or effect of capitalism or to reduce women's appropriation of fashion to consumerism. Fashion serves more than a functional or a decorative purpose. It is a practice through which one constructs and presents a 'bodily self', a visible identity (Craik, 1994, p. 1).[10] It offers women an opportunity to mark out an identity within certain social and economic constraints, identities that appear to be within reach. Anne Hollander notes that in France in the 1700s, the painter Antoine Watteau sketched people staged in casual poses that had 'the same compelling chic as those created by modern fashion photographers ... both ideally elegant and perfectly natural at the same time ... it has looked perfect, but *attainable*'. According to Hollander, Watteau's sketches of people 'in theatrical costumes, shown mingling with ordinary clothes and unaffected gestures, bring up the modern idea that all clothing is costume, permitting people to fancy themselves playing various parts for each other and for their own satisfaction (1989, p. 211). Similarly, the photographs of Ann Southern posing in her back yard in the latest beach wear, lounging in bed with a box of chocolates, and chatting on the phone wearing white pyjamas presented an image of attainability to Mexican women who, in spite of their economic status, could imagine themselves as modern. And, the democratic availability of fashion made it possible for many of these women to fantasise themselves as a working woman *and* a mother like Joan Crawford or a sexually transgressive woman like Mae West.

As Hollander explains it, 'the cinematic effect of a particular movie star is never merely a function of her body, her skin color, her acting ability, or her dress'. Hollander notes that 'the Garbo spell, for example, is a matter of light and shade creating an emotional atmosphere analogous to the spell of Vermeer's women, an uncanny evocation of female inwardness' (Ibid., p. 445). Hollander suggests that through fantasy, female viewers could envision themselves, as acting out the parts their favorite female stars acted out on screen, parts that were prohibited them in their lives of domestic and working responsibilities; the performance of a 'this-moment' character, which is linked to temporary guises, passing fads, perverse fantasies, and extreme whims, like fashion itself. (Ibid., p. 211)

Thus, it wasn't that Mexican women necessarily wanted to look like Garbo, or Mae West, or Ann Southern, or that these women imagined that by wearing Davis's hairstyle or West's slinky black dress, they would be immediately transformed into a Hollywood movie star. What they imagined, perhaps, was the possibility of being 'like' these stars, of being extravagant or being fashionable, or, being modern.

It is a given that Hollywood films and Hollywood movie stars dominated Mexican film culture in the 1930s. One might argue that this domination resulted in an 'Americanisation' of Mexican culture or that the privileging of 'modern' US femininity in the promotion of beauty and fashion styles might be seen as an 'Americanisation' of femininity. However, such a perspective assumes that femininity is a fixed object that is available for consumption. It also assumes that Mexican women desired to be American and believed that by wearing a particular dress or hairstyle, they could be 'American.' Jackie Stacey considers that same question in her study of British women's relation to Hollywood movie stars in the 1950s.[11] Her study of female spectators' memories of stars points to 'an increasingly interactive relationship between self-image and star ideals with the opening up of multiple possibilities of becoming more like the screen ideal through the purchase of commodities associated with particular stars'. She defines this process as 'mimetic self-transformation' (1994, p. 236). Rather than seeing this transformation as participating in an 'intensification of female objectification' or as evidence that British women were simply buying into the 'Americanisation of British culture', Stacey argues that British women's desire to be and look like Hollywood movie stars indicates 'the use of *American* femininity to rebel against what they perceived as restrictive *British* norms' (Ibid., p. 238).

Similarly, for Mexican women, dress was a tool readily available to women across various social boundaries that could be used to fashion oneself according to individual interests and desires and in response to different kinds of models. In Mexico, women used fashion as one means of responding to radical cultural and social transformation. Women selected different modes of dress for different roles: domestic chores, working outside the home, entertaining. They used fashion to articulate their social roles, to define their femininity and to assert an individual identity. And they made use of fashion to satisfy aesthetic, imaginative and erotic desires. Perhaps some Mexican women used fashion as a way of rebelling against what they saw as patriarchal structures of femininity. Perhaps others saw dress as a way of promoting their sexuality. Certain women may have chosen dress styles that advertised professional or economic success. And some women may have *wanted* to project themselves as 'Americanised'.

At the same time, transnational modernity might have made certain Mexican women somewhat uneasy. These women could turn to other models of femininity for inspiration such as *la Adelita* or *la china poblana* that were linked to official national discourses promoting post-revolutionary nationalism that appeared in *historietas* (comic books), *fotonovelas* (illustrated short novels) and Mexican films of the 1930s. These models pictured 'the revolutionary girl who was new to commercial storytelling but closely related to the heroic women of national myth as reconstructed between 1920 and 1940' (Rubenstein, 1998, p. 9). They were exploited by the state and by state-supported artists and intellectuals to promote and project a particular kind of national identity. They were featured in the state-commissioned murals painted by Diego Rivera and David Alfaro Siqueiros and they appeared in state-supported films such as *Redes* (Emilio Gómez Muriel, 1934) and *Vamanos con Pancho Villa!/Let's Join Pancho Villa* (Fernando de Fuentes, 1935). Advertisements and articles featuring *la china poblana* in magazines such as *Mexico Moderno/Modern Mexico* advertised an exotic, folkloric Mexico to potential North American tourists.

First immortalised in popular *corridos* (epic songs of historical narratives) *la Adelita*, the legendary heroine of the Mexican Revolution (loosely modelled after las *soldaderas* or women who followed their men from battle to battle and often fought alongside them) appeared in films such as *La Adelita*, *La Valentina* (M. Lucenay, 1938) and *Con los Dorados de Villa/With Villa's Veterans* (R. de Anda, 1939). The *Adelita* figure was also the protagonist of numerous *historietas*, such as *Adelita y las Guerrillas*. In a promotion for the introduction of this popular serial, written and illustrated by José G. Cruz, the author of numerous *historietas* of the 1930s and 40s, Adelita is pictured as a dark-haired, voluptuous Mexican beauty, dressed in a sombrero, a peasant blouse, with a pistol attached to a belt loaded with bullets which immediately identifies her as a revolutionary icon. However, in her updated, modern version, she also wears a short

La china poblana as a fashion statement. Mexican movie star Esther Fernandez in *Allá en el Rancho Grande* (1936)

skirt and high-heeled dancing shoes which define her most definitely as a modern woman.

Another popular female stereotype was *la china poblana*, described above. *La china poblana* was immortalised in the wildly popular film, *Allá en el Rancho Grande* (Fernando de Fuentes, 1936). (De Fuentes' film is noted for introducing the popular Mexican cinematic genre, the *comedia ranchera*, a musical genre that was set in the context of the pre-revolutionary *hacienda* and incorporated elements of comedy, tragedy, popular music and folkloric and nationalistic themes.) *La china poblana* also appeared in *la historieta de aventuras rancheras* (comic book serials mythologising life on the Mexican *hacienda*, or large ranch) such as *Los bandidos de Rio Frio, Los Plateados, Los Charros del Bajío,* and *Juan Gallardo* (Aurrecoechea and Bartra, 1994, p. 154).[12]

In all of her manifestations in popular culture, *la china poblana* wore the supposedly traditional costume of her grandmother – long, flowered skirt and embroidered blouse – and kept her hair in long braids. At the same time, *la china poblana* and other Indian archetypes appeared on the society pages of newspapers, in national and regional beauty contests, and adorned the bodies of well-known Mexican celebrities. In fact, the wearing of these 'costumes' emerged as a 'fashion statement' among society women from all over Mexico. An article in *Modern Mexico* announced that 'Indians are chic! They have an innate flair for right posture, striking design, becoming lines. The Park Avenue Fashion leader might well envy the tilt of their straw hats, the swing of their red zarapes' (September 1940, vol. XIII, no. 4, p. 17). Famous women, such as the painter Frida Kahlo, wore folkloric costumes daily in public.

For some Mexican women, figures such as *la china poblana* may have functioned as a kind of 'domestic exotic'. For others, she served as the archetype of a 'national Other' who could be identified with politically through dress. However, although the popularity of these national costumes must be seen in the context of the state's promotion of *indigenismo* discussed above, their attraction for some women may have merely been as a statement of a 'fashion style'. Fashion styles do not mean the same thing to all women and have no meaning in and of themselves; their significance is produced in relation to the social body they adorn and in relation to the social context in which they are appropriated and infused with meaning. In their choice of fashion styles to appropriate and stars to adulate, women reveal 'their personal tastes, their subjective preferences; they affirm their own individuality with respect to their familial and social environment' (Lipovetsky, 1994, p. 186).

In his discussion of the function of Hollywood films in transnational contexts, Ulf Hedetoft describes a process in which 'two national contexts meet within the public communicative space of the movie theatre, producing a new national text framed by a more universalised "transnational imaginary" of American origin' (2000, pp. 278–9). Women's appropriation of Hollywood movie stars as models of the modern woman in the context of developing nationalism in Mexico in the 1930s needs to be understood within this notion of the 'transnational imaginary'. The idea of the transnational imaginary forces us to rethink the construction of modern nationalisms and national identities.

While mass culture in Mexico in the 1930s *was* indebted to US and European discourses of modernity, Western ideologies were not simply imposed on post-revolution-ary Mexican nationalism. Instead, Mexican subjects drew on those ideologies and discourses that captured their imagination to fashion their own modern Mexican lives. A kind of push-and-pull dialectic shaped the course and form of the modern Mexican state: if the state actively asserted a modern national identity as the crux of the new nation; many women also vigorously claimed a 'modern' identity that was unavoidably transnational.

Notes

1. Despite the increase in Mexican film production, only 6.5 per cent of the films which premiered in Mexico City in the 1930s were Mexican. See de la Vega Alfaro (1995), p. 84.

2. The political objective of *indigenismo* was the 'incorporation' of the Indian into the state's nationalist project. For an analysis of *indigenismo* see, for example, Knight (1994), pp. 59–60, and Dawson (1998), pp. 279–308. Despite this official veneration of the Indian, it was the *mestizo* that defined the 'quintessentially national, redefinition of relation between nation and homeland' (Lomnitz, 2001, p. 40). In his long essay, *La raza cosmica (The Cosmic Race)*, written in 1925, Jóse Vasconcelos, director of the Ministry of Public Education (SEP) from 1921–4, writes of the coming of a new age wherein a fusion of races and classes in Latin America would culminate in the creation of a new race, the *mestizo*. Essentially, the *mestizo* was an Indian whose blood had been 'whitened'. By the 1920s, light-skinned *criollos* and *mestizos* comprised the economically and politically dominant classes while darker-skinned Indians 'still occupied the lowest rung of society [and] *mestizo* culture regarded its Indian heritage as a source of shame and its European aspects as superior' (O'Malley, 1986, p. 118). See also Bonfil Batalla (1996).

3. *Cardenismo* is the term used to define the political and social strategy and set of policies administered under the presidency of Lázaro Cárdenas (1934–40).

4. As Maxine Molyneux puts it, in Mexico, 'the regulation of women, the female body, and sexuality were thus inscribed in the processes of state making' (2000, p. 46).

5. While women did achieve some constitutional rights, it is generally agreed that the Revolution did not alter the essential patriarchal structure of Mexican society and women assumed their new roles within another patriarchal system 'provid[ing] a quick way to restore the population's physical and "moral" health, to make the most efficient use of their meager economic resources, and to create responsible workers for the rebuilding of the economy' (O'Malley, 1986, p. 138).

6. In her study of the relation between popular fashion and Hollywood films of the 1930s Sarah Berry sees popular fashion 'as an aspect of women's negotiation of modernity and post-traditional identity' (2000, pp. xii–xiii).

7. One of the first film reviews published in Mexico by Luis G. Urbina in *El Universal* on 23 August 1896, confirms the public's fascination with the new diversion: 'What a wonderful way to enjoy oneself! There, inside, is China with its houses of strange turrets ... over there is the temple of Buddha with his paunch ... there is Egypt with

its plains of dry yellow earth and its burning sky' (quoted in Gonzáles Casanova, 1995, p. 79).

8. Ramona Curry notes that this, combined with her 'bawdy dialogue and body language', marked her as lower class (1996, p. 8). In her analysis of Mae West's significance in US popular culture, Ramona Curry argues that West played a role in resolving two apparently conflicting discourses: as an attractive commodity within the economic discourse of a capitalist industry, and second, as a sign of transgression against cultural norms in a discourse on movie morality.

9. Women were very active in journalism in the 1920s and 1930s. A number of feminist and leftist journals aimed at women were published including *Mujers*, *Rebeldía*, *La Mujer*, *El Hogar*, *La Voz de la Mujer* and *Luz*. Women journalists wrote regularly for communist newspapers and also for mainstream magazines such as *La Revista de Revistas* and *El Universal Illustrada* (Soto, 1990, p. 81).

10. Jennifer Craik challenges the notion that fashion codes are imposed upon individuals by the forces of the market. Instead, she wants to consider women's continued fascination with fashion, the pleasures fashion provides especially for women and the ways in which women use fashion to articulate identities (1994, p. 16).

11. Stacey suggests that 'with the expansion of consumer markets in Britain' and the resulting contraction of the perceived distance between Britain and the United States during the 1950s, the 'positioning of Hollywood stars as distant idols is gradually, if unevenly, transformed' (1994).

12. This particular image is reproduced in Aurrecoechea and Bartra (1994) *Puros Cuentos III: Historia de la historieta en Mexico, 1935–1950*, p. 196).

9

Dress, Class and Audrey Hepburn: The Significance of the Cinderella Story

Rachel Moseley

They make me feel so *sure* of myself.
(Hepburn on Givenchy's clothes for her. *Honey*, April 1967, p. 119)

Dress and adornment become tangible means of gaining some control over the social order. (Roach and Eicher, 1965, p. 187)

The Cinderella story – that tale of aspiration and social mobility through stylish trans-formation – has been an enduring staple of feminine popular culture. From the childhood fairytale we read at bedtime, to the woman's film of the 1940s and beyond (for instance *Now, Voyager,* [Irving Rapper, 1942]; *Pretty Woman* [Garry Marshall, 1990]) to the makeovers beloved of contemporary women's magazines and television, the idea that a woman might succeed and progress if only she had the right look (and the con-duct to complement it) has endured. This motif, which describes the intersection of clothes, style, power and status, was central to both the key films of Audrey Hepburn's Hollywood career and to her own story as a woman and as an actor, and has defined her star persona. Further, it emerges as a structuring discourse in accounts of the star's appeal given by British women who admired her at the height of her career in the 1950s and 1960s.[1] In this chapter, I explore the construction and circulation of Audrey Hepburn as a 'woman's star', through discourses of romance, fashion, beauty and trans-formation, and consider the significant ways in which selfhood, in her films, is articulated through dress.

As I suggest in the introduction to this collection, there are important distinctions (but also connections) between the terms we use to describe the coverings we place on our bodies, distinctions and connections which, frequently, we understand and operate within quite unconsciously. One might think, for instance, that 'clothes' and 'fashion', as two such terms, occupy opposite ends of this sliding semantic scale; yet in the accounts of their favourite star given by the women who spoke to me in my research, it became quite clear that as a 'technology of gender' (de Lauretis, 1987), fashion operated both as fashion (in constructing Hepburn as icon and them as 'fash-ionable'), but also functioned as clothing and as dress in very significant ways.

While the opening image of *Breakfast at Tiffany's* (Blake Edwards, 1961), which introduces Hepburn as Holly Golightly in a full-length black Givenchy evening gown and pearls, has become iconic in itself and shorthand for edgy glamour, it is interesting to think about exactly how the dress operates in this scene. Holly walks through a deserted New York street at daybreak. She is entirely alone – physically vulnerable, shoulders bared, in a sheath skirt, kitten heels and rather noticeable jewellery. Nevertheless, the garment which envelops her (in conjunction with the dark glasses which she wears) radiates a protective power of its own. In its conspicuous glamour, it signifies 'status' and forbids approach, acting as both attraction and armour. As Warwick and Cavallaro have suggested, fashion operates simultaneously as boundary and margin (1998, p. xvii); in acting as both social armour and signifying system, clothes, through Hepburn, act both to distinguish the star and her female admirers, but also to connect them to the social, offering them power and protection simultaneously. In discussing Audrey's British Cinderellas of the 1950s and 60s, I hope to show the ways in which star style, for the women who spoke to me, offered pleasure, power and, occasionally, pain.

A Woman's Star

Hepburn was constructed as a star 'for women' throughout her career, both through the generic identity of her films and as a result of her construction in and through discourses conventionally associated with the feminine. In the Hepburn oeuvre, romantic comedy – perhaps the ultimate feminine genre – predominates; the romantic resolutions, however, are less than easy. The bittersweet denouement of *Roman Holiday* is clear, but the 'happy' endings of *Sabrina* (Billy Wilder, 1954), *Funny Face* (Stanley Donen, 1956) and *My Fair Lady* (George Cukor, 1964) are tinged with uncertainty. The wedding sequence in *Funny Face* (tellingly, the only one of her career), is only a fantasy musical number in soft focus, and while Hepburn 'gets her man' in *Sabrina* and *My Fair Lady*, her status in relation to those men, as I discuss below, remains uncertain. In this sense, then, her films have more than a little in common with the 'woman's film' of the 1940s, as theorised by Mary Ann Doane (1987).

Perhaps the clearest feminine discourse of the Hepburn persona, though, is the concern across her films and her 'real' life with fashion and beauty, and the related 'transformation' or makeover scenario which often accompanies it. The long-standing professional relationship and personal friendship between Audrey Hepburn and Paris couturier, Hubert de Givenchy is well known and documented; Givenchy dressed Hepburn, on screen and off, from the beginning of her screen career to the end of her life. There were only a few on-screen occasions, late in her career, when she changed into 'off-the-peg' clothes, the most significant of which was *Two for the Road* (Stanley Donen, 1967), in which she wore the designs of new, young designers including Paco Rabanne, Mary Quant and Foale and Tuffin. Indeed, the significance that Givenchy's clothes held for Hepburn is indicated in the epigraph to this essay, a comment made in

Glamour provides protection for Holly on the streets of New York in *Breakfast at Tiffany's* (1961)

an interview where she was discussing this style change: they made her feel safe and confident. It is significant, then, that Hepburn still regularly tops polls claiming to determine 'the world's most stylish women'; the couture styles with which she is most readily associated (the elegant Givenchy dresses in *Sabrina* and *Breakfast at Tiffany's*, for instance, or the simple black trousers and tops of *Sabrina* and *Funny Face*), might be described as 'timeless' or 'classic'. Hidden in 'neutral' terms such as this, however, are dimensions of class and status which should not be overlooked, and to which, indeed, Hepburn's own comments allude. A 'classic' dress is stylish, not fashionable (i.e. not tied specifically to the moment) and is, of course, in the meanings it carries, profoundly *classed*.

Fashion, then, as narrative device and as visual pleasure, is central to Hepburn's persona. Early in her life, Hepburn had a career as a photographic fashion model, and by the time of *Funny Face* in the late 1950s, the association with couture built up through knowledge of her 'real life', in conjunction with the importance of style in her films to that point, produced a highly self-reflexive film. *Funny Face* is a transformation narrative romantic musical comedy, in which Hepburn plays Jo, a Greenwich village bookstore assistant, 'discovered' by photographer Dick Avery (Fred Astaire). The name is a clear play on that of photographer Richard Avedon who photographed Hepburn many times, and who acted as Special Visual Consultant on the film. Jo is transformed, initially against her will, into a couture model by the staff of *Quality* magazine, and the team set off for Paris to shoot the new collection of a Paris couturier (for which, read Givenchy).

Jo's disdain for fashion and beauty culture in *Funny Face* is an inspired device; the film plays heavily on the visual tropes associated with fashion photojournalism, from the opening credits which feature close-ups of a made-up face illuminated on a photographic light box, to the opening musical number, 'Think Pink!', which features disembodied images of pink fashion and beauty accessories – toothpaste, a bag, an earring – similar to those which might be found in the pages of a women's glossy magazine. The pleasures of such a 'feminine' aesthetic for a reader competent in the codes are self-evident. This, in conjunction with a central character reluctant to participate in the culture of commodified femininity, offers the female viewer a satisfying set of contradictory pleasures – allowing her to 'have it both ways', and to engage in and deny the film's conventional pleasures simultaneously.

This moment of acknowledgment of the importance of fashion and the female viewer in Hepburn's persona was possible as a result of earlier films which offered similar, if less self-conscious, pleasures. Even in her earliest Hollywood films, when Givenchy was still uncredited as the designer of the key, quite literally show-stopping, dresses of the production, fashion functioned as attraction and produced an aesthetic which offered a very clear address to a competent feminine gaze. *Sabrina* is a case in point; in this, the second film of Hepburn's Hollywood career, she plays Sabrina Fairchild, the daughter of a Long Island chauffeur. There are many moments in this film (and in those which follow) where the organisation of the *mise en scène* is orientated towards the display of Hepburn's clothes (albeit in an entirely unsexualised fashion), but the most significant instance occurs on her return from Paris, where she has spent two years ostensibly learn-

The display of fashion detail for a feminine viewer in *Sabrina* (1954)

ing *cordon bleu* cookery. The more significant learning experience of her stay, however, turns out to be that of 'how to be *in* the world, and *of* the world', as she puts it: she has grown up. As I discuss in more detail below, this transformation is one told through dress, and the moment where this becomes clear is one at which Hepburn's dress – her new-found, grown-up, couture style – is displayed for the audience and predominantly, I want to argue, for a feminine audience, one which is competent in reading sartorial codes.

Preparing him for her return from Paris, Sabrina tells her father 'I shall be the most sophisticated woman at Glen Cove station.' On the change in location to Long Island, there is a slow pan upwards from a close-up of a toy poodle in a diamanté collar atop a stylish set of luggage. The pan takes in the length of Sabrina's body, sheathed in her Paris suit, and comes to rest on her rather consciously posed head, encased in a white skullcap hat, chin rested on finger, arms casually crossed. From here, the camera pulls back and watches her parade up and down the platform from afar, displaying the details of her outfit for the spectator. It is very difficult to read this sequence as constructed for an imagined male spectator, for a number of reasons. First, this gaze at the new Sabrina is not mediated by another character; indeed, it is only after this display for the spectator that one of the love interests of the film, David Larrabee (William Holden), roars up in his sports car, does a double take at Sabrina and then screams to a halt to offer her a lift. A space is allowed before this focalisation, for an admiring gaze which is not specifically gendered male. Indeed, the camera pan allows one the

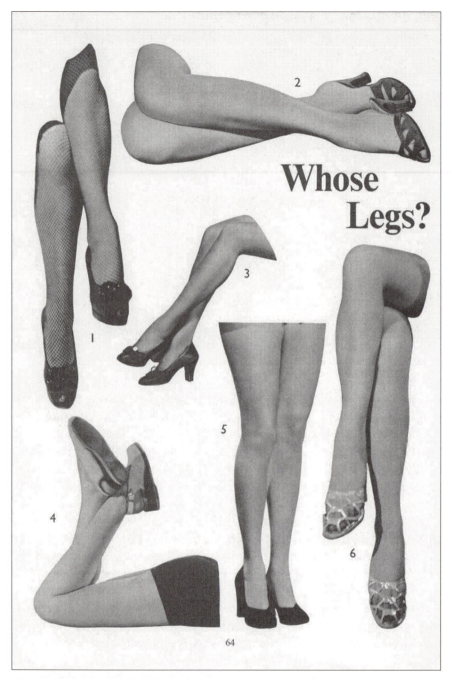

'Whose legs?': A young Audrey Hepburn, disembodied and fetishised, in the pages of the British *Picturegoer* annual (1951)

Can You Identify these Heads and say to which Legs they belong?

1

2

Iт's puzzle corner again. This time we've dismembered, more or less gracefully, we hope, half a dozen delightful young lovelies.

On this page you find the heads and all you have to do is name them. Incidentally, you should find that easy enough to do. Now comes the more difficult part. Can you fit the legs on the opposite page to the right heads?

You won't find clues much use to you, so we won't give any. This is something of a test of observation, and we have an idea that this is one in which the male of the species may well put up a better average than the feminine reader.

If you have any difficulty—and you probably will—turn to page 144 for the correct pairings.

We can tell you that the ladies so summarily dealt with are a mixed bag of British and American starlets—all of whom have been in the news during the past year.

3

4

5

6

65

time to take in all the details of Sabrina's outfit, from the tiny split in the hem, to the stitching, to the tailoring of the jacket and the design of her hat, finishing with a full-length display of the *ensemble*. Hepburn was never constructed as a starlet sexualised through dress and performance for the male gaze as many of her contemporaries were; indeed in an early British *Picturegoer* annual (1951), Hepburn appears, disembodied, with a number of other young actresses, in a game called 'Whose Legs?', where the reader is invited to match the legs to the face. In this feature she appears in the short skirt and fishnet tights which she wore as the cigarette girl in *Laughter in Paradise* (Mario Zampi, 1951). The incompatibility of this representation of Hepburn, body parts separated and fetishised, demonstrates the power and persistence of her non-sexualised star persona. One can imagine that the scene at Glen Cove station might have been presented quite differently had the part of Sabrina been played, say, by Marilyn Monroe or Jayne Mansfield with their very different body types, performance styles and star personae.[2]

The centrality of fashion, then, in Hepburn's films, is closely tied to the transformation or 'Cinderella' narratives which underpin them. This story of romance, growing up and transformation through dress appears around Hepburn not only through the characters she played on screen, but also in what was known and disseminated about her 'real' life through press and publicity. First, of course, is the larger narrative of her own trajectory as it is often told. The journey from the hardships she endured in occupied Holland, running messages, which she hid in her ballet shoes, for the Resistance, surviving on turnips and flour made from tulip bulbs (Woodward, 1984), to discovery and Hollywood stardom must be the ultimate Cinderella story. The significance of clothes to the Audrey Cinderella story comes to light in Givenchy's own recollection of his first meeting with her: as she tried on his designs, he remembers, 'the change from the little girl who arrived that morning was unbelievable' (Collins, 1995, p. 173). The clothes transformed the little girl into a woman, made her into Audrey Hepburn, in his story.

The transformation, or Cinderella story, then, is always bound up with dress, from the first versions of the fairytale to those of the present day (*Pretty in Pink* [Howard Deutch, 1986]; *Pretty Woman*; *She's All That* [Robert Iscore, 1999]). Around Hepburn, though, and indeed as I will go on to examine, in the personal accounts of women who admired her, it acquires an extra dimension. For Hepburn's Cinderella characters in films from *Roman Holiday* (Cinderella-in-reverse) and *Sabrina* to *My Fair Lady*, the story of their transformation, growing up and acquisition of status is told precisely *through* their clothes. Their dress fulfils not only social functions (in producing them as respectable and properly attired, which, of course, it also does), but it also carries and expresses the weight of their emotional development, and frequently, acts as protection. Dress is here, as Warwick and Cavallaro suggest, not simply a supplement, but a necessary part of the person (1998, p. xv). It tells a parallel, if amplified, emotional story, and this is true not only of Hepburn's characters. This particular Cinderella story, in which dress plays such a significant part, is a discourse which also structures accounts told of the star and of their own histories, by women who admired her, growing up in the 1950s and 60s.

Audrey's Cinderellas

The Cinderella story around Hepburn is one of transformation through dress but also through education, and in this sense it intersects with the *Pygmalion* story (upon which, of course, *My Fair Lady* is based). A story of growing up and social 'coming out', this star-specific version of the basic tale is intricately bound up with the issue of class, and how one might transcend it, acquire it, or appear to have it, through dress and education (this is true, too of *Roman Holiday* when the princess becomes 'ordinary' for a day – though of course in reverse). In the Hepburn story then, clothes play a significant, transformative role. Not only do they render Cinderella 'fit' for her new social setting, they also put her on display and simultaneously cover and protect her. The moment of the newly made-over Sabrina's public appearance at Glen Cove station expresses this dilemma completely through the possibilities of costume, performance, music and *mise en scène*. The scene described above is accompanied by a reprise of 'La Vie en rose' which we have heard earlier through Sabrina's open window in Paris, played on an accordion. Here, though, it is more fully orchestrated and thus suggests the fulfilment of an earlier, unexpressed potential: she has grown up and emerged into the world. While the camera position and movement puts Sabrina, in her Paris suit and with her new short hair, clearly on display, at the same time the clothes – the tightly tailored long dark suit, the close-fitting hat – cover her and act as protection, as armour – they make her appear confident. Hepburn's performance here perfectly expresses the contradiction: her pose suggests her new sense of self, and yet the subtle movement of her eyes reveals her slight discomfort (and pleasure) in being so openly on display. Part of what is at stake in the contradiction expressed here in the coming together of clothes and performance, is the insecurity and impossibility of adequately performing class – a question lingers over whether 'class' can ever really be acquired, or whether it can only ever be performed, more or less successfully. This, of course, is the question of habitus, in Bourdieu's sense (1990). While Hepburn's Cinderellas are always fit and deserving of their transformation and the romance with their 'prince' which accompanies it, the slight instability, registered in Hepburn's performance in this, and other scenes, returns in the insecure denouements of her Cinderella films. While Linus Larrabee (Humphrey Bogart) decides eventually that he wants Sabrina, and meets her finally aboard a ship bound for Europe, there is little sense of a resolution, or even the suggestion of an impending marriage. There is romance, certainly, but it is, quite literally, cast adrift from the ties of family, status and class which have hindered their relationship to this point. Similarly, while transformed flower seller Eliza Doolittle (Hepburn) returns to Professor Higgins (Rex Harrison), the man who made her, at the end of *My Fair Lady*, her status remains unclear: 'Where the devil are my slippers?' his final line. Will she be his wife or his housekeeper? The class anxieties attendant on Hepburn's Cinderellas, for all their new-found finery, finally remain, and return in the stories of their own growing up and coming out told to me by women who admired this star in the 1950s and 60s.

Despite her couture associations, Hepburn emerges as a remarkably available and attainable star in terms of models of femininity – at least for the British women I spoke to. Undoubtedly, this is partly the result of her perceived 'naturalness', both as a 'person' – she was frequently understood not to be acting, but simply to be 'being herself' – but also in terms of her beauty and her style. Hepburn featured frequently in the fashion and beauty pages of magazines for young women, and on the fashion advice pages of British film fan magazines at the height of her career (for instance that of Pat Gledhill in *Photoplay* and of Gillian Giles in *Picture Show*).[3] In these features, her particular kind of beauty was produced as natural, 'individual' and thus democratic and achievable, and similarly her style of dress was represented as appropriate to be copied by young British women.[4]

While her on- and off-screen clothes were largely couture, the simplicity of her look meant that they could be easily sourced or made, through adapting patterns, by young women who admired her style. The Hepburn look which has come to be known as 'student' or 'Bohemian' chic – slim black trousers, black turtle or polo neck and flat black ballet shoes, is perhaps the key example of this kind of achievability of style. I heard a number of accounts, in the research I conducted with British working-class women who admired Hepburn's look, of hunting for an equivalent to this outfit, and in particular, of its being both modern and fashionable, but also appropriate in the late 1950s and early 1960s. This may have been for a special family occasion where their desire was both to stand out, but also to 'blend in', or even to carry them through an event, where, as I discuss below, they felt out of their social depth.

All of the women who helped in my research on Hepburn's enduring appeal told me Cinderella stories, unprompted, of their own growing up and coming out into the world. All of those stories were told through their memories of dress, of the clothes they wore which eased their path and thus, as in the Cinderella narratives of Hepburn's characters, clothes are profoundly tied to the acquisition of subjectivity, and of a classed subjectivity at that. Hepburn's persona was a particularly resonant one, it seems, for young British women growing up and moving on in the 1950s and 60s.

In a particularly apposite account, Liz told the story of playing the part of Sabrina in an amateur dramatic production of *Sabrina Fair* by Samuel. L. Taylor, upon which the Hollywood film was based. She recalled with pleasure being 'discovered' and chosen to play the part and the process of making, with her mother, the 'smart outfits' which would be her costumes in the play. Particularly interesting in this account, is the way in which she contrasts her moment of discovery with her 'ordinary' job as a shorthand typist from which it allowed her, temporarily, to escape.

A number of interviewees spoke to me, in recalling their memories of Audrey Hepburn, about their weddings, and in particular, their choice of wedding dress and going-away outfit. For many, the choice of a dress 'just like she would have worn' was a guarantor of the meetness of their appearance on their own special 'Cinderella' day, perhaps the ultimate moment of coming out into the world and being on display in many women's lives – their own happy ending. Similarly, Barbara, a woman who had grown up in the Midlands in the 1950s, talked very interestingly about an Audrey-style outfit which she had made herself, similar to something the star had worn in *Breakfast at Tiffany's*, for a trip abroad, and the experience of being 'on display' in it. It had:

nice little shoes to match, I think I even had a bag to match as well! ... Because it was
a big thing then, when you went on the aeroplane you dressed up. ... you didn't go in
your jeans, or whatever, you actually dressed up when you went on a plane, 'cos it was
such an important thing, you know. ... I remember coming back off that holiday, and
er, we got rained in, the runway was washed out, so we were actually stuck there for
twenty-four hours, and they put us up in – I remember sitting in the airport, trying to
be comfortable in this dress [laughing] and the belt was – oh! And I'd actually – I was
actually pregnant, I'd – well I was only just pregnant, I didn't know I was pregnant until
I was on holiday, and the second week, I started getting morning sickness, so, and I felt
so uncomfortable, I remember this great big belt, and trying to be – sitting nicely in the
airport, you know!

While this woman clearly enjoyed the memory of dressing up, Audrey-style, to go on
holiday, and of being suitably dressed for the occasion, her recollection is tempered by
the memory of feeling constrained as she 'sat nicely' in the airport. Similarly Janet, recalling the Audrey Hepburn-style clothes she had bought and made, talked to me about
getting a good job in an office, but working for a man whom she felt was her social
superior. This account is a clear story of 'discovery and display' in true Cinderella fashion,
and she recalls being taken out by her boss to an event where she felt out of her depth,
and trying to ensure that she was properly dressed:

And I can remember buying, erm, and I thought I was the bee's knees – I bought what
they called – now I don't know what they used to call it – it was a straight edge-to-
edge coat, and it was reversible, it was beige on one side and it was cream on the other
side, so you could wear it either way, and I bought new cream shoes and a cream
handbag, and the shoes were a bit tight, and I made the mistake of taking them off
while I was in the theatre, and I couldn't get them back on again! [shudders and laughs
at the memory] Oh, God I was crippled! I was *crippled*, I, I don't think I've ever felt so
miserable in all my life – as I tried to *hobble* back to the station [laughs] – oh, dear God!

Ironically, the event in question was an evening at the theatre in London's Drury Lane
to see the opening of *My Fair Lady*! Again, the remembered pleasure of the clothes
which enabled this woman to 'pass' socially – which protected her from what she felt
to be the investigative gazes of those around her – is tainted with the memory of the
discomfort of wearing them. In reading accounts such as these, I think it is possible to
understand the 'pain' of the clothes which were also remembered and recalled with
great pleasure and in enormous detail, as symptomatic of the anxiety of 'being found
out' – a phrase which I encountered repeatedly – which prompted and accompanied
the wearing of them. The dress which Janet described is both enveloping and protective (the coat), and yet simultaneously, the shoes emerge in her account as precarious
as well as perfectly co-ordinated, and as the items which threaten to 'give her away' –
just as the glass slipper in the original Cinderella story. For Barbara, it was the wide belt

which proved uncomfortable – significantly, the item of clothing which, literally, holds an outfit, and all that it expresses and conceals, together.

Delight in and fear of discovery is at the heart of the Cinderella narrative; double-edged, it is based on an oscillation between the pleasure of being discovered and put on display, and the anxiety of exposure. This is true for Hepburn's characters, and clearly this discursive structure resonated with the women who told me their own Cinderella stories in the process of remembering their admiration for Audrey Hepburn. Similarly, the clothes with which the women at the centre of this story chose to dress themselves produced visibility and display, leaving them open to an investigative gaze, but also provided a literal and metaphorical cover which protected them from exposure, in both physical and social terms. The right clothes – dress, then – can function as social armour. In this way, fashion becomes dress in very particular ways around Hepburn's Cinderellas: as a 'European' star who was held as an ideal of femininity and widely emulated, Hepburn offered a way of being which enabled the British women I spoke with to negotiate a path between fashionable modernity and respectability, to use clothes as both ornament and protection. Remembering and talking about clothes and fashion provided the women in my study with a vocabulary through which they could tell their own stories of growing up and social mobility, just as in Hepburn's films dress articulates subjectivity and carries the emotional charge of the narrative. For Hepburn's Cinderellas, dress truly does tell the woman's story (Gaines, 1990).

Notes

1. This chapter is based upon a larger research project which explored the enduring appeal of Audrey Hepburn through textual analysis and audience research. All the interviewees cited in this chapter are British, white and grew up working class in the 1950s and 60s, though many now consider themselves to have become middle class, either through marriage, or education, or both; the anonymity of all interviewees is preserved by the use of pseudonyms. See Moseley (2002) for a full account and interviewee profiles.

2. It is interesting to note that Truman Capote, writer of the novella *Breakfast at Tiffany's* upon which the 1961 film was based, was unhappy with the choice of Hepburn as his high-class call girl Holly Golightly. He wanted Marilyn Monroe for the part; had his wish been granted, it would have been a very different film.

3. See also Christine Geraghty's discussion of Kay Kendall's appearance on 'Gillian's' page in *Picture Show*, in the next chapter.

4. It is notable that despite her general 'appropriateness' as a fashionable feminine ideal, the slim black trousers worn by Hepburn in films such as *Sabrina* and *Funny Face*, where shown, were accompanied by a note of caution, and the suggestion that they might be worn under a skirt. See Moseley (2002), chapter two.

10

Paris, Hollywood and Kay Kendall

Christine Geraghty

The Constant Husband (Sidney Gilliat, 1955) was in many ways a watershed film for the British star, Kay Kendall. Filming took place in the spring and early summer of 1954, when *Genevieve* (Henry Cornelius, 1953) and *Doctor in the House* (Ralph Thomas, 1954), hugely popular British comedies, had already brought her to the attention of the public and the critics. Although there had been problems before over suitable parts for her, it was the last film she made before the very public falling out with Rank Organisation in December 1954 when she was suspended from her contract for turning down a number of proffered parts, including the second Doctor film (*Daily Herald*, 22 December 1954). It was also the film on which she met and fell in love with her future husband, Rex Harrison, who was already a major star. But *The Constant Husband* is also significant from the point of view of image and fashion, the aspects of Kay Kendall's later career which are the subject of this essay. It was in this film that elements of Kendall's individual style most clearly seem to be shaping her costumes; it is perhaps not an accident that the costume designer, Anna Duse was someone who knew Kendall in her childhood and had taught her dancing (Golden, 2002, p.15). The turned-up collar, the pushed-up sleeves, the heavy jewellery, the vivid colours, all seemed to be the culmination of touches which had marked earlier, smaller parts in black-and-white films such as *Lady Godiva Rides Again* (Frank Launder, 1951), on which Anna Duse had also worked, as well as the two colourful comedies. Kendall's next role as a theatre star who moves into television in *Simon and Laura* (Muriel Box, 1955) gave the opportunity for glamorous dresses (the responsibility of Rank's leading costume designer, Julie Harris). After that, Kendall's clothes, on and off the screen, would mainly be in the hands of the Hollywood studio, MGM, and Paris fashion houses such as Balmain and Givenchy.

I do not want to argue that Kendall's style took the wrong turn when she moved out of the British star system nor that the big battalions suppressed her own individuality. As we shall see, the change suited her in more ways than one and it is of course hard to see how things would have turned out for her had it not been for her early death in September 1959. But in this essay I want to look at the way in which fashion and style helped to create her image in this later part of her career. I have argued elsewhere that, in the male-dominated British cinema of the mid-1950s, Kendall was significant for presenting the possibility of an independent, stylish heroine of the New Look. In these comedies of the companionate marriage, she used clothes and fashion to personify not the 1950s' housewife and mother but the modern woman who made her own money and knew her own mind (Geraghty, 2000). With the move to Hollywood and the entry into the heights of celebrity which the liaison with Harrison brought, a different approach developed. This essay examines this shift in two different areas – in the biographical material in the press and elsewhere which commented on her use of fashion,[1] and in an examination of two of the films she made with MGM, *Les Girls* (George Cukor, 1957) and *The Reluctant Debutante* (Vincente Minnelli, 1958).

It is important to note that Kendall's body was not that of the ideal 1950s' film star, if we take Bardot and Monroe as typical pin-ups of the period. Kendall turned down parts in *Value for Money* (Ken Annakin, 1955) and *As Long as They're Happy* (J. Lee Thompson, 1955) and felt justified when they were played by a completely different type, Diana Dors. Her height and slimness made her look more like a catwalk model than a film star. Indeed, after the disastrous *London Town* (Wesley Ruggles, 1946), Kendall, according to her biographer, 'applied for and got many modeling jobs in the late 1940s. Photos show her to be the height of New Look elegance in off-the-shoulder gowns, full, sweeping skirts, peasant blouses and dirndls' (Golden, 2002, p. 39) and it was at this stage also that she had her hair cut into a distinctive short style that worked with the clothes. The discrepancy between her own appearance and that of the classic film star was drawn attention to by Kendall herself who publicly expressed dissatisfaction with her looks and her body. In a number of interviews in the late 1950s, she told a tale of the late 1940s when, she claimed, a Rank executive told her '"You are too tall and you photograph horribly"' (*American Weekly*, 5 January 1958; Lewin, 1957?). Height was always an issue for her. '"I have legs like a kangaroo"' she told another US reporter during the making of *Les Girls*, adding that '"I'm the same height as Gene Kelly without heels so I guess he'll have to stand on a box"' (*Hollywood Citizen-News*, 2 February 1957). For a 1950s' film star in Hollywood, less than substantial breasts were also a problem; *The New York Times Magazine* reported her measuring herself up against contemporary icons and complaining '"I feel so vitriolic about ladies with enormous bosoms ... They give anyone who is my height and slightly flat-chested a bad name"' (15 September 1957). As late as the summer of 1959, she was quoted in *Life* magazine as complaining that '"my feet are too big, my bosom is too small. I have huge hips and an enormous bottom ... I look like a female impersonator – or rather an angular horse"' (quoted in Golden, 2002, p. 147).

There were a number of ways to deal with this body and turn it into an element that worked with rather than against her star image. One was to use its contradictory elements productively. Thus, *Picturegoer* headlined a major feature on her as 'Two Takes on Kay Kendall'. Ostensibly, the two takes were by her father and grandmother who both contributed articles but the contradictory elements were immediately foregrounded in her father's piece, headlined 'Oh What a Spitfire', which began

> Tall and elegant – a big star in films. That's how picturegoers know her. But I've known another Kay Kendall – a thin, little, live-wire, always getting into scrapes. An angel one minute and a minx the next. A tomboy you wanted to smack one moment and love a few seconds later. (10 December 1955)

This re-working of Kendall's physical awkwardness (the article is full of stories of her physical scrapes and accidents) into the characterisation of her as a tomboy supported stories of her as a rebel against the establishment, inside and outside the film industry. As her status grew, however, the emphasis on height and physical risk-taking transmutes into an appreciation of her as a comedienne capable of using her body to comic effect. Thus, a review of *Les Girls* drew attention to her unconventional presence by calling her 'a lanky beauty of thoroughbred features' but linked this to her skills as 'a comedienne who can be funny in the mere tilting of an eyebrow' (quoted in Golden, 2002, p. 117). The clowning element, first given scope in the trumpet episode in *Genevieve*, was acknowledged in the response to her comic skills in *Les Girls*; the British trade paper *Today's Cinema* welcomed 'our own Kay Kendall, whose drunken haywire comedy may not please everyone but is richly hilarious' (5 November 1957).

But the other way of dealing with this problematic film star body was to recognise it as indeed the perfect body for a model. Press interviews and pictures thus dwell on Kendall's love of clothes, emphasising both her own personal style and the expensive designer clothes appropriate to an internationally known celebrity. On the one hand, Kendall apparently rejects the glamour of Hollywood starlets' 'extremely low cut dresses' in favour of simple 'tweeds or sweaters or skirts' (*Los Angeles Times*, 12 January 1958). But simplicity too could be glamorous when it was Humphrey Bogart giving the advice to stick to 'a simple sweater, skirt and flat shoes' (Golden, 2002, p. 144). Anne Sharpley sought out the 'real Kay Kendall' and concluded that she had changed from being 'the one-time "one of the boys"'. Kendall was now a fully fledged star, going to lunch and the theatre with Vivien Leigh and 'Betty' Bacall and asking, disingenuously, '"It's not wrong to wear a mink coat, is it?"' (*Evening Standard*, 25 February 1959).

In many ways, designer clothes from Paris fashion houses solved the problem of her tomboy body and allowed her to combine simplicity with glamour. On her return to London from the US, an interviewer reported that she was 'gay and vivid, in a Paris model coat with a silk lining' and praised her for managing to be glamorous in the controversial fashion item, the sack dress (Lewin, 1957?). A link was made between the clothes she wore in her MGM films and her off-screen appearance. In London, at the gala performance of *My Fair Lady* in 1958, she wore a Balmain gown created for *The Reluctant Debutante* but gave it her own signature by dying the boa pink (Golden, 2002, p. 133). For her final film, *Once More with Feeling* (Stanley Donen, 1960), the Givenchy gowns were designed solely in black and white and Kendall drew a fashion lesson from them for her own style. In an interview with *Hollywood Citizen-News*, she commented on how her own style was affected by these film wardrobes: 'I was a little frightened of black and white at first, because I love colors. I rotate orange, yellow and navy blue through the seasons but this is such fun for a change' (16 June 1959).

One feature of the later years, however, is the way in which fashion seems to be used as a prop to deflect attention from how ill she was. Being as thin as a model could then be understood as the result of a diet, as Muriel Pavlow later recalled (Golden, 2002, p. 144). Photos and reports of the clothes she wore in the last stages of her illness movingly suggest a defiant use of style to create an image that was the essence of simple

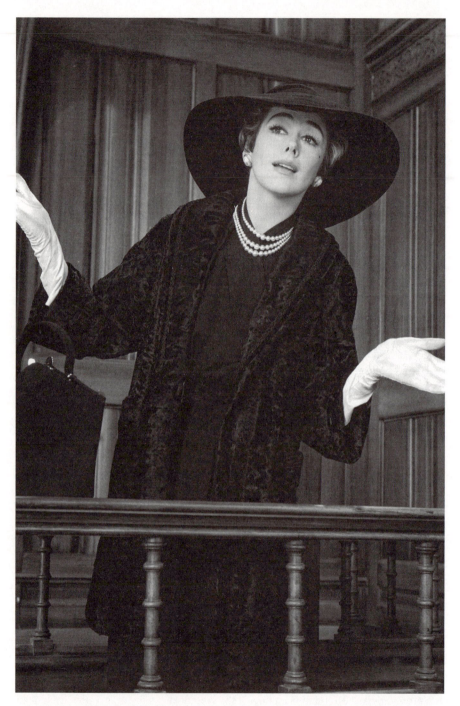

Lady Sybil (Kendall) dressed for glamorous respectability in court in *Les Girls* (1957)

chic. When she came out of the London clinic in June 1959 to finish shooting *Once More with Feeling*, she was 'in her black Givenchy dress and Cartier brooch' (Ibid., p. 146). So strong is this connection between Paris fashion and the cover-up of her illness that her friend, Dirk Bogarde recalled in a 1995 interview what she had worn on the last night that he saw her in the spring of 1959: 'a white chiffon dress, a Balmain, with autumn leaves and orange and beige on it. Very, very simple with beautiful shoes and that great mane of hair' (Ibid., p. 142). The accuracy of this description, which does not feature in Bogarde's autobiography, is less important than the image it conjures up of the wearing of a Balmain dress as an act of bravery as her body gave way.[2]

Les Girls is a musical comedy, directed by George Cukor who had a reputation for working sympathetically with screen actresses. It centres on a trial for libel brought by Angele (Taina Elg) against Kendall's Lady Sybil Wren. It tells the stories of a trio of dancers – the third is Joy (Mitzi Gaynor) – who are working for and fall in love with Barry (Gene Kelly). Although the trial takes place in London, the three different versions of the story given at the trial are set in Europe, mainly in Paris which features in the elaborate set of the quarter in which Barry and the girls live. The film focuses on the lives of the three dancers but the narrative is resolved though the man; Barry's evidence to the court reveals elements of the story which the two women had not known and, by discreetly avoiding the question of his relationship with them, he restores the marriages they had made when the act broke up. The film was better received in the trade press than elsewhere. *Hollywood Reporter* called it the 'gayest, maddest, merriest, musical spin' (2 October 1957) while the British *Today's Cinema*, reporting on the film as the choice for the annual Royal Film Performance, suggested that it had 'unlimited scope for all the glitter, personality, dancing and prodigal production that Hollywood can provide' (5 November 1957). The film was seen as a US breakthrough for Kendall with her drunk scene gaining particular praise in the *Hollywood Reporter*. The *Motion Picture Herald* described her as 'a British actress whose billing on this side of the water will have important meaning hereafter' (5 October 1957) while the British *Kinematograph Weekly* exulted that Kendall had 'proved that she can not only hold her own with, but outstrip, leading American and Continental actresses' (7 November 1957). Kendall did indeed win a Golden Globe for this performance.

The British pressbook for the film emphasised the 'lavish wardrobe for Kay's debut' and 'Fashions for "Les Girls"'. The critical comment emphasised art direction and costumes as an integral part of its appeal as a musical. The *Motion Picture Herald* included these in its list of what had made the film 'a souffle of gaiety, wit, color, movement, song, dance, fashion, romance'. *Hollywood Reporter* felt that 'the gowns by Orry-Kelly seem to be both attractive and chic, a neat trick when you can manage it' while *Kinematograph Weekly* found the 'wardrobe breathtaking and [the] décor dazzling'.

The Hollywood costume designer, Australian Orry-Kelly, had shared an Academy Award for his work on *An American in Paris* (Vincente Minnelli, 1951) and would win another for *Les Girls*. In the overall organisation of the women's wardrobe, there is a contrast between the clothes worn for public show (at the trial, in the performance numbers) and those worn when the trio is off stage. Over the three days of the trial, Angele and

Sybil wear glamorous clothes which fit the older, richer selves they have become through marriage. They appear in dark colours (black, brown, dark red) with contrasting jewellery, often pearl necklaces and earrings; they wear distinctive hats with sweeping brims or high crowns and are swathed in furs. The dance costumes are also co-ordinated and are rich and dramatic. Despite Kendall's concerns about her inadequate body and the publicity photos in which she looks ill at ease in a skimpy costume, there is relatively little flesh on display in the film. In the first sequence, 'Les Girls', black, white and red predominate; initially, the trio appears in enveloping white coats with red lining, then in black, shoulderless, cocktail dresses split up the front to show off the legs which are also emphasised by red shoes. Only at the end are the three revealed in sparkling showgirl costumes though even then their figures are obscured by diaphanous, fur-trimmed stoles. In their second song, the comic 'Ladies in Waiting', the three wear a parody of seventeenth-century French dress with powdered wigs, white lace and hooped skirts which split at the back to reveal legs and bottom, topped with a blue bow. Complementing the stars throughout the theatre scenes are the chorus girls who provide a vivid background in black-and-white, African-inspired outfits or the more traditional red showgirl costumes.

For the off-stage scenes, the trio's clothes are similarly co-ordinated though in a less rigorous way. The clothes are less formal, often separates with fitted tops or jackets worn over casual skirts or trousers. Patterns worn by one actress re-appear on another; thus, Joy's black-and-white striped jacket is reprised in the dress which Angele wears for her romantic date on the punt with Barry. The palette generally tends to be lighter with softer colours predominating. Colours complement each other with one character, normally Joy, providing a splash of darker colour against the lighter tones of the other two. This situation is reversed though in the final party in Paris when Angele and Sybil wear co-ordinated evening dresses in turquoise, blue and green while Joy, who has taken on the role of Barry's main (and final) love interest, wears a white gown, with a light blue underskirt and matching ribbon trim. Thus, the off-stage wardrobe of the three women indicates that they continue to work as a trio but in a looser way.

The costumes though also allow for individual touches which relate to who is telling the story at any one point. Thus, in Sybil's account, Angele is presented as a sexy, Continental type with saucy hats, tight-fitting dresses in black lace and tops which tend to slip off the shoulder. By contrast, when Angele tells the story her clothes become demure and provincial while the drunken Sybil parades around in her see-through nightdress, clutching bright red carnations. The same clothes can take on different meanings depending on narration. In Sybil's tale, Angele dons her dull grey-and-white dress and schoolgirl hat when she despairs of Barry's love and decides on suicide; in Angele's own version, the same outfit merely reflects her faithfulness to her fiancé and the good nature which leads her to try and help Sybil.

A more consistent marker of difference though is nationality, which is related to character. Angele's more flirtatious style indicates her French nationality. Sybil's clothes are

'Les Girls' in ensemble costume surround Barry (Gene Kelly), backstage in *Les Girls*

generally in tones of beige, white and cream and she wears full, pleated skirts, leather belts and soft tops. Each of the women gets a separate number with Barry but it is significant that, while the other two perform either stage numbers or romantic duets, Kendall's turn is a comedy number, 'You're Just Too Too', in which she is dressed in a smart olive trouser suit with a green scarf at the high neck. In general, then, her style is a casual version of the tailored, respectable clothing suitable for the character's eventual marriage into the British aristocracy. Joy's clothes, on the other hand, reflect her US nationality. She wears more easygoing separates, a check shirt and red slacks or a camel-hair coat for going to the market, and is often in trousers. In her smarter outfits, Gaynor displays a sleeker silhouette than Kendall with pencil skirts or a simple black dress which hugs her figure. An all-American 1950s' girl, Joy holds out for marriage and in the end gets the man. Although *Les Girls* is reasonably even-handed in its treatment of the three women, Joy's wardrobe does indicate the practical commonsense and unproblematic sexiness which will lead to the final revelation of her as Barry's wife and the instigator of his courtroom intervention.

The film's wardrobe is thus constructed around two approaches which offer a model of how Kendall herself was served by *Les Girls*. On the one hand, the costumes work to blend the three women into a single entity so that the girls fit into their surroundings and their musical numbers with ease and grace; on the other hand, the clothes have individual touches which serve to emphasise character and particularly nationality. The clothes were thus an important part of the way in which Kendall herself in *Les Girls* became part of the industry's design process, the 'prodigal production' which *Today's Cinema* associated with Hollywood, but also retained her individuality as a British female star.

The Reluctant Debutante was a less prestigious production than *Les Girls* although it was directed by one of Hollywood's most experienced and established directors, Vincente Minnelli. Set in London, the film was shot in Paris from a script adapted from his own play by William Douglas Home, a playwright who had been rather left behind by the upheavals taking place in British theatre in the late 50s. The story is set firmly in the British class system. Once again, Kendall plays an upper-class society belle, Lady Sheila Broadbent, who in a fit of one-upmanship, decides to launch her American stepdaughter, Jane (Sandra Dee), into London society. The film featured a husband and wife partnership between Kendall and Harrison as Jimmy Broadbent but also set Kendall's character at odds with the commitment to love, regardless of class or money, represented by Dee's innocent yet down-to-earth teenager. Their quarrel is resolved when the 'unsuitable' suitor, David Parton, inherits an Italian title and is therefore rendered desirable on all counts.

The film's reviews emphasised both fashion and the star couple as strong elements of the film's appeal. *Kinematograph Weekly* felt that the film had 'a compelling feminine interest' and an 'irresistible women's angle' (11 December 1958). The film continued Kendall's success in establishing herself as a major star in the US. *Variety* pronounced that 'It's really Miss Kendall's picture and she grabs it with a single wink', maintaining that she had created 'one of the best female comedy turns in years' (6 August 1958), while *The New York Times* praised her as a 'super-slick comedienne' who makes 'small talk into a minor art as she voices it' (15 August 1958). As with *Les Girls*, fashion was part of the appeal to the female audience with *Variety* suggesting that, 'topping everything, as far as the female patrons will be concerned, will be Pierre Balmain's wardrobe creations for Miss Kendall and the feathery frocks are sure to cause a stir'.

The credits indeed proclaimed that the wardrobe was by Pierre Balmain of Paris and the story gives plenty of scope for the display of beautiful gowns, worn at the balls and dinners which are the relentless staple of the coming out process, as well as for a parade of more casual wear, suitable for gossiping over elegant breakfasts. The costumes, although they are often themselves elaborate, are placed in a more simple wardrobe design than that of *Les Girls*. The major contrast is between Lady Sheila's wardrobe and that of Jane whose costumes are credited to a different designer, MGM's Helen Rose. Jane's clothes are generally girlish and neat. She arrives at the airport in a grey suit, velvet collar and matching hat; her gowns are in the palest of pastels, with embroidered bodices and full, floating skirts. Such clothes emphasise Jane's youthfulness and virginity (which Lady Sheila is trying to defend) though they do little to suggest the modern teenager which the script also hints at.

Kendall's wardrobe, on the other hand, is successful in establishing the style and character of Lady Sheila. The clothes work as simple but glamorous statements of fashion *and* as comic props and thus pull together Kendall's star image of fashion plate and comedienne. The first two outfits, both a dramatic pinky-red, establish Kendall as the main focus of attention. In the early scenes, she wears a simple suit with one large button at the top of the jacket, a collarless boat-shaped neckline and a slim skirt worn with white gloves and a matching hat with a wide brim. The colour is also picked up in the set design, since it co-ordinates with the cyclamen on the office desk and a lampshade in the Broadbents' apartment. The effect is elegant and dramatic, a look maintained in Kendall's first chiffon ball gown which is in a similar red. The slim, shoulderless dress looks simple but, as Sheila moves through the ball, details of the draped front and the fall of material from a bow at the back are revealed. There is also a hint here of what is to come in the satin stole with a fur trim which dramatically complements the dress.

The use of a strong colour for these early costumes establishes Sheila/Kendall as the main focus in the image, the character who creates the action and works with the *mise en scène*. A montage of ball scenes then features two more gowns and as the film progresses the colours associated with Sheila become more muted – beige, grey, white – as the contrast between the elegance of the clothes and the exuberance of Kendall's clowning becomes more apparent. The high spot in the middle section of the film is the use of costume in an extended sequence in which Sheila and Jimmy host a dinner, try to keep Jane under surveillance at a ball and, on their return home, deal with the consequences of her attraction to David. Sheila's dress for this sequence, which frequently breaks into farce, is a plain, high-necked, pinky-grey beige chiffon, buttoned up the back, with long

(Overleaf) The boa which 'did everything but talk out loud'. Kendall as Lady Sheila in *The Reluctant Debutante* (1958)

sleeves and a full skirt. This rather strait-laced effect is, however, offset by dramatic accessories – elaborate jewellery and a huge matching boa. The latter, although at first sight an elegant accessory, in fact becomes a comic device, which reflects the mental state of the wearer; the feathers provide a shimmering, undulating commentary which is always, though, slightly behind the movements of the agitated owner. At dinner, when the wrong guest arrives, Sheila's startled head peers up as if from a nest of feathers; when she chases fruitlessly round the ballroom, the swaying of the boa emphasises her zigzagging movements; at home, in debate with Jimmy, it falls in a long curve down her back or drops away from one shoulder as she waves her arms; it falls in two long columns down her sides when she tries to address David in a dignified fashion. The boa is useful as a feminine weapon when Sheila taps Jimmy with one of its wavering ends and as protection when she hides her face with it, on overhearing what she thinks is a fierce fight between the two men. Finally, it provides a cover for her when she falls, fully dressed, into exhausted sleep. No wonder Minnelli is reported to have 'changed its [the boa's] position in the script to a sequence requiring the maximum action' and remarked that '"The boa proved the most effective prop I have ever worked with . . . It did everything but talk out loud"' (*Picture Show*, 14 February 1959). The film ends, though, with Sheila restored to elegance, receiving guests at her own ball in a slim, grey, halterneck dress with white gloves, a diamond in the V of the neckline and more scattered in her perfectly groomed hair.

The Reluctant Debutante offers a good example of the way in which Paris fashion fed back into discourses about dress via film stars such as Kendall. One example of this practice, discussed more generally by Moseley (2002) in relation to Kendall's contemporary, Audrey Hepburn, is the long-running fashion column by 'Gillian' in the British film magazine *Picture Show* which translated the 'looks' associated with particular stars and designers into patterns and accessories more accessible to the readership. This involved encouragement from upcoming and established stars such as Heather Sears and Leslie Caron who, readers are assured, make their own clothes at home (31 October 1959); practical tips such as making a peasant-style blouse from handkerchiefs (29 May 1954) and descriptions of what stars wear, on and off the set. The column emphasises the virtues of restraint and being sensible which is couched in the language of femininity – clothes can be glamorous as long as they are not too revealing, are comfortable to wear and fit the concept of the modern housewife. Some films are difficult to work into this discourse; a discussion of *Imitation of Life* (Douglas Sirk, 1959) is accompanied by advice from Lana Turner – 'Don't overdo the glamour' – which rather contradicts the example set by her costumes in the film. *The Reluctant Debutante*, on the other hand, provided good material for Gillian's column.

The magazine reviewed the film as a 'pleasant, romantic comedy . . . charmingly acted' (7 February 1959). In the same issue, Gillian features Sandra Dee in an article entitled 'Be Your Age' which warns teenagers against the 'scruffy look' and commends Dee for looking 'pretty and feminine' in the film. The following week (14 February), the column devotes its whole page to the film, using Balmain's designs for Kendall to argue against the vogue for 'the sack'. The column quotes Balmain on the 'pleasure' of designing for Kendall's 'tall, willowy type of figure'. Balmain compliments Hollywood designers, including Orry-Kelly and Helen Rose, for helping to 'set fashion style for women all over the world' and, crucially, for keeping 'fashion styles within bounds that have made them copyable'. This is picked up in a detailed description of the 'red woolen two-piece' Kendall wears at the beginning of the film, emphasising the fashion details of the '*uncollared* neckline' and the '*loose* belt ... around the normal waistline, tying in a bow at the front' (original emphasis). This outfit is deemed appropriate for readers to copy, being both up-to-date and wearable. It avoids the fashion excesses of the waistless 'sack' but has the imprimatur of Balmain and Hollywood. The evening dresses though are a different matter. Balmain emphasises that a floor-length dress 'makes a woman more alluringly feminine' and the column agrees that they are 'just lovely to look at'. But Gillian warns that 'one is not likely to gain inspiration for one's own wardrobe from them'; clearly, too much sophistication and glamour makes the translation into appropriate wear for the feminine reader too dangerous.

Hollywood and Paris were thus crucial to the way in which fashion was constructed as part of cinema's appeal. I have discussed Kendall as an individual star but her success in these two late films tells us something more generally about how costume was used by Hollywood and Paris in the star-making process. *Les Girls* represents the process by which Kendall is slipped into and supported by the Hollywood machine. Her costumes help to create her character by complementing and contrasting with those of the other girls. Her star image is reinforced by the differences but it is more important that she fits the total *mise en scène*. She works as part of the system ('Les Girls' and *Les Girls*), not outside it. Having achieved this, *The Reluctant Debutante* offers a rather different approach. Kendall again fits the *mise en scène* but this time Minnelli builds the film around her so that her costumes define the entire look of the film.[3] She becomes not just a character but the key element of the decor, a splash of scarlet or a floating feather. In her British films, Kendall's costumes carried the stamp of her rebellious personality; in *The Reluctant Debutante*, that individuality remains but is underpinned by Hollywood and Paris. It has been smoothed into place as carefully as the chiffon and satin she wears with such style.

Notes

1. In using quotations from Kendall's interviews, I am not suggesting that these give us unproblematic access to her own thoughts, although part of her image was an apparent openness and willingness to confide. Indeed, the repetition of 'spontaneous' comments in a number of interviews confirms the possibility of using such material to look at the image it creates. See Golden (2002) pp. 91 and 146 for examples of interviews separated by two years, in which Kendall makes a similar reference to looking like Danny Kaye.

2. This would seem to be another dress from *The Reluctant Debutante*. One of the difficulties about looking at and writing about Kendall in this period is indeed that her early death inevitably and poignantly overdetermines what one sees, an experience which was clearly much more difficult for those who knew her.

3. Characteristically, Jean Wagner's 1959 review of the film for *Cahiers du cinéma* said nothing about the clothes but praised Kendall as a puppet in Minnelli's brilliant control of the *mise en scène*.

11

Hot Couture: Brigitte Bardot's Fashion Revolution

Ginette Vincendeau

The fashion industry may in vain spend fortunes, but this witch, this sphinx only needs buy a pair of trousers and a man's sweater at Madame Vachon in Saint-Tropez, for all the young women of the Côte d'Azur to adopt this outfit, and for this outfit to become fashion. (Jean Cocteau, 'The Brigitte Bardot case', Cocteau, 1979, p. 69)

Introduction

Brigitte Bardot: the long blonde hair, luscious pout, wasp-like waist, shapely breasts and long legs. The archetypal French sex goddess – revealed to the world in Roger Vadim's 1956 *Et Dieu ... créa la femme/And God Created Woman* – has remained a celebrated object of male desire for generations. But the Bardot appeal equally endures as the evocation of a hedonistic lifestyle – dancing the mambo, sunbathing in Saint-Tropez, riding in open-top cars, hair and silk scarf floating in the wind. It is often asserted that Bardot was, in the late 1950s and early 1960s, 'the most photographed woman in the world', and evidence suggests the most widely imitated, from the Barbie doll to Barbarella (Servat, 1996, pp. 15–16). While Bardot posed for a notoriously sexualised bust of Marianne, the emblem of the French Republic, stars like Mylène Demongeot, Annette Stroyberg, Jane Fonda, Catherine Deneuve and many others (see Crawley, 1975, pp. 78–9, for an entertaining portrait gallery), adopted her clothes and hairstyles. Later, pop star Madonna paid tribute to Bardot's 'sense of style' and said how she longed 'to be able to wear her tight sweaters and pointy bras'.[1] In the 1990s, model Claudia Schiffer pastiched Bardot's look, as did, in the early twenty-first century, singer Kylie Minogue and model Kate Moss.

A lot has been written on Bardot's looks and performance, her complex sexual persona combining the sex kitten with the sexual predator, her impact on French cinema, her international image and work for animal rights and her fraught relationship to feminism (see in particular: de Beauvoir, 1960; Morin, 1972; Rihoit, 1986; Vincendeau, 2000; Merck, 1994; Burch and Sellier, 1995; and, last but not least, Bardot herself in her startlingly frank autobiography [Bardot, 1996 and 1999]). Building on this work, but also on the history of women's fashion in France, this chapter traces Bardot's early career as a model, her elaboration of an idiosyncratic and highly influential style on and off screen – concentrating on the 1950s and early 1960s, the most innovative period of her career in fashion and cinema terms, and attempts to understand her extraordinary impact.

Brigitte before Bardot
The model *jeune fille*

Brigitte Bardot[2] was born in 1934 into a wealthy Parisian family, the elder of two sisters. Like many young women of her class at the time, she studied ballet, from which she gained the ability to dance (which many of her films exploited), and her distinctive walk, poised and sexy in equal measure. Brigitte's elegant mother was well connected in the world of Parisian couture (for a while she had a boutique in Paris's plush 16th arrondissement). Contrary to many accounts that see Brigitte accidentally 'discovered' as a model, it is clear that Madame Bardot *mère* worked hard to push Brigitte into a modelling career (Rihoit, 1986; Bardot, 1996). In 1948, she convinced her friend Jean Barthet, a reputed hat designer, to use the fourteen-year-old Brigitte to model his hats while dancing to music from *Swan Lake*. The Barthet *défilé* led to various photo assignments for traditional women's magazines such as *Jardin des Modes* and *Modes et Tricots*. In turn, this led to her being spotted by Hélène Lazareff, the editor of the more modern and prestigious *Elle*. Brigitte's first cover for *Elle* was on 2 May 1949 (she was then fifteen). It was followed by many others. One of these early *Elle* covers attracted the attention of film director Marc Allégret.[3] Allégret sent his young assistant, aspiring journalist and photographer Roger Vadim, to contact Bardot. The rest, as they say, is history, although several years would elapse until their joint breakthrough in *Et Dieu ... créa la femme*, during which Bardot combined modelling with a run of low-profile movies, and small parts in quality films such as René Clair's *Les Grandes manoeuvres/Summer Manoeuvres* (1955).

Influenced by Christian Dior's New Look of 1947, French fashion of the 1950s was glamorous in a highly feminised but mature and structured way: tailored jackets pinched at the waist with full skirts and petticoats (Dior's so-called *femme-fleur*) or more sober long, fitted skirt, making up what *Elle* called the 'ultra-perfect feminized suit',[4] and highly structured evening gowns. Hair was short and permed, clothes matched by hats, bags, high-heeled shoes. Each occasion and time of day had its outfit: afternoon ensembles, 'town' suits, cocktail dresses, evening gowns. These were the clothes of Brigitte's mother and of her mother's friends; they formed the sartorial horizon of the world in which she grew up. Their declension of rigidly set tasks and times of the day implied a repertoire of appropriate roles for bourgeois femininity.

The fashions Brigitte modelled in the late 1940s and early 1950s were a young version of these women's clothes. One of her early *Elle* covers (24 March 1952) shows this graphically, as she poses behind a grown woman, both wearing identical flowery dresses. On 29 December 1952, a double-page *Elle* spread entitled '*Jeunes filles* of 1953: this is *your* fashion', elevates Bardot to juvenile role model: 'Brigitte opens her door. She shows you "her" fashion, which is also yours.' There was some irony in this, since *jeune fille* implies virgin; Brigitte had married Vadim just a week earlier, on 20 December 1952. In the three years since meeting her, the rakish, bohemian Vadim had swept Brigitte off her feet and relayed Madame Bardot in the building up of Brigitte's – and his – career, networking and placing photographs of her through his friends in *Elle*, *Paris-Match* and other key publications such as *Jours de France*. Vadim is often presented as Bardot's Svengali with *Et Dieu . . . créa la femme*, but his most important role may well have been this more obscure but crucial building up, which demonstrates his shrewd understanding of the developing power of the mass media in 1950s' France. By December 1952, his efforts were beginning to pay off and Brigitte made a modest foray into movies, with two films – *Le Trou normand* (released 7 November 1952) and *Manina, la fille sans voile* (Willy Rozier, 1953) (released in North Africa in December 1952).[5]

The double-page spread in the 29 December 1952 *Elle* illustrates Brigitte's version of early 1950s' bourgeois young women's fashion. Photographed in her apartment, she wears flat ballet shoes and her long light brown hair is neatly done up in a ponytail, with a set wavy fringe. Two profile shots show her, pouting, dreamily looking at herself in a mirror or gazing at toy animals. In one picture she wears a demure coat for walking the dog, a knitted hat from which the ponytail sticks out, and a crocheted mohair shawl. Patterns given at the back of the magazine indicate the reader is assumed to be a mother. Brigitte is quoted as borrowing her grandmother's petticoats – pursuing the childhood theme but also hinting at what will become a trademark: the recycling of clothes and taste for romantic garments and material. The predominance of profile shots emphasises her child-like looks, her short, turned-up nose and full, pouting lips.[6] At the same time, the right-hand page of the spread features her younger sister Mijanou kneeling on the floor to fix the back of her ball gown. In a *mise en abyme*, the corner of the page shows Brigitte's first *Elle* cover (in which she appears in a similar pose and gown), while the background of the main shot is decorated with portraits of Brigitte, one of them, the reader is informed, drawn by Vadim. Apart from the relentless image buildup, the sexy ball gown highlights her hourglass figure: the woman is about to leave the *jeune fille* behind.

Manina: the girl in the bikini

Bardot's second film *Manina, la fille sans voile* (literally 'Manina, the girl without a veil', in the US *The Girl in the Bikini*), explicitly trades on the display of her body. Her sensational figure is showcased by a bikini with a strapless,[7] diamond shaped bra, out of which she constantly seems to be about to pop, while her hair is long and loose (though not yet bleached). No more ponytail or hair-clips. The film is at pains to emphasise her harmonious relationship to the sea and the rocky beach, while the framing exploits her body in a variety of pin-up poses (such as high-angle shots over her breasts). *Manina* is shot in Corsica, then becoming a major tourist destination, and Bardot and her bikini crystallise sociological and fashion moves away from the bourgeois home towards Mediterranean holidays. Bardot was not the first woman to wear a bikini, a garment officially 'invented' by Louis Réard in Paris in July 1946. However, she was the first to narrativise it in a film's leading role, and the impact of the film in the US, when it was released after *Et Dieu . . . créa la femme* had made Bardot internationally famous, was in part connected to the display of her navel, then forbidden by the Hays Code. This would seem to support Valerie Steele's contention that 'sexual curiosity is expressed sartorially by the attraction to novelty – what has been called "neophilia"' (1988, p. 280). The only other outfit Bardot wears in *Manina* is a wide skirt with a low waist worn with her shirt tied under her breasts. With this garment Bardot combined the erotic display of her midriff (showing her navel again) with the use of bold-patterned 'ethnic' Provençal print, contrasting with the dark clothes worn by her mother in the film, and the traditional prints with small flowers worn by women in Provençal films from the 1920s to the 1950s (Peyrusse, 1986).

The display of her body now becomes a major part of Bardot's image. After *Manina*, she turned into fully fledged sex kitten[8] at the Cannes Film Festival of April 1953, where she stole the limelight in another bikini, even without a major film to her name. Here again Vadim helped, by ensuring that she was abundantly photographed. Thus her success was firmly rooted in fashion spreads and glamour photography. From then on, her body was central to her films, in particular in 1955: *Futures vedettes/Sweet Sixteen* (Marc Allégret), *La Lumière d'en face/Light Across the Street* (Georges Lacombe), *Cette sacrée gamine/Naughty Girl* (Michel Boisrond) and the British *Doctor at Sea* (Ralph Thomas, 1955), which gave rise to tabloid frenzy in the UK, where a life-size cut-out pin-up in *Réveille* sold out overnight (Crawley, 1975, p. 40). She was on the threshold of major stardom.

Bardot's New New Look
That wedding dress

Bardot attained major stardom in 1956 with *Et Dieu . . . créa la femme* and retained it until Jean-Luc Godard's *Le Mépris* (1963) which, like Louis Malle's *Vie privée* (1961), both reflected on her stardom and effectively marked the end of it (Sellier and Vincendeau, 1998). In parallel with her career, Bardot's trajectory from demure *jeune fille* model to iconoclastic fashion leader is book-ended by two weddings. In December 1952 she had married Vadim – in church – in a sober white velvet dress. Designed by Yvonne Trantz,[9] the dress had a Mao collar, fitted bust and long straight skirt with draped fabric around the hips. Brigitte's brown hair was pinned up, her face surrounded by a fine white veil. By contrast in June 1959 she married her second husband Jacques Charrier in loose, long blonde hair, wearing a pink and white check *vichy* (gingham) dress with *broderie anglaise* trimmings around the collar, cuffs and pockets, designed by Jacques Estérel. One of the most famous French post-war garments, the dress was deemed iconic enough to be part of a 1988 exhibition of 'French elegance in the cinema',[10] even though it was not worn in a film.

The Bardot-Charrier wedding was a colossal media event. There was a stampede of photographers, journalists and delirious crowds in the town hall at Louveciennes, near Paris, which by law had to be open to the public. The dress was instantly copied, provoking a craze for gingham that helped revive the flagging *vichy* industry in the Auvergne.[11] The impact of the dress was clearly a function of Brigitte's celebrity, then at its zenith. It also stemmed from its bold challenge to the codes of class and femininity which underpinned 1950s' fashion – especially given the solemnity of the occasion.

As designer Fred Salem put it, 'To be married in a gingham dress was very avant-garde, and it created a small scandal in bourgeois families' (quoted in Rihoit 1986, p. 192). How 'scandalous' the dress was is relative, since it was rapidly assimilated into the mainstream (if not as a wedding dress). I will use it as a guide to discuss the meaning and importance of Bardot's 'sartorial revolution' at the turn of the 1960s.

Dressing the sex kitten

Bardot's clothes of the late 1950s are both markers and symptoms of her sex-kitten image. Like the tartan, flat shoes and berets of her earlier pictures, gingham checks connote simple domesticity as in kitchen tablecloths,[12] and childhood: school overalls and nursery decorations – with pink and white obviously girls' colours. As with the bikini, Bardot was not the first to wear gingham – Janine Darcey wears a belted gingham dress in Jean-Paul Paulin's 1942 Cap au large (a poster can be seen in Peyrusse, 1986, p. 239), and the April 1950 Molyneux collection included a gingham summer dress (Amouroux, 1991, p. 175). Bardot herself, long before her wedding to Charrier, modelled garments and accessories in gingham, including high-heeled shoes on the cover of Elle 1 August 1955). But Bardot (whose initials BB spell baby in French), particularly emphasised the fabric's childhood connotations. Magazine spreads and archive pictures of the wedding and honeymoon – in Saint-Tropez naturally – show a veritable declension on the theme: a blue-and-white gingham Bavarian-style dress,[13] Capri pants, shorts, a gingham top with broderie anglaise bra, tucked inside tight shorts and Brigitte's hair in plaits. Brigitte would cling to gingham as a vision of youth for some time – a 1970s' nude shot shows her, from the back, looking through a window framed by gingham curtains.

Broderie anglaise too connoted Catholic babyhood and childhood (christening gowns, Sunday dresses) as well as romantic underwear and nightdresses. In fact, the success of the wedding dress also led to something of a broderie anglaise craze, seen in many of Brigitte's frothy dresses and petticoats. The following year, Saint-Tropez boutique designer Christine Vachon launched a line of broderie anglaise clothes modelled by Brigitte.[14]

Bardot's looks were the natural ally of her youthful fashions. Her large eyes, short nose and full lips – made fuller by the famous pout – retained, and traded on, a childhood aura, while her silhouette was always youthfully slim. By contrast with the more mature stars of her era, such as Monroe and Martine Carol, the tall and slim Bardot never seems to have experienced weight problems. In a 'competition' published in the Easter 1957 issue of Cinémonde, Bardot – at 1 metre 68 centimetres – is seven centimetres taller than Carol, but slimmer. Although Cinémonde's readers awarded 139 points to Bardot, against 169 to Carol, with hindsight we know that Bardot had already become number one French sex symbol and fashion guru. Indeed, the summing up of the competition repeatedly describes Bardot as forcefully young: 'She is more aggressive', 'She has the insolent air of very knowing young people'. It also asserts that 'Her looks are unique ... but all the young women in France see themselves in her'.[15] The apparent contradiction (unique yet universal) characterises Bardot as emblem of youth also in the sense of a generation. To her overtly feminine dresses, she added the then radical clothes of American youth, in particular the jeans popularised by James Dean in *Rebel Without a Cause*, which were making the switch from workwear to a leisure garment (Chenoune, 2000, p. 16), as well as the duffle coats of the 'beat' generation, adding a layer of bohemian rebellion to her image.

In demographic terms, those who, like Bardot, came of age in the 1950s were the first to see themselves as a generation, preceding the Baby Boom children by ten years. Their rising economic power was not, however, matched by social freedom. As a result they found an outlet in consumption and the adoption of new kinds of behaviour, from delinquency to *cinephilia*, a phenomenon explored by many cultural historians (among others: Monaco, 1987; Steele, 1988; de Baecque, 1998). In her films of the 1950s Bardot's clothes 'speak' the assertiveness of the pre-Baby Boom generation, both in themselves and by contrast with those of older women. In *Et Dieu ... créa la femme,* she wears jeans and a white polo shirt, in *La Vérité/Truth* (Henri-Georges Clouzot, 1960), she hangs out in the cafés and hotels of the Latin Quarter clad in tight trousers and sweater, flat shoes and a duffle coat. In *En Cas de malheur/Love is My Profession* (Claude Autant-Lara, 1958), her older lover (Jean Gabin) buys her the kind of ski outfit Bardot had modelled a few years earlier,[16] contrasting with his wife's formal dresses. In *Une Parisienne* (Michel Boisrond, 1957), she goes to an upper-class hunting party in jeans and throughout the film wears a younger and funkier version of the attire worn by the older mistresses her husband prefers to her (this being the comic basis of the film): a suede coat against their mink, simple soft dresses against their more complicated

Bardot's subversion of 'office clothes' in *Une Parisienne* (1957)

outfits, loose hair against their short set perms and hats, Jacques Estérel to their Balmain, as the credits make clear.

At the same time as they connoted youth – in the child-like and the teenager sense Bardot's clothes were ostentatiously sexualised, carefully designed to show off her figure. As Kaja Silverman has noted, since the late eighteenth century, fashion shifted from men and women to women only, and from a class to an erotic role, contributing to the construction of woman as spectacle. 'The cinema [gave] complex expression to the male fascination with female dress' (1986, p. 142). In comedies and dramas alike, Bardot, like a doll, is constantly dressed and undressed, drawing attention to both her clothes and the erotic zones of her body: her generous bosom, her amazingly narrow waist, her slender hips and bottom, her long and slim legs. That this description evokes a Barbie doll is no accident. Launched in March 1959, Barbie was based on a German doll, 'Lilli', which itself was created as 'a shapely femme fatale, embodying the glamour and sexiness of the stars of the moment, Marilyn Monroe and Brigitte Bardot'.[17] Although Barbie's proportions, life-size, would produce a grotesquely exaggerated female silhouette, Bardot, in her combination of curves and slimness, came close to the Barbie 'ideal'. Indeed, the very first Barbie wore a Bardotesque striped swimsuit and blonde ponytail.

The Estérel wedding dress typically partakes of the eroticisation of Bardot's body in sharply delineating her torso, with its tightly shaped bodice and nipped-in waist, while the billowing skirt draws the eye to her legs. If, as Camille Paglia claims, Bardot's mouth

Voulez-vous danser avec moi? (1959): Brigitte Bardot combining the innocence of gingham with the sexual innuendo of the can-can petticoat

was blatantly 'vulvar',[18] the frothy petticoat of the Estérel dress, like a French can-can dancer's skirt, metonymically refers to her sex. One of Bardot's most famous photographs, taken by Sam Lévin in the late 1950s, shows her holding up a lacy petticoat to display her legs, like a French can-can dancer.[19] This is echoed in a famous dance scene in *Voulez-vous danser avec moi?/Come Dance with Me* (Michel Boisrond, 1959), in which the camera isolates the swinging movement of her wide gingham skirt and frothy petticoat around her legs. Beyond the obvious Frenchness of the can-can, it has been argued that there is a national specificity in the emphasis on underwear in the representation of French (and European), as opposed to American stars (Boyer, 1990, p. 36). When not in wide skirts and petticoats, Bardot wore pencil skirts and dresses cut close to the body, like her red dress in *Et Dieu . . . créa la femme* and her outrageously stretched grey skirt and pink cardigan in *Une Parisienne*. Similarly, her trousers, whether Capri pants, jeans or micro-shorts, shared tightness as common denominator – in her memoirs she expresses bafflement at the 'feminist' taste for baggy trousers (Bardot, 1996). Her clothes thus relentlessly drew attention to, celebrated and sexualised her sensational body.

Bardot's clothes promoted and confined her to the role of sex kitten, to a sexuality that was both triumphant and infantilised. In this vocabulary, hair played a significant part. Its blondeness first appeared in 1956, in black and white in *En effeuillant la marguerite/Plucking the Daisy* (Marc Allégret) and in colour in *Et Dieu . . . créa la femme*. In France it was widely perceived as a bow to Americanisation in following the Monroe model. But it was also, as in the 'dumb blonde' stereotype, a marker of youth (Dyer, 1979b). Edgar Morin first pointed out that the young Bardot's hair connoted both the sexual woman in its abundance and the little girl in its fringe and ponytails (Morin, 1972, p. 29). But Bardot's most famous and influential hairstyle was the so-called *choucroute* (sauerkraut), or in another, even less elegant phrase of Brigitte's, the *chignon-bordel* (the chignon as total mess). Appearing from 1959,[20] this consisted of piling up hair on top of the head while letting the rest hang loose, any old how – as shown in *Marie-Claire*, which offered a 'step-by-step guide to Brigitte's *choucroute*' which, needless to say, is completely and intentionally incomprehensible.[21] The *choucroute* combined the child-like – a little girl with tangled hair, sometimes even including bows – with the sexual maturity of a pompadour high coiffure. Unruliness and abundance combined invitation with defiance – it is a hairstyle that says both 'fuck me' and 'fuck you'. The importance of the *choucroute* to Bardot's appeal is illustrated by its continued popularity. For instance in 2003, a website advertised the 'sexy, tousled Brigitte waves that are essential for the purest form of the look', while a fashion spread in *The Times*, entitled 'Echoes of Bardot' features gingham 'mini-dresses' as well as the advice 'hair is big and soft'.[22]

Bardot adopted and promoted fashion that liberated the body (and hair) from the constraints of rigid couture outfits, leaving behind bourgeois conventions – illustrated in the distance between her two wedding dresses. In this sense she revisited the post-World War I fashion 'revolution' led by Chanel, which saw the victory of looser and shorter dresses over the corseted Victorian clothes of the *belle epoque*. Yet, historians of 1920s' fashion also point out that the triumphant discourse of liberation that greeted, and later interpreted, these fashions must be modified. The supple but clinging clothes of the 1920s, simpler and more practical, nevertheless demanded a more 'perfect' body, which began to be catered for by the emerging beauty industry (Roberts, 2003, pp. 81–3). Similarly, Bardot's clothes are always seen as evidence of new, liberated lifestyles. Yet at the same time in their merciless exposure of female flesh, they firmly put in place the tyranny of the body-beautiful, with the attendant industries now in full swing.Slimness, which in France had been the privilege of the upper classes before World War II (Veillon and Denoyelle, 2000, p. 40), now became an imperative across the board.

Making new designers' fortunes

As in the post-World War I period, Bardot's sartorial revolution after World War II affected body and outfits. It also deeply affected the fashion industry. Another hallmark of the Bardot style was its simplicity and apparent cheapness: cottons rather than satin and silk, suede rather than mink, 'ready-mades': jeans, petticoats, men's T-shirts or shirts, sailors' jerseys, work overalls. She ignored accessories – she wore few jewels, often went barefoot and with no handbag, hats or gloves, or else cheap straw hats and plain scarves. Her clothes looked casual, just thrown on, though still sexy: her grey dress in *Et Dieu ... créa la femme* is an overall, but she wears it tight, the sleeves rolled up and buttons half-undone. In that film, in answer to the inquisitive look of a snobbish woman on a yacht who gazes at her plain red dress (contrasting vividly with her own flowery and expensive concoction), she insolently replies, 'I bought it on the harbour; I'll give you the address'. Although Saint-Tropez had been a fashionable spot for decades, Bardot and *Et Dieu ... créa la femme* made it world famous. Boutiques catered for local celebrities and wealthy *vacanciers* with a range of summery clothes in light fabrics and pastel colours. One of these was Christine Vachon, championed by Bardot.

Once she left home and modelling, Bardot vociferously rejected traditional couture as 'for grannies' (in Steele, 1988, p. 278). Instead, she plumped for a new breed of trendy young couturiers such as Jacques Estérel and Louis Féraud, whom, like Estérel, she made famous when she bought a white cotton dress in his Cannes shop in 1955 (Chenoune, 2000, p. 18). The Féraud dress, before Estérel's wedding gown, spawned a craze; Féraud said: 'Within a week, every woman up and down the Côte d'Azur was wearing my little white dress. We sold 500 of them in a matter of days.'[23] He went on to design Bardot's clothes for *Une Parisienne*, *Les Bijoutiers du clair de lune/The Night Heaven Fell* (Roger Vadim, 1958) and *En cas de malheur*. Bardot also championed designers such as Fred Salem, as well as Hélène and Willy Vager, who worked, respectively for Marie-Martine and Réal – both favourites of the Parisian *jeunesse dorée*. Bardot recounts how, in 1958, 'while window-shopping in Faubourg Saint-Honoré, I stopped in wonderment in front of a shop filled with delightful dresses. A happy chance had made me discover "Réal", who, for more than twenty years, would dress me on and off screen' (Bardot, 1996, p. 211).[24]

Bardot's choice of labels was emblematic of major shifts in the fashion industry. At the Liberation of France, Paris successfully fought a fierce battle to remain the world centre for fashion against attempts to move it to New York, Dior's New Look greatly contributing to this victory (Steele, 1988, pp. 268–75). However French couture soon had to fight another threat to its hegemony, the rise of *prêt-à-porter*, which throughout the decade slowly rose from a marginal to a central force in French fashion (Chenoune, 2000, pp. 15–17), connected in particular to its ability to cater for young consumers (Delbourg-Delphis, 1981, pp. 205–6). The new designers like Féraud and Estérel, as well as Courrèges, Cardin and Saint Laurent, were not cheap, but they inhabited a halfway space between *haute couture* and *prêt-à-porter*, and were, crucially, keen to dress the younger generation. Although 'fashion had always privileged the idea of youth to impose its rule' (Veillon and Denoyelle, 2000, pp. 37–8), a concerted move to put the very young woman centre stage and marginalise the mature woman, in a reversal of time-honoured practice, took place around 1958–9 (Ibid., p. 41). Simultaneously, design influence came from other sources than the 'laboratory' of couture, registering street and film fashion (Ruffat, 2000, p. 32) and *stylistes* such as Emmanuelle Khanh and Michèle Rosier opened shops, while others began to work for department stores such as Galeries Lafayette and the cheaper Prisunic. Thus the young couture outfits and *prêt-à-porter* designs were assimilated within a mass market. Bardot's clothes, made by expensive designers, nevertheless appeared cheap and, being made of industrially produced material (gingham, *broderie anglaise*), were easily reproducible. She was thus at the epicentre of the modernisation of fashion.

Bardot, like the New Wave cinema, was a symptom of a country undergoing an unprecedented economic boom (de Baecque, 1998). Her exuberant youth and joie de vivre, as expressed by her clothes, can also be seen as an index to the return to abundance after war-time privations, in the same ways as, at the Liberation, 'flamboyant fashions [such as Dior's New Look] had been a way of denying the humiliation of defeat' (Steele, 1988, p. 267). As Rihoit put it, 'One can see the Bardot phenomenon as a popular reaction, on an astonishing scale, against the persistent shadow of the war' (1986, p. 39). Is it too far-fetched in this respect to see the emphasis on her mane as a response to *les femmes tondues*, the shorn women who were punished for having slept with the enemy? Nowhere is this sense of Bardot as denial of the war years better expressed than in her emphasis on summer and the outdoors. From her second film *Manina*, as we have seen, she was associated with the Mediterranean – and then, forever, with Saint-Tropez (Servat, 2003). Her look and clothes were carefully crafted to stress the *natural*, even though it was based on the artifice of bleached hair (to evoke bleaching by the sun), holidays in the most expensive area of France, a luxury hedonistic lifestyle which re-established a new 'distinction' (in Bourdieu's sense) as summer holidays were becoming the norm. Bardot's championing of 'the natural' also prefigured the nostalgia for the artisanal and the ethnic, in a denial of the industrial dimension of modernisation that was gathering speed. In this respect it is indicative that Bardot's championing of cotton dresses took place in a decade which saw the phenomenal rise of synthetic fabrics, especially nylon whose production in France went up twenty-fold between 1949 and 1961 (Ruffat, 2000, p. 32). French *vichy* against American nylon: Bardot was fighting for French national identity in this way too.[25]

Whereas Bardot's initial rival Martine Carol, always made-up in classic glamour style, provided advice on her make-up technique in film and women's magazines (Chapuy, 2001, p. 66), Brigitte was overtly the opposite. On the release of *Et Dieu ... créa la femme*, *Cinémonde* asked, 'Do you want to look like BB?', advising: 'For eyes, above all no artificial effect. ... To give the impression of freshness, lips are cyclamen pink and they do not contrast too much with the foundation which must be very pale, transparent, natural'.[26] Ultimately, Bardot's image of transparency, cheapness, 'do-it-yourself' and naturalness spelt the fantasy of a classless society – a society in which a new youth generation was erasing the older class divisions, in the same way as clothes now transcended social occasion and spoke only of youth. Here again Bardot typified wide sociological currents: in October 1952, a huge sample of women interrogated for a poll reported they dressed 'to shop in winter, see parents and friends, go to a ceremony or wedding, go out on Sunday'. In June 1960, a similar mirror sample reported the obsolescence of these distinctions.[27]

Revolution or Consensus?

From 1963, as Bardot's film stardom waned, so her fashion appeal diminished, even though, through the 1960s, she appeared in Courrèges, 'pop art' fashion, Paco Rabanne and Yves Saint Laurent.[28] In the 1970s, she championed Jean Bouquin's 'hippie chic' (Servat, 1996, pp. 22–3). She continued to wear tight jeans, sailors' jerseys and bikinis. But just as her highly sexed behaviour lost its appeal in the permissive age, her fashion sense was no longer innovative.

But back in the late 1950s, Bardot's star image offered a powerful fantasy of sexual liberation – one that was not yet possible for most women, but which was intensely desired. The decade in which Bardot came of age, the 1950s, spanned the most contradictory period in women's history in France. For the first time politically adult (French women were finally granted the vote in 1944), and on a wave of economic growth, women were turned towards the future while the young generation – men and women – was becoming a real economic and cultural force. Both combined to demand, and a decade later obtain, change beyond recognition. At the same time, women in the 1950s were both the victims of the 'patriarchal settling of scores' (Burch and Selllier, 1995) of the post-Liberation period, in which a wounded French masculinity needed to bring women back into the fold, and prisoners of their biology under the sway of pro-natalist policies, in a country which was morally under the twin influence of Catholic conservatism and communist puritanism. This is why Simone de Beauvoir's *The Second Sex* (1949) was greeted with such ferocious derision and hostility (Chaperon, 1999, pp. 269–81). Female sexuality was the – often unacknowledged – terrain of the most vicious ideological battles, while this was also the decade of an extraordinary rise in erotic literature and the revival of the Marquis de Sade. In their combination of the child-like and the hyper-sexual, Bardot's clothes perfectly expressed this contradictory period, both the delirious joy of the new and the tight grip of patriarchy.

Bardot's sartorial challenge, which echoed the move from aristocratic *haute couture* to democratised *prêt-à-porter*, served the interests of the capitalist economy, while she took full advantage of the developing mass media. She promoted a paradoxical vision of femininity, a fantasy of the modern, yet unthreatening woman. As philosopher Antoinette Fouque put it, 'She signified sexual liberalism, not liberty for women' (1996). Which is why, unlike in the 1920s, when the fashion changes provoked a vicious backlash, Bardot's gingham wedding dress and her other clothes were embraced and copied. They generated consensus, not controversy. Thanks to the economic boom of the *Trente Glorieuses*, women entered the public sphere for good. But their visibility was at the price of relentless scrutiny and ever more stringent imperatives in terms of body shape. In the summer of 1959, however, as incarnated by a radiant Bardot in pink-and-white gingham, the joy and fun of the new fashions were truly irresistible.

Notes

1. Interview with Madonna in *Vanity Fair*, 1985, quoted in <www.mgross.com/MoreThgsChng/interviews/madonna1.html>, accessed February 2004.
2. Brigitte Bardot is her real name, not 'Camille Javal', contrary to a tenacious legend which attributes to her the name of her character in *Le Mépris/Contempt* (Jean-Luc Godard, 1963).
3. Marc Allégret had a reputation as a discoverer of young female talent, having launched the young Simone Simon in his 1934 *Lac aux Dames/Ladies Lake*. His 1955 *Futures vedettes* (*Future Stars*), featured Bardot as one of the rising '*vedettes*'.
4. *Elle*, 5 March 1951.
5. The film was not released in France until March 1953 in France as the result of a much publicised legal action by her father on the grounds of the film revealing too much of her body.
6. Several commentators at the time pointed out the resemblance of the young Bardot to Simone Simon (see note 3).
7. Although, mysteriously, posters for the film add the straps on to the bikini.
8. One of the documentaries about Bardot claims the term was coined for her – I have not found corroboration of this.
9. *Elle*, 29 December 1952.
10. 'L'Elegance Française au cinéma', Musée de la Mode, Palais Galliera, 26 October 1988–8 January 1989. The catalogue was published in English (Delpierre, de Fleury and Lebrun, 1988). The Jacques Estérel file at the Musée de la Mode, Palais Galliera, indicates that Estérel agreed to make a replica for the exhibition.
11. Marie Le Goaziou, *La France au fil de l'aiguille* (Rennes: Editions Ouest-France, 2002). See also, 'Le Vichy. L'Histoire d'un tissu', <ggc.free.fr/vichy_toile.htm>, accessed January 2004.
12. Eli Siegel evokes the hominess of gingham (and its link to American history), in his 1953 poem 'The Persistence of Fabric', <www.elisiegel.net/poetry/tro1290.htm>, accessed January 2004.
13. This is featured on the cover of the June 1959 *Paris-Match* containing photos of the Bardot–Charrier wedding.

14. *Elle*, 22 April 1960, features Bardot in a *broderie anglaise* shirt and a headline announcing: 'Brigitte launches *broderie anglaise* in Saint-Tropez'.

15. 'Brigitte Bardot contre Martine Carol', *Cinémonde* no. 1182, Easter special issue, 4 April 1957.

16. Archive footage of the young Bardot modelling ski outfits can be seen in a *Without Walls* documentary on Bardot, Channel 4 Television (1994).

17. The Lilli doll came from a cartoon in the tabloid *Der Bild*. The doll was designed by Max Weissbrodt and manufactured by the firm O. M. Hausser. From 'Dear Prudence', an article on the Lilli doll. <home.alltel.net/pennlee/bildlilli.html>, accessed February 2004.

18. Camille Paglia, interview on Bardot in *Without Walls* documentary.

19. One version of this picture can be seen in Crawley, 1975, p. 25. The obsession with these is obvious in, for instance, a website devoted to Bardot's petticoat pictures: <www.pettipond.com/bardot.htm>.

20. Servat (2003) claims it appeared in November 1960, in the photographs of Brigitte with her newborn son, Nicolas. However, her hairstyle in, for instance, the 1959 *Voulez-vous danser avec moi?* is close to the *choucroute*.

21. 'La Choucroute de Brigitte Bardot', *25 ans de Marie-Claire de 1954 à 1979*, Numéro special, 1979. No exact date is given for the article, but it coincides with the release of *Vie privée* (February 1962).

22. <www.drivingwithdawn.com/archives/2002/12/brigitte_bardot_hair_is_back.shtml>; *The Times*, 28 July 2003.

23. Quoted in 28 December 1989 obituary, <news.bbc.co.uk/1/hi/world/europe/581320.stm>, accessed February 2004.

24. It is not easy to verify exactly how many films they worked on, as a number of Bardot films have no acknowledged costume designer. However, Réal are credited as having designed Bardot's clothes for *Vie privée*.

25. I thank Steve Allen for helping me clarify this point.

26. *Cinémonde*, 22 November 1956, p. 22.

27. In Jacques Estérel cuttings file, Musée Galléria.

28. *Elle*, 7 December 1967 (no page number). Bardot features in a Paco Rabanne ensemble and in a faux-bullfighter costume by Yves St Laurent.

12

'Sean Connery *Is* James Bond': Re-Fashioning British Masculinity in the 1960s

Pam Cook and Claire Hines

Within the context of the cinematic James Bond's extraordinary resilience as a cultural phenomenon, there remains the equally interesting question of Sean' Connery's status among many fans and aficionados, and in the public imagination, as the definitive Bond. Despite 007's shape-shifting over more than four decades, no other actor has achieved the degree of authenticity attributed to Connery's interpretation – although each of the others has their own following.[1] In theory, James Bond could be played by any sufficiently mature, urbane and athletic actor – and there are rumours that when Pierce Brosnan retires, a non-British actor might take on the role of the British secret agent.[2] Indeed, 007 has already appeared in American form.[3] This is less of a travesty than it appears; after all, the special relationship between Bond and his CIA counterparts is a consistent theme throughout the franchise, and a primary element in a spy's job description is their ability to disguise themselves successfully. In a sense, the way has been paved by Brosnan, who is the most 'transatlantic' of all the Bonds, not least in his accent. However, if this were to happen, it is predictable that the desire to re-establish an original James Bond, most likely in the form of Sean Connery, would intensify.

This article sets out to explore what it is that makes Sean Connery the perfect, the quintessential James Bond. Bond is a post-modern phenomenon, on one hand, an international icon whose origins are indeterminate, on the other, a figure whose Britishness is a defining characteristic, and an essential element in marketing the films – but always an ironic cipher whose existence appears to be predicated on his chameleon-like lack of identity. He constantly re-invents himself – rather like an actor. 007 can, and does masquerade in a variety of roles in the line of duty, yet he remains himself: Bond, James Bond, as he frequently reminds everyone. He is identified by a name, and a number – perhaps a nod to his military background as a commander in the Royal Navy – and his back-story is minimal. It has been argued that the star persona – that is, the loose set of attributes that make up what we understand as a star's identity, creating a recognisable brand name – informs and inflects the characters they play, investing them with special qualities and setting up audience expectations (Dyer, 1979). Clearly, it is important to get the relationship between star and character right, if audiences (and advertisers) are not to be alienated or disappointed. Choosing the right actor to play

007 is a complex and hazardous business, especially as this is a subject on which just about everyone, whether they are fans or not, has an opinion. In cinematic terms, there is no character without the star/actor persona. Yet rather than just being a character, James Bond has become the equivalent of a star persona in his own right, in that he possesses a limited set of characteristics that are carried over from film to film, and that are mobilised in advertising and marketing campaigns. The cinematic 007 is a brand name that extends far beyond the Bond films themselves – indeed, the films are only a part of the global Bond phenomenon.[4] When Pierce Brosnan advertises Omega watches, he does so courtesy of his role as James Bond. It is possible, then, that James Bond transforms the accepted relationship between star and character by conferring star status on the different actors who play him, rather than the other way round. If that is the case, it would seem important that the actors who depict Bond should not be top-rank stars such as Tom Cruise or George Clooney, since their high-profile personas would outshine that of the special agent himself.

The implications of this are, of course, that in playing 007, an actor aiming for major international stardom risks being identified with the role to such an extent that all his other performances are tarred with the Bond brush – and, indeed, despite having become a global superstar with almost seventy films to his credit, Sean Connery's seven outings as James Bond still define his acting career for many people, causing him to distance himself from those films.[5] On the other hand, playing James Bond can help revive an acting career – as with Roger Moore, for example – or represent a nail in the coffin, as with George Lazenby, or transform an actor into a star, as in the case of Pierce Brosnan. Connery's and Brosnan's careers as 007 mirror one another to some extent: Connery kick-started the series, making an international name for himself in the process, while Brosnan revived the franchise, achieving worldwide recognition which has gained him considerable power in the industry. Brosnan's turn-of-the-century action hero has travelled some distance from Connery's suave 1960s' dandy – but that is the subject of another article. Here, we want to investigate how the working-class Scot Sean Connery was fashioned into the English gentleman-spy James Bond, contextualising our analysis in the cultural history of the 1960s. Our focus will be on the re-invention of British masculinity in the period, under the impact of consumer capitalism, and how that was manifested in both fashion and cinema. We shall also look at the connections between James Bond and the US male lifestyle magazine *Playboy*, launched in 1953 by Hugh Hefner with a view to re-styling the American man.

Producers Albert Broccoli and Harry Saltzman went to considerable lengths to find the right British actor to play Ian Fleming's sophisticated special agent, who had been popularised during the 1950s in the risqué James Bond novels and a cartoon strip that first appeared in the *Daily Express* in 1958 (Jones, 1999, p. 62). In the early 1950s, at the height of the Cold War, the highly publicised scandals of British communist double agents Guy Burgess and Donald Maclean, explicitly linked to their homosexuality, had cast doubt on the trustworthiness of the British Establishment. Burgess and Maclean came from the upper echelons of society, and were Cambridge men. In the context of contemporary research studies into male and female sexuality by Alfred Kinsey,[6] which had revealed some surprising statistics about the incidence of homosexuality in married men, and the lack of sexual gratification experienced by many married women, the implications were that all was not well with the 'normal' heterosexual marriage that formed the bedrock of the post-war consumer economy. At the same time, state legal intervention into formerly private arenas such as prostitution, homosexuality and abortion was attempting to reform and liberalise sexual morality in the direction of individual freedom and choice (see Hall, 1980). Against this background, James Bond emerged as both catalyst and symptom. His relationship to the British Establishment in class terms was not that clear, but his aggressive heterosexual masculinity and his inclination for slightly kinky rough-and-tumble distanced him from what was increasingly perceived as an effete, snobbish and outdated upper class. As a maverick risk-taker and sexual adventurer, Bond flouted the hierarchical, military-style rules and regulations of his stuffy superiors. While his patriotic allegiance was not in doubt, his rebellious tendencies made him vulnerable, both to exotic female spies and to the authoritarian system for which he worked.

Bond was a hero for the times, a transitional figure encapsulating the changes and contradictions facing British society in the throes of modernisation. The expansion of post-war consumer capitalism had produced groups with increased spending power, among them young working-class males, whose newly acquired wealth created a market for styles and fashions that would reflect their challenge to the status quo. Stars such as Elvis Presley, Marlon Brando and James Dean, dressed in T-shirt and jeans or black leather, articulated this youthful rebellion, which expressed total antipathy to the suits, shirts and ties of the conservative older generation. In Britain, a new style of actor emerged in response to the influence of the disaffected American male: the Angry Young Man, initially incarnated by Richard Burton in Tony Richardson's 1959 film *Look Back in Anger*,[7] who was driven by hatred of the British class system and the elitism of British society in general. In the late 1950s and early 60s, British cinema began to feature muscular, virile, working-class rebel heroes, personified by the likes of Albert Finney, Richard Harris and Stanley Baker, whose bodies were put on display for erotic contemplation, and whose hedonistic, amoral attitudes threatened the polite surface of the public-school ruling class. In this context, James Bond represented a bridge between tradition and modernity. Although not a working-class hero, his opposition to the British Establishment was clear in his tendency to break ranks and his disregard for authority. His aspiration to the lavish lifestyle and privilege of his superiors, coupled with his amorality and proclivity for sexual violence, reflected an impatience with, and occasionally contempt for, British middle-class hypocrisy. In many ways, then, beneath his urbane sophistication, James Bond possessed many of the attributes of a rebel hero, masquerading as a member of the Establishment and producing a kind of ironic commentary on its shortcomings.

In the wider social arena, Bond encapsulated the strengths and weaknesses of Britain on the world stage, and its need to modernise. With the decline of the ruling classes, the Empire and the traditional heavy industries, Britain attempted to reinvent itself as a democratic, technologically innovative nation, vying for a place at the forefront of developments in aerodynamics, the chemical industries and electronics. During the 1950s and 60s, Britain's trade and cultural links to both Europe and the US were consolidated by ambitious projects such as Concorde, and by the increase in imported ready-to-wear men's fashions from continental Europe, particularly from France and Italy, which challenged the domination of American popular culture in the British marketplace. The latter had inspired many of the youth subcultures, and had also transformed traditional dress for older men by creating a more casual fashion for open-necked shirts, often worn without a jacket. New synthetic fabrics such as Dralon, Orlon and Terylene, when mixed with wool, produced lightweight garments which kept their shape and were easy-care, allowing for greater freedom of movement. These lighter fabrics were to completely transform the military-style, formal tailored suits worn by the English City Gent, which were already being parodied by the street fashions of groups such as the Teddy Boys, who merged English style with elements of American iconography. This period heralded an era of intensified male consumerism in fashion and commodity consumption which had a dramatic impact on attitudes to male dress, and helped to establish Britain as a major force in the burgeoning global consumer economy, led by the US (Costantino, 1997, pp. 78–93).

In the international context, Bond represented a cosmopolitan European–British style in contrast to those youth subcultures inspired by US popular culture and music.[8] Indeed, although relatively young (he is described by Ian Fleming in *Moonraker* as in his mid-thirties), his military background and experience placed him at some distance from both teenage youth culture and the twenty-something Angry Young Man. At the same time, he was definitely not part of the older generation, and his style and expensive tastes identified him as a well-heeled bachelor with no strings – in other words, he spent all his money on himself. Despite being disposed to conspicuous consumption when it came to fast cars and other boys' toys, his dress style was defined by its understated elegance, presumably in order to allow him to merge into the background when necessary.

How, then, did Sean Connery, whose previous cinematic roles had been confined to Celtic working-class villains in films such as *No Road Back* (Montgomery Tully, 1956) and *Hell Drivers* (Cy Endfield, 1957), land the part of the suave James Bond against competition from a prestigious line-up of British actors that included Trevor Howard, Cary Grant, Richard Burton, Patrick McGoohan, Roger Moore and David Niven (see Macnab, 2000, p. 197)? This list is interesting in itself – the inclusion of the Irish McGoohan, the Welsh Burton and the Scottish Connery demonstrates how the bias towards upper-class Englishness that characterised British male stars until the 1950s was breaking down, producing a more inclusive definition of Britishness, in class and regional terms. However, Connery's Scottishness could have been perceived as a drawback, particularly in the all-important American market: despite landing a contract with Fox, and appearing as romantic interest in *Another Time, Another Place* (Lewis Allen, 1958) and Disney's *Darby O'Gill and the Little People* (1959), his career in the US had not taken off. Yet in some respects he possessed the ideal attributes to play Bond. He had an athletic physique,[9] and a certain grace of movement, thanks to some dance training. Due to his experience as a male model,[10] he was used to posing in suits. He also had a dark, brooding quality that seemed to match Fleming's description of his hero in *Moonraker*: '[A] rather saturnine young man ... something a bit cold and dangerous in that face ... Looks pretty fit ... [a] tough-looking customer' (quoted in Jones, 1999). Connery's relaxed physicality and predatory sexuality, the obverse of the 'stiff upper lip' brigade, was exactly the right image for the cool, modern version of British masculinity represented by the cinematic Bond, who would break with the past and project a vision of Britain at the forefront of technological and economic progress. This image drew on traditional British class stereotypes, while redefining them for the modern world.

Connery's Scottishness can thus be seen as a key element in that process of revision, displaying a new version of Britishness that would be viable in world markets, without sacrificing the hallmarks of quality and superior standards of craftsmanship that traditionally characterised British products. It also carried with it connotations of the history of Scottish antagonism to English imperialism, a factor that would appeal to American audiences in particular. Connery has always insisted on his Scottish roots – something which has endowed his persona with a degree of authenticity (see Macnab, 2000, p. 199). One might speculate, then, that he brought some of this authenticity to his performance as 007, and that it has contributed to his reputation as the 'best' Bond in many people's eyes. The authenticity seems to reside less in his ability to accurately portray the English gentleman-spy, than in his skill in re-defining and updating British stereotypes.

Another significant element in the choice of Connery was the fact that, although he

Designed for action: Sean Connery dressed to kill in *Dr No* (1962)

was an established actor, he was still relatively unknown to cinema audiences. This meant that his persona would not eclipse that of Bond himself, the true star of the films.[11] The working-class Connery had to be tutored in style, manners and dress sense for the role. Terence Young, the director of the first film, *Dr No* (1962), who was an Old Etonian and ex-Guardsman, and whose background was similar to that of Fleming's Bond, acted as mentor, taking the actor to his tailors in London and Paris and encouraging him to go out in the evening wearing Bond's clothes, so that he became accustomed to 007's urbane image. In addition to acquiring the special agent's expensive tastes, Connery was required to enhance his slightly receding hairline with a toupé, and his bushy eyebrows were plucked (see Broccoli, 1998, p. 171). Connery has recognised Young's decisive role in defining Bond's stylish and sophisticated on-screen image through a process of familiarisation which lent polish to the aggressive masculinity and rugged exterior that the actor brought to the role.[12] The biographical details for Connery in *Dr No*'s British pressbook continued to emphasise his working-class origins and confident physicality following 'a succession of rough-and-ready jobs requiring plenty of physical activity and stamina', promoting 'James Bond – Milkman' as a populist figure.[13] Bond's was an image constructed through wardrobe and studied by Connery, whose performance in *Dr No* was described by the *News of the World* as 'fitting Fleming's hero like a Savile Row suit', a comparison which forecast both the actor's identification with the role and the continued attention paid to Bond's attire in subsequent additions to the film series.[14]

The immediate cultural impact of the first Bond films was astonishing. Connery was so successful in creating Bond as an international style icon that the image quickly became a trademark, with multiple tie-ins to men's fashions and accessories. As well as the many licences granted to manufacturers eager to label their products with the lucrative '007' or 'James Bond' logo, the style was reflected in contemporary articles and advertisements in men's magazines, which proliferated in the 1960s. In 1966, American *GQ* devoted an editorial to Connery's interpretation of the Bond style, while *Playboy* magazine, which had a long-standing association with Ian Fleming and his James Bond, displayed an approach to male fashion that shared a number of features with the Bond films. The publication of an original Fleming novella entitled *The Hildebrand Rarity* in its March 1960 issue meant that *Playboy* became the first American magazine to print a Bond story, an alliance sustained by the serialisation of a further five Bond adventures during the 1960s.[15] In addition to the growing popularity of Fleming's work, his publication in *Playboy* was also a result of publisher Hugh Hefner's self-confessed admiration for both the 'tall, Continental-suited, profoundly British, profoundly sophisticated' author and his creation.[16] It was an appreciation that, *Playboy* suggested, was based on mutual esteem since Fleming was said have to been convinced that 'James Bond, if he were an actual person, would be a registered reader of *Playboy*', as the reader was offered a hero who lived the fantasy lifestyle that the magazine recommended.[17]

Playboy's articles were to take men's fashion seriously, introducing the reader to the importance of sartorial style within the consumerist, sexualised and liberated lifestyle that it promoted. A typical article in the January 1965 issue on 'The Progressive Dinner

Party' illustrated the magazine's propensity to combine fashion with other elements of the playboy lifestyle. The article constructed a fictional narrative of the evening's events, while a series of photographs depicted the party's 'host' and guests engaged in a number of sociable activities including dinner, conversation and dancing, followed by breakfast in a suitably 'exurban hideaway'. Surrounded by women, the playboy host's party attire was described in detail:

> Host is impeccable in Italian olive-colour nubby-silk dinner jacket with black satin lapels and sleeve cuffs, black mohair-and-worsted trousers with satin extension waistband and side stripes; jacket $85, trousers $35, both by Lord West. Formal shirt is of cotton broadcloth, has narrow pleats, double cuffs, by Excello, $9. (Mario and Green, 1965, p. 107)

Functioning as more than a dinner jacket, the host's 'impeccable' attire was intended as a fashion statement, and as an aspirational style for others to copy. Despite its libertarian approach to (hetero-)sexuality, *Playboy* was reluctant to put the nude male body on display, a reluctance shared by men's magazines even today. Cultural commentators have put this down to the difficulty associated with 'forcing men to look at themselves self-consciously as men', since it is a look fraught with overtones of homo-eroticism – a threat to the aggressive heterosexual masculinity advocated by both *Playboy* and the Bond films (Mort, 1986, p. 41). In surrounding *Playboy* Bond with hordes of glamorous desiring women, the intention was to make it clear that they were the natural objects of male attention. This disavowal of effeminate homosexuality made it possible to redefine consumerism, previously associated primarily with women, as a legitimate masculine activity, as heterosexual male readers and viewers could consider fashion with their sexual identities more or less intact. Even so, the sheer force of the disclaimer indicates the enormous effort required to overcome the 'problem'. The attention to detail exhibited in such articles about male fashion, and in the costuming of the cinematic James Bond, smacks of a dandyism which seems to be at odds with the virile man of action. Such fetishism threatens to distract from the serious business at hand, whether that be the seduction of beautiful women, or saving the world from evil.

Connery's besuited frame achieved the status of an icon during the 1960s, and despite the fact that he wore many different outfits as the secret agent, it is this image of 007 in a suit that has endured, and has become synonymous with the Bond films. The suit also remained an integral item in the wardrobe of *Playboy* magazine. It has been argued that the garment is 'symbolic of traditional manliness', displaying qualities associated with 'self-restraint, and focusing energy on . . . goal-directed behaviour', traditional masculine characteristics which the playboy bachelor transformed, imbuing them with hedonism, style and sexuality (Bruzzi, 1997, p. 69; Rubinstein, 1995, p. 58). Yet for others the modern suit is erotic in itself, revealing the contours of the broad-shouldered, idealised male body established by classical Greco-Roman culture (see Hollander, 1994). As the 60s progressed, the international box-office success of Connery's Bond offered *Playboy* a tangible vision of its model hero, and a special 'James Bond issue' of the mag-

Dandy Jim: Sean Connery as *Playboy* Bond in *Goldfinger* (1964)

azine published in November 1965 contained both an interview with Sean Connery, and a pictorial essay on 'James Bond's Girls'. Connery's comments were indicative of the new attitudes to male fashion fostered by both the magazine and the Bond films:

> I think I've got seven or eight suits now; I took them all from the films – plus a couple I bought a while ago in a moment of weakness. Something came over me and I went out one day and spent £300 [$840] on two suits.[18]

Connery's willingness to spend his disposable income on his wardrobe supported the ethos of affluence presented by *Playboy*, while his admission that he had experienced a 'moment of weakness' endorsed the acceptability of such reckless spending. The masculine identity associated with *Playboy* Bond was defined by an aggressive individualism signified by a sophisticated style based on conspicuous consumption, sexual promiscuity and an easy familiarity with the brand-named products represented as the necessary accessories for his bachelor lifestyle. The suit, which underwent a radical transformation during the 1960s, played a vital role in shaping this identity.

As a version of the gentleman-spy, Fleming's Bond was well dressed, in a simple, classic style: dark suit, white shirt and black silk tie and shoes. The understated style of the modern English gentleman seems to have originated with the dandy Beau Brummell in the early nineteenth century, who was instrumental in creating a new, urban male identity which aspired to aristocratic and upper-middle-class status, but was available to anyone who could afford it. Brummell and his followers revolutionised male dress, creating a fashion for an unadorned look that depended on superb cut and fit, and new pliable fabrics, for its effect. Despite its simplicity, however, this look was blatantly erotic: the dandies' tight, figure-hugging breeches and cutaway jackets displayed the sleek male body in all its graphic beauty. Many of the features of this dandy fashion philosophy can be detected in the Bond image. As described by Elizabeth Wilson,

> [t]he role of the dandy implied an intense preoccupation with self and self-presentation; image was everything, and the dandy a man who often had no family, no calling, apparently no sexual life, no visible means of financial support. He was the very archetype of the new urban man who came from nowhere and for whom appearance *was* reality. His devotion to an ideal of dress that sanctified understatement inaugurated an epoch not of no fashions for men, but of fashions that put cut and fit before ornament, colour and display. The skin-tight breeches of the dandy were highly erotic; so was his new, unpainted masculinity. The dandy was a narcissist. He did not abandon the pursuit of beauty; he changed the kind of beauty that was admired. (1985, p. 180)

The nineteenth-century dandy's look was a reaction to the highly decorated male fashions of the time, whose effeminate take on masculine identity was deemed inappropriate to the more restrained, serious ethos of the Industrial Revolution. It was a classless, upwardly mobile fashion that relied on classic British tailoring combined with innovatory materials and techniques. It was accompanied by a fastidious attention to style detail, and to personal hygiene, redefining these trivial, 'feminine' preoccupations as legitimate, serious male pursuits. The dandy did not subscribe to the contemporary work ethic; rather, he lived by his wits, and worked on himself, as pure image. The dandy was a style icon, but he also embodied an ironic critique of the emerging middle class.

As a transitional figure, who resolved social change and contradiction on the level of image, the Regency dandy has much in common with Connery's Bond, whose sartorial style was a response to the traditional dress of the English Establishment, as well as to the 'peacock revolution' of the burgeoning counter-cultures. Youth fashions of the 1960s were characterised by mimicry and pastiche. They appropriated styles and iconography from different periods and cultures, mixing them together to produce new, clashing configurations which were deliberately iconoclastic. The 'peacock revolution' referred to colourful, decorative styles for men, which allowed them to enjoy and consume fashion, while displaying themselves to attract women. At its most extreme, this peacock style was exhibited by rock stars such as Mick Jagger, who sported a flamboyant, long, frilled tunic reminiscent of eighteenth-century 'effeminate' dress. The bi-sexual, or 'unisex' fashions of the period challenged gender boundaries while being compatible with heterosexuality. At the same time, French designers such as Pierre Cardin, completely revamped the design of the conventional city suit and the way it was produced, revolutionising tailoring methods to produce ready-to-wear designer garments for the young, fashion-conscious male (see Costantino, 1997, pp. 94–107).

While he participated in the 'peacock revolution' to some extent, notably in his desire to dress to attract women, Connery's Bond positioned himself firmly against the strident iconoclasm of the counter-cultures, and even the milder version exhibited by the Beatles, whose low-necked, collarless suits were inspired by Pierre Cardin.[19] In *Dr No*, Connery

> ... wore Turnbull & Asser shirts with French cuffs, specially made by Michael Fish (who went on to open his own hugely influential shop, Mr Fish); he wore a Nehru jacket, and razor-sharp suits made for him by Anthony Sinclair in London's Conduit Street. Connery was both smart and casual, and the knitted short-sleeved shirt he wore when helping Ursula Andress out of the sea has been a casual-wear classic ever since.
>
> He was influential in other ways: because he always favoured two-piece tropical weight suits that offered serious mobility, men bought them in their hundreds of thousands; because he wore a white tuxedo, it began filling the pages of countless fashion magazines. (Jones, 1999, p. 62)

Connery's outfits were a mixture of old and new, bespoke and off-the-peg: Michael Fish was one of the new young designers leading the 60s' sartorial revolution. He had trained with traditional outfitters in Jermyn Street, and worked for exclusive shirt-makers Turnbull & Asser, before opening his own ready-to-wear shop just off Savile Row, the bastion of fine English tailoring. Designed by Anthony Sinclair, Connery's jackets were cut a little fuller, allowing Bond room to carry his gun while still following the contours of his figure. Michael Fish provided similarly sympathetic tailoring, supplying Connery with double-cuffed shirts using buttons rather than cufflinks in order to allow Bond to dress and, of course, undress, more easily.[20] 007's suits may have been custom-made for him, but they were mass-produced and bought in their thousands through the burgeoning men's fashion retail outlets. The 'smart casual' look, which extended to the suits and the formal tuxedo, courtesy of Connery's relaxed body language and habit of posing with his hands in his pockets, evoked the dandy's and the playboy's refusal of the puritanical work ethic. Yet this casual air was something of a masquerade, since in the line of duty, Connery's Bond was required to be quick on his feet in order to extricate himself from sticky situations. Fortunately, the suits were made in lightweight fabrics, allowing for maximum mobility. Like the dandy, Bond lived, and survived, by his wits. On many occasions, it was his own survival, rather than that of the Western world, that seemed to be most at risk. In this respect, he resembled the modern-day super-heroes who exist solely for the purpose of resolving major crises which threaten destruction on a global scale. In Connery's case, it was often explicitly his genitalia, and by implication his heterosexuality, that were under threat.[21] His sharp suits, and his 'smart casual' demeanour, on one hand revealed his body and sexuality, rendering him vulnerable to homosexual and female desire, and on the other masked his ability to muster a repertoire of survival tactics. Thus the suits both empowered him, and revealed his weaknesses. Those weaknesses were necessary to his sexual allure, while making it clear that he would never be able to survive without the array of state-of-the-art technological gadgets developed by the best scientific minds Britain had to offer.

It is not difficult to regard Connery's Bond as an anachronistic throwback to a traditional type of white, heterosexual masculinity, an example of unreconstructed manhood arising just when the radical social changes heralding the modern women's movement, and the gay and civil rights movements were making waves. He can also be seen as a conservative reaction to Cold War politics, and to the growth of continental Europe as a world power at a time when Britain's relationship to the EU was on the agenda. However, such readings do not exhaust the available meanings in Connery's Bond persona. It is precisely his (often cringe-making) regressive qualities, and his lack of political correctness, that underpin his enduring appeal. His sadism and habit of treating some women as disposable objects are counter-balanced by an occasional chivalric tendency, and by a penchant for strong, independent women who present a challenge to his manhood in that they are not necessarily immediately available, and are his equals in professional skills and sexual expertise. While they do generally submit to his charms, they give him a run for his money, and his ability to be 'up to the job' is constantly tested. The crude racism of the 1960s' Bond films, completely unacceptable in social terms, is tempered by a comic-strip quality that removes it from the realms of reality, allowing audiences to enjoy forbidden fruit in safety. These tensions are often played out in sartorial terms: in *Goldfinger* (1964), for example, Bond's superiority is established by the understated elegance of his wardrobe in contrast to the more florid attire of the villainous Goldfinger or the untidy disarray of his henchman Oddjob's outfit, itself a gross parody of the classic English city suit. In this cartoon universe, Bond's aura of 'cool' resides in his ironic awareness of himself as fiction, as pure image. Connery's knowing performance encapsulates this sardonic distance, while endowing 007 with a certain authenticity, courtesy of his physical attributes, his working-class origins and his Scottish nationality. The success of his rendition of Bond lies in a particular combination of rebel hero, dandy and heterosexual playboy that offers the pleasures of identification while enabling an ironic take on white, heterosexual masculinity itself.

Sean Connery Bond Filmography
Dr No (Terence Young, 1962, UK. Eon Productions)
From Russia with Love (Terence Young, 1963, UK. Eon Productions)
Goldfinger (Guy Hamilton, 1964, UK. Danjaq/Eon Productions)
Thunderball (Terence Young, 1965, UK. Danjaq/Eon Productions)
You Only Live Twice (Lewis Gilbert, 1967, UK. Danjaq/Eon Productions)
Diamonds Are Forever (Guy Hamilton, 1971, UK. Danjaq/Eon Productions)
Never Say Never Again (Irvin Kershner, 1983, UK/USA. Woodcote/Talia Film Productions/Producers Sales Organization)

TV Documentary Material
Brits Go to Hollywood: Sean Connery (Christopher Bruce, 2003), Channel 4,
22 November 2003.
'Inside *Dr No*' documentary, special feature on *Dr No* DVD, UA/MGM, 2000.

Notes
1. See for example 'Bond 1 – Sean Connery',
   <www.geocities.com/Hollywood/Boulevard/5584> accessed 2004.
2. Australian Hugh Jackman is one of those tipped to play the next Bond.
3. American television network CBS broadcast a one-hour adaptation of *Casino Royale* on 21 October 1954 as part of its weekly thriller series, *Climax!*, in which Bond was played by Barry Nelson, an American actor best known for his starring roles on Broadway. See Chapman, 1999, pp. 40–2.
4. In addition to the international box-office success of the Bond films, and Bond's circulation as a popular cultural icon, related merchandise and product tie-ins have included a mini-industry of music, clothing, cars, toys, alcohol, books, cosmetics and memorabilia, updated with the release of each new film. See 'A View to a Sell', *Time*, 11 November 2002, p. 70, with reference to *Die Another Day* (Lee Tamahori, 2002).
5. See the Channel 4 documentary *Brits Go to Hollywood: Sean Connery*.
6. Alfred Kinsey's report on *Sexual Behaviour in the Human Male*, published in 1948, was followed by his report on *Sexual Behaviour in the Human Female*, published in 1953.
7. Based on John Osborne's 1956 Royal Court Theatre production, starring Kenneth Haigh as Jimmy Porter.
8. However, some of the subcultures, such as the Mods, defined themselves in terms of European (i.e. Italian and French) styles as well.
9. Connery won a bronze medal at a Mr Universe contest in London in the early 1950s (see Macnab, 2000, p. 197).

10. As well as posing as a model for students at the Edinburgh College of Art, Connery also worked as a photographic model for a men's mail-order catalogue firm. See Sellers, 1999, pp. 25–6.
11. The tag line 'Sean Connery Is James Bond' was first used on the posters for *You Only Live Twice* (1967), trading on Connery's identity as Bond, in contrast to *Casino Royale*'s spoof treatment of the character.
12. See 'Inside *Dr No*' documentary, special feature on *Dr No* DVD, UA/MGM, 2000.
13. These jobs are said to have included 'cement mixer, bricklayer, steel bender, a printer's assistant and a lifeguard'. See *Dr No* Pressbook, BFI microfiche.
14. See *News of the World*, 7 October 1962.
15. This included two short stories, *Octopussy* (printed in March and April 1966) and *The Property of a Lady*, published in *Playboy*'s tenth anniversary issue, while April, May and June of 1963, 1964 and 1965 featured serialisations of *On Her Majesty's Secret Service*, *You Only Live Twice* and *The Man with the Golden Gun* respectively, each within a short time of their initial publication in hardback editions.
16. See 'Playbill', *Playboy*, March 1960.
17. Ibid.
18. '*Playboy* Interview: Sean Connery', *Playboy*, December 1965, p. 80.
19. Note 007's ironic reference to the Beatles in *Goldfinger*, just before he's knocked unconscious!
20. See 'Inside *Dr No*' documentary, special feature on *Dr No* DVD.
21. Among many references to physical castration, the laser sequence in *Goldfinger* remains a classic.

13

Luisina Brando's Costuming in María Luisa Bemberg's Films: An Excessive Femininity

Denise Miller

Luisina Brando was the favourite actress of popular Argentine feminist film-maker, María Luisa Bemberg. This chapter examines Bemberg's use of the middle-aged Brando's acting persona and Argentine fashion in her direction of *Miss Mary* (1986) and *De eso no se habla/We Don't Want to Talk about It* (1993). In these films, Brando performs a glamorous, comic femininity which, as Doña Leonor in the last film, reaches an 'excess'. In the latter film what constitutes 'truth' and what fantasy question each other. Doña Leonor indulges her fantasies in an increasingly extravagant 'dressing up' until actual fashion has been left behind. That the question of fantasy as opposed to 'truth' is made explicit through costume makes explicit the questions around Brando's performance (and Bemberg's display) of a constructed femininity. The excesses of her costume put on show some feminist film theoretical questions around masquerade as fabrication. This chapter asks how Brando's costume is made to stand out against her *mise en scène*, yet, in its construction of our comic, sympathetic identification with her, refines her persona's 'class' (refining the spectator's appraisal of her from 'kitsch' to 'camp'), and pre-empts a voyeuristic gaze. Initial brief analysis of Brando's role, performance, 'looks' and placing within her *mise en scène* in Fernando Ayala's *El año del conejo/Year of the Rabbit* (1987) will enable us to gauge their comic refinement, briefly in *Miss Mary* and extensively in *De eso no se habla*. Through Brando's costuming in the latter film, the chapter then considers masquerade as a strategy through which a male gaze is emasculated, and a woman-to-woman address is reinforced.

Luisina Brando

Brando – who moves easily between stage, television and film, and quickly between comic and tragic registers – has appeared in films by many distinguished Argentine directors in which (up to 1993) she always plays a sexually vibrant woman, moving herself 'like a cat in front of the camera'.[1] Brando is stereotypically 'feminine', having a curvaceous figure and abundant thick dark brown hair. Her mobile face and dark eyes, combine with her physical features, deep, husky voice and graceful movements and gestures to suggest not a simmering, but a flaunted, sensuality. Before her prize for Best Actress in Bemberg's *Señora de Nadie/Nobody's Wife* (1982), Brando had won three awards, two of them Best Actress Awards, one for the stage and one for film.[2] However, Brando is little known outside Argentina. Neither is she among Argentina's top noted actresses.[3] As answer to this paradox, Clara Fontana suggested her 'type-casting to the lower middle class'; Fontana pointed to the roles that (even) Bemberg made her play.[4]

María Luisa Bemberg

The feature film-making of María Luisa Bemberg spans the years 1979 to 1995. In her later films especially, an opulent *mise en scène* frames the female leads whose sensuality is displayed and celebrated in a *mise en scène* of femininity. Bemberg's first two features were made during the Dirty War of 1976 to 1983, in which 'thousands' of people were 'disappeared' by the military. Bemberg's final four films were made in the period of restored democracy that witnessed the trial of the generals who had headed this Dirty War. What could not be talked about in the first three years of Bemberg's film production was excavated for public witness in the subsequent three.[5] In all of Bemberg's films that repressive force and logic which allowed the military machine to 'disappear' the other is implicated in the patriarchal repression of the feminine in home and state. *De eso no se habla* allusively talks about the inadmissible: that censorship enacts many kinds of 'disappearance' in Argentina: 'We Don't Talk about That'. Thus the fact that in it Brando's costume is foregrounded is a wider than feminist refusal to let women disappear.

Brando was an early asset: 'I choose my actresses . . . especially for the expressiveness of their face. Brando's mobility . . . enables her to evoke different moods brilliantly' (*La Plata*, Buenos Aires, 29 November 1981). Costume was likewise essential to Bemberg's project. She elected a top designer in Buenos Aires. Graciela Galán, designer for the Paris Opera, was wardrobe designer for both films in which Brando 'starred' for Bemberg. In Galán's costumes and under Bemberg's direction, Brando's expressive acting achieved a comic refinement evident in none other of her film roles.

El año del conejo

Pepe (Federico Luppi) encourages Norma (Brando) to have a breast implant in the vain hope of spicing up their love life. They separate. Norma becomes a successful businesswoman and meets up again with her husband. Now their love life improves. The plot and the tone of this film are vulgar. Accordingly, Brando's performance reinforces a brash *mise en scène*. This is exemplified in an early scene in which, arguing with her husband, she is getting ready for bed. She is shot from behind and reflected face-on in a three-way mirror. Ayala's screen takes in a wide *mise en scène* – dominated in the foreground by a messy array of bright, 'tacky' objects on Brando's dressing table – that signifies her 'low' class. Brando moves and holds herself in a brittle way. At one point her reflection shows her head held upwards in a gesture reinforcing the raising of her eyes to heaven. Her eyes (like her head) do not move, so that her stare, arrogant and harsh, is of a piece with the rough way in which she next brushes her loose, long hair and with the brittle timbre of her voice. Finally, she coarsely slaps cold cream on her face. Apart from the raising of her eyes to heaven, she does not take her eyes off herself.

Miss Mary

In *Miss Mary*, Brando likewise represents a loose and lower-class woman. Here she clashes with the sexually repressed, lonely governess, Miss Mary (Julie Christie), and the uptight and arrogant Señora, Mecha (Nacha Guevara).[6] Perla (Brando) offends the good taste of the aristocracy – disrupting the tone of the film – by flaunting her brash sexuality to win the rich widower, Pacheco. Now, however, her vulgarity is tempered by a kind of sorrowful joy.

Perla first appears (conflicting with Miss Mary and Mecha) halfway into the film. They oppose (looking at each other) over a wedding table. Brando recounts a joke at the expense of the recently deceased Pacheco. An establishing shot outlining her audience's seating positions – Miss Mary at one end of the table, Brando at the other, facing Alfredo (Mecha's husband) – begins her monologue. To her left is the admiring Ernesto (Mecha's brother); further to the left, at the top end of the table looking down it, is Mecha. This is Brando's scene. Her tale – an 'I said, he said' anecdote – (by its invitation to mimicry) allows for acting up and for display. It begins with, 'He was so mean', and is punctuated throughout with her physical gestures. She is all hands and eyes. The light catches her dark eyes (whose shine is echoed in pearl earrings and necklace) in their frequent movements around the table, while her hands percuss the emotional effect of her tale as well as the exaggeration in the telling. When she lifts her drink, her red nails – rhyming with the redness of the red car in which she arrived, and which, rushing into the tranquil and pastel colours of the *mise en scène*, has created an 'outstanding' disturbance – are prominent. At the end of her, 'He sat down and he said . . .', she folds her arms in a mannish way.

Perla looks for recognition, across the table, left to right, and out of the front of the screen. Although she mostly looks at the men, this is after a first attempt to gain, with an eyeline match to the studiously oblivious Mecha, the latter's approval. Brando reacts by playing up her role of careless abandon. Thus, part of her own motivation for vulgar 'display' (notwithstanding that the men are captivated) is tempered here by Brando's comic, yet sorrowful, wish for female recognition.

The *Mise en Scène* of Femininity: Brando, *De eso no se habla* and Argentine Fashion

The comic physicality of Brando as Perla anticipates that in *De eso no se habla*, where her sexual presence and comedy are part of her hyper-femininity and the way in which she carries her 'fashion'. The comedy of costume works here towards the utterance of serious, even tragic, statements. The narrative begins with the realisation that Doña Leonor (Brando), a prosperous widow in small-town Argentina, cannot escape the fact, even if she censors all mention of it, that her daughter Charlotte is a dwarf. Charlotte grows up. Handsome Italian, Ludovico d'Andrea (Marcello Mastroianni), falls in love with her. They marry. He gives her love but cannot bring her happiness. The film ends with Charlotte's escape to the circus that her mother has fruitlessly kept at bay.

That Bemberg's direction refines Brando's natural liveliness with grace (and sadness) is seen immediately. The opening sequence narrates Doña Leonor's displeasure at the whispered rumours concerning Charlotte, to whose birthday party we cut back and forth from Doña Leonor's brooding gaze at herself in a three-way mirror (a direct quotation to that of Ayala)? At that party, one other mother has tried to comfort her but was rejected. For this, Doña Leonor earns the curse that God will punish her again. After the credits is a cut (in silence) to a close-up of a glass dish on a dressing table. We are in a middle-class home, where everything is in its place (behind the casket, the items of ornamentation and brushes etc. catching some light, suggest some degree of wealth). The clatter of beads into the dish, however, suggests discord. The camera moves upwards from the dish, to the right (along her arm) to bring into mid-close-up and into the right half of the frame, the profile of a middle-aged woman (Brando). As the camera moves up to the woman's face, the subdued light of dressing-table lamps, displaced by shadows, remains in the outline of her hair and on her forehead. An indistinct reflection of her in the mirror is occluded as she bends her head down and further into the frame. Brando's hair is tied back, and at the mirror she is mostly still. Her simple, classic black dress with white collar, works with the drab and heavy colours of the *mise en scène*. Eventually, the camera pulls back, ninety degrees to the right and behind, to reveal her in an over-the-shoulder, middle-distance shot, reflected three ways again in the mirror that she faces. The effect is of a woman in mental pain. The subdued *mise en scène* is abruptly obliterated with the change of scene to the bright outside light of the children's party whose primary colours are accompanied by sounds of festivity and children laughing (so that two *mise en scènes* of femininity are contrasted in the first two shots of the sequence).

In the scene's second bedroom component, Brando, in elegant long black negligee, sleeps on a shiny, deep red eiderdown. Her prone body is picked out in a white light shining from above to frame her black torso, and naked arms and shoulders. This sensuous lighting of her body continues as Brando's movements direct the camera off the bed, towards the wardrobe, into the corridor. We witness a heavy grace yet flourish in her movements, especially in the way she walks. Now framed mid-distance in the corridor, she puts on her coat with one fluid, graceful movement of it over her shoulders, before she swivels on her heel and swings through the door. This action, quietly excessive in its repressed, vigorous movement, rhymes a previous action in the party scene: there she sashayed into the frame to remind one mother that – whereas she refuses to admit that her own child is 'handicapped'– this mother's child, being deaf, cannot hear her. The rhyming of comic flourish with expression of deep grief involves us sympathetically with Doña Leonor.

The tender, yet comic grief of Bemberg's opening provides the foil to an increasing excess of costume and gesture with which, as a coquettish, socially aspirational woman, Doña Leonor clothes and expresses herself. As 'excess' and fantasy are vital to Bemberg's construction of Brando's *mise en scène*, she chose a wardrobe designer who prefers to imagine rather than imitate.[7] Galán's play with the 'make-believe' of what is both feminine and fashionable is made clear when we situate *De eso no se habla* – a film that progresses through three epochs: the 1920s, 1930s and 1940s – within its period of Argentine fashion. These were the times before mass production when, at the same time that Argentine classes could be easily distinguished by their dress, there was a freer expression of idiosyncrasy.[8] Argentine fashion journalist Susana Saulquin notes, 'A large proportion of women of the highest classes ... dressed for other women, to demonstrate their superiority' (1997, p. 226). Bound up with aspiration is envy; character traits we see feeding into Doña Leonor's ideas of fashion.[9] Furthermore, in the film, the fantasy of competition that is fed by envy, spirals. According to Galán, Doña Leonor gets more exaggerated as the film progresses, because the situation – Charlotte is growing older, but not growing – gets more desperate. Thus she dresses Charlotte in an increasingly 'out-doing' way. She is to be the best *señora burguesa*. This 'grotesque' fantasy reaches its apogee in two dresses. First, her choice (for Charlotte) of frothy white wedding dress; the baroque excesses of this dress – layers of white froth – are decorative surfaces under which Charlotte is hidden. 'Tender' though this dress is, it obliterates Charlotte as an individual. Nevertheless, that it is tender is exemplified against Doña Leonor's blue dress, which (second), representing her own best at Charlotte's wedding, is worn assertively, not tenderly.

Analysis of the sequence in which we first see this blue dress – as Doña Leonor finishes preparations for the wedding – will exemplify the sensual qualities both of its texture and of Brando's performance within it. The sequence begins with a mid-distance shot of Charlotte's white nightgown laid out on the bridal bed. From this, there is a cut to Brando in mid-close-up, behind a wedding cake. The camera pulls back, revealing a shiny blue dress, in whose contradictions the comic tone is established. It is gloriously puffy but cut around the cleavage so that Doña Leonor is power-dressed and sexy. Her extravagant white hat slopes coquettishly on one side. Her actions begin a comedy of incongruity. She looks around to establish that she is alone, reaches forward, takes the sugar bride and groom off the cake and stuffs them into her mouth. When another character (Mohamé, her shop-boy) enters into the right of the frame, the shiny quality of her dress (upon which extra lighting is thrown) stands out against his drab brown suit. Mohamé has entered to entreat her to visit the sick mayor. She rushes off, desperate to persuade him to accompany Charlotte (beside whom, in his wheelchair, he will hardly tower), up the aisle. The camera – tracking her running to the mayor's house – moves back from close-up to reveal her sensuous curves, pointed up by the shiny quality of the material. The shine picks out so clearly the slippery texture of the material that our visual experience of it is made tactile.

Once in the mayor's sick room Doña Leonor acts the part of coquette. As she approaches the side of the mayor's bed, she sidles. She is in control again. Now, in motivating the camera's movements, she displays herself in three actions to the spectator across the screen. In the first of these actions, the camera follows Brando's arm – made sensuous by a light rippling along her muscles – as it reaches from left to right across the screen to stroke the mayor's head. The next cut gives a full-frontal view down Doña Leonor's cleavage. As the following cuts confirm that this is, first, from the crippled mayor's point of view, then from that of his fey assistant, the spectator point of view is made impotent. Doña Leonora is saying, 'He's getting better, isn't he?' in a deep voice which enjoys its own authority. The second action begins when Doña Leonor agrees to

Self-delighting, masquerading in *De eso no se habla* (1993)

Her fantasy of class, or, stating what she wants (*De eso no se habla*)

take the mayor to the toilet. Now a comic music begins, dramatising her putting on a role, and her own consciousness of the comedy she is performing. The exaggerated gestures in which Brando rights the mayor's hat, appraising it for effect, suggest her awareness of audience. She further shows a consciousness of the camera as, third, she moves directly into its lens (and in placing her backside against it places herself up against Bemberg's camera) before swaying down the corridor along the trajectory of its view in which only the blue dress shines out.[10] The excessive sumptuousness of costuming is so enjoyed here that it effaces our awareness of any other element of the *mise en scène*. Doña Leonor's swaying action indicates her knowing enjoyment of effect. She also gets what she wants: the mayor agrees to accompany Charlotte up the aisle.

Doña Leonor's dress confirms how it was the middle classes in 1930s' Argentina who had more psychological space (as well as just enough wealth) for a wider expression of fashion. Saulquin says, 'The high classes tended to the conservative because threatened by upward mobility, whilst the lower classes tended through economic insecurity to imitation and to uniformity' (1997, p. 187). Middle-class women 'dressed themselves for themselves, out of pure pleasure in dress and to affirm themselves' (Ibid., p. 226). Bemberg is interested in the middle class to which Brando's snobbish character belongs and the upper class to which she aspires. Wealthy women, travelling between Britain, France and Buenos Aires, had an important influence on upper-class fashions in Buenos Aires, which became dedicated to high couture.[11] According to Galán, however, aspiring, snobbish and middle-class women would have got their fashion ideas from magazines which were six to seven years behind Europe. Furthermore, the women in this film are from a poor small town. With poorer cloth than their middle-class counterparts could get in Buenos Aires, and with some exercise of fantasy, these snobbish women will have got their dressmakers to attire them as they imagined the socially and fashionably eminent of the metropolis to dress. This was something that Bemberg and Galán were keen to portray. Galán's method of research and design is revealing.[12] She confirmed that all fashion designs for Brando were based on primary documentation. In Buenos Aires, she scoured the San Telmo Sunday antiques market for magazines of the 1930s, mainly *Para Ti*. She also looked at photographs from the 1920s and 1930s, as well as at *Chabela*, from which she adapted one design for Brando's white and (heightened because bright) red dress with the magnificent white collar, worn at Charlotte's public piano recital. Comparison reveals Galán's comic exaggerations.

Bemberg's 1990s' film would also carry the connotations of a 1940s' and 1950s' vulgarity that the upper classes associated with Eva Perón's (Evita's) social aspirations.[13] Evita's tour to Europe (1947) shows a restrained elegance in which nonetheless the hat signifies an excess of glamour. Trailed by the paparazzi, dominating the public scene like no-one before her, this 'poor girl from the sticks' constructed a femininity that was 'possible' to the socially aspirational, but risible to those who, threatened by her embrace of the poor, considered themselves of a superior class. By the time she returned from Europe in August 1947, she had polished her appearance. But the hats still feature an excess, with which, paradoxically, poor women identified. Brando's character carries these connotations in that she too – socially aspirational – is not quite 'the real thing.'

By the way she wears her hat (*De eso no se habla*)

Hats on and hands up! (*De eso no se habla*)

The outrageous excess of Evita's hats feature prominently in a scene where Doña Leonor competes with other women. This scene – showing how Doña Leonor's pretensions are to the upper class that comprised women who dressed for (but to outclass) each other – occurs in the priest's office. Doña Leonor wants Charlotte to play the piano at the town's charity show. Neither priest nor the other women are prepared for this 'shame'. Galán confirms that the women's hand-made hats demonstrate their fantasies and competition at play. While their debate (in which every woman has her say) ensues, the camera moves across each woman to the right, foregrounding their hats: the rhyming shots eventually focus the confrontation between Doña Leonor and one other woman (with whom, as the mother of the deaf girl, the film has earlier placed her in deadly rivalry). This then becomes a confrontation between Doña Leonor and the priest, in which the camera (by close framing) makes issue of her hat. By the way she wears her hat, Doña Leonor gets the better of the women and the priest (who is shot from behind to reveal his baldness):

Brando has performed in her hat in a way which we cannot see Evita do, winning us over to laughing with, rather than at, her scheming. Thus Brando positions us in feminine identification with her (albeit an identification with her competition with other women), while the hats have 'stood out' from the *mise en scène*.

Bemberg's *Mise en Scène* of Femininity: Integration or Display?

While Perla stands out from a 'cool' background, only Doña Leonor controls her spaces and the men (and women) within them through her sexual play and costumes. Her sumptuousness of costume is foregrounded to the extent that it does not blend in with, but dominates the *mise en scène*. The feminist film theoretical position on costume is that it foregrounds the feminisation of history.[14] In making her costumes increasingly stand out, Bemberg makes this issue explicit. Integration would not be consonant with Bemberg's challenge to the 'disappearing' of women. This challenge is made self-conscious (when later – at the wedding banquet itself – Brando is burying the dead mayor in a bath of ice) by the director's placing of the bulb above Brando's blue dress, which then shines out from the dark. This refusal of integration goes against the grain of costuming in classical Hollywood cinema of the 1930s and 1940s, which, in expressing the assumption that its visual apprehension should not deflect from the (male Oedipal) narrative momentum, registered on screen at the same time that it receded (Gaines, 1990, p. 182). The spectacle of women's dress rather than folding into, propels, narrative in the scene where Doña Leonor uses her sexuality to manipulate the mayor.

Feminist Glamour/Masquerade as a Strategy

Through Brando's humour, Bemberg exceeds feminist film theoretical expectations, however, by making Brando (increasingly) glamorous. If Mary Ann Doane correctly suggests the 'simple gesture of directing a camera towards a woman has become equivalent to a terrorist act' (in Penley, 1989, p. 216), glamour (as excess of femininity) becomes problematic, as is its capture on the screen. Bemberg is not a 'terrorist'. First, glamour makes women visible, so makes 'significant the insignificant' (Barthes, 1978). Thus, Bemberg's costuming of Brando addresses a paradox of feminist film criticism which as B. Ruby Rich complains, 'insists on our absence even in the face of our presence' (1998, p. 87). Second, we have seen Doña Leonor use costume to empower herself. Here her glamour recalls the pre-second wave feminism of Garbo and Dietrich who obtain power through enjoying how others see them.[15]

A third counter to terrorism is that when (feminine) visibility becomes excessive, it highlights itself as a construct: in this case, Brando's vocal masculinity contrasts with the excessive feminine code of her dress, suggesting that dress constitutes a performance of femininity. Fourth, Bemberg's direction of Brando suggests Luce Irigaray's argument that woman can empower herself by mimicking the role of femininity ascribed to her (1985, pp. 68–85). Masquerade becomes an offensive strategy (rather than a defensive mask) and sends up femininity as a male construction of women. The key, interinvolved strategies of 'taking on' one's femininity – of 'standing out' and 'playfulness' (Ibid., p. 76) – are exactly those that analysis has suggested of the excessive femininity of Brando's costuming. Doña Leonor's triumph in the scene of the hats shows her character putting playfulness and standing out to work, and the two scenes with the sick and then the dead mayor respectively have made Bemberg's play with the outstanding blue dress explicit too. Appositely, women 'should take on the way in which they have been defined as lack ... they should signify that ... a disruptive excess is possible on the feminine side' (Ibid., p. 78). Excess is disruptive, not in renunciation of the feminine 'style', but in the questions it asks of its appraisal. If masquerade reveals what is hidden, the question becomes one of reading. Brando's performance – inviting both emasculated and comic modes of appraisal – makes us see her masquerade, her costume, as offensive. This appraisal is more than visual. Irigaray (Ibid., p. 79) suggests the feminine mimicry of feminine style should make sight 'tactile'. In making her dress tactile (a tangibility effected by the camera's slow revelation of its shine on her body as she walks to the mayor's sickbed), Doña Leonor's dressmaking and Bemberg's film-making return us – as does Jane Gaines (Gaines and Herzog, 1990, p. 23) – to the anthropological meaning of the word fabrication: to possess. The blue dress celebrates (and parodies) both tactile desires to feel and to have, which transgress the silencing and containing of woman.[16]

Excess Wit: Kitsch or Camp?

The offensive masquerade in Brando goes beyond her loud costumes, extending to her comic gestures and mannish voice. It is not so much that glamour empowers her, as her sense of it (her performance of it and her playing up of her sexiness) has. Thus is the offensive effect of masquerade doubled. But Bemberg's humour is problematic. For the blue dress, Galán looked for a 'ghastly, cheap, kitsch' material. Her models were 'Menemistas' (the famously kitsch, blonde, made-up and over-dressed women of President Menem). The intention was for the audience to laugh at Brando's social pretension (in other words, to laugh at her class).[17] In this blue dress, however, Brando's performance outwits the intentions even of Bemberg and Galán. In it Brando as Doña Leonor comes closer to what in the 1960s in Argentina was a combination in fashion-conscious women of 'hyper-sexiness' and refinement (Vrljicak-Espain, 1992, p. 103). Her performance of her character's sensuous love of display – counteracting the 'ghastliness' of the costume – is 'camp,' invoking a tender recognition that affectionately laughs with, rather than at (as is the case with 'kitsch' which laughs at the artistically vulgar).[18] Camp is consonant with Brando's 'refining' performance in the opening scenes of De eso no se habla which engages our tender identification with her grief. Nevertheless, the tenderness and refinement of camp do not obviate theatricality. We have seen Brando's performance heightened in 'actions and gestures of exaggerated emphasis' by which performances of camp are defined.[19] The same can be said of her comic display of costume. Finally, the humour means that women are not only looking at, but laughing with, each other.

Woman-to-Woman Address

Brando performs her femininity to other women largely through her dress. If in the picnic scene of Miss Mary, Perla, with her red nails and pearl earrings, performs to other women within the diegesis, in De eso no se habla, Doña Leonor's sense of performing to the camera is vivid: she flaunts her blue dress to the spectator. In the scene when she takes the mayor to the toilet, Doña Leonor genders this look as female in three ways. First, the male point of view, rendered weak, is emasculated. Second, this begs the question to whom and for whom was she performing. Third, Doña Leonor positions herself – knowingly – in front of the woman director's camera. All three of these strategies have a comic effect, which, reinforcing the complicity between the female spectator and female actress, demonstrates how, according to Gaylyn Studlar (1990), costume is a way of acting on and controlling the gaze. While women comically shown as dressing for and against each other may not be the most feminist statement, the result is nevertheless other women's comic pleasure and a negation of men.

Conclusion

Bemberg's directing and dressing of Brando refines her lower-middle-class persona, yet makes her vitality and glamour increasingly excessive. Brando's 'looks' are directed at women within and across the screen, who applaud the celebration of her costume. At the same time fashion is used ironically to comment on women's fantasies. We have not been looking at fashion so much as a fantasy of what is fashionable. In Bemberg's last film Brando performs a fantasy of class. The result is a feminine dress that is overblown, magnificent and sometimes hilarious.

We are looking at a glamour which stands out – is made feminist and funny – by its filmic analysis as a strategy. Doña Leonor's transgressions lie in using masquerade strategically, rather than defensively, to have what she wants. Bemberg's feminist 'glamour' delights in its oxymoronic qualities. Through her costuming of Brando she constructs an excessive feminine glamour through which she defies the 'disappearing' of women, both celebrating and analysing one woman's sensual enjoyment of herself as spectacle. Thus she confirms the identification of her spectator with the 'feminine' at the same time that she questions of gender construction. Thus Bemberg – through Brando – uses costume to make feminist statements.

Bemberg's women defrock their men and masculine walls tumble in her *mise en scène* of femininity. But Brando plays her glamour in a tragicomic way to bring out the full sense of desperation that motivates it. We are never laughing at the woman within the costume. In this way, Brando exceeds Bemberg's directing, as well as the comedy of Galán's costume.

Notes

1. In *Los Andes* (Mendoza, 25 April 1982).
2. The Molière Prize (1977) for Tenessee Williams' *The Glass Menagerie*; and for Sergio Renán's *Sentimental*, from the Critics Association of Argentina (1979).
3. There is little documented information concerning Brando. Much of my sense of her persona was gleaned in Argentina from '*chismes*'/gossip.
4. Personal interview (Buenos Aires, 4 September 2000).
5. *The Report of the Commission on the Disappeared: Nunca más/Never Again* (1984) – listing 8,960 cases of disappearance based on testimony – marks the definitive official confirmation of a 'cleansing' in Argentina (the actual figure is thought by the Commission to have been much higher).
6. The credits welcome 'the guest appearance of Luisina Brando'.
7. I interviewed Galán in her Buenos Aires apartment (2 September 2000). Galán stated her preference for designing for the opera, in which – as the art form least rooted in reality – she can use her fantasy.
8. 'Economic development caused a multi-class system, in which fashion closely intimated the prestige of class' (Saulquin, 1997, p. 72).
9. Saulquin (Ibid., p. 192) suggests, 'Imitation, emulation and a little bit of envy' is particularly part of the Argentine's Spanish inheritance.
10. French feminists call to women to speak with their bodies. Nicole Ward Jouve (1991, p. 83) quotes Hélène Cixous: 'Write yourself: the body must be heard.'
11. Until 1947 there was a liberal importation of French, English and Italian clothes into Argentina (Saulquin, 1997, p. 72).

12. Galán showed me her designs (and reviews on which they were based) for Brando in *Miss Mary* and *De eso no se habla*. Galán did not consult the few Argentine documentary surveys of fashion. Nevertheless they confirm Galán's comments regarding middle-class women's creative fantasising about fashion.

13. Eva Duarte (1919–1952) – a radio actress – came to prominence in 1945 by her marriage to Colonel Juan Perón (elected president the following February). As first lady, she began the re-definition of her image whose star glamour became inseparable from her role as politician. With her highly publicised tour to Europe (1947), her image was refined, her transformation completed. She travelled with her own photographer, hairdresser and the head seamstresses from Henriette and Naletoff, the couture houses that designed her wardrobe. Today, critics and lay people alike talk of her 'performances'.

14. See Cook (1996) and Bruzzi (1997).

15. There is an irony of difference between them and Doña Leonor: the former were stars, whereas the latter can only fantasise about becoming one.

16. Carmen Vrljicak-Espain (1992, p. 10) cites Baudrillard's contention that the final aim of fashion 'consists in dramatizing an intimated desire for transgression'.

17. In contrast, Mastroianni was to be dressed up as an up-to-date, very rich, European.

18. Jack Babuscio (1977, pp. 122–3) notes these distinctions between the respective humours of camp and kitsch.

19. Cleto (1999, p. 9) quotes from a dictionary of late Victorian slang. Brando's heterosexual performances of camp are also consonant with an Argentine appropriation. Camp has a particular, distinguished history in Argentina. It was not only (out-of-date) fashion magazines that fed Argentine women's fantasy. More topical images (received from Hollywood) were more fanciful. That these images were fundamental is evidenced in Manuel Puig's novels, *Betrayed by Rita Hayworth* (1968), set in the 1930s, and *Heartbreak Tango* (1969), set in the 1940s, which parody popular culture – in which women particularly partake – as camp.

Bibliography

Adrian, (no date) *Special Collection: Adrian Papers*, New York: Fashion Institute of Technology.

Alexander, K. (1991) 'Fatal Beauties: Black Women in Hollywood', in Gledhill (ed.) *Stardom: Industry of Desire*, pp. 45–54.

Amouroux, H. (1991) *1945–1950, La France du Baby-Boom*, Paris: La Découverte.

Ash, J. and Wilson, E. (eds) (1992) *Chic Thrills: A Fashion Reader*, London: Pandora.

Aurrecoechea, J. M. and Bartra, A. (1994) *Puros Cuentos III: Historia de la historieta en Mexico, 1935–1950*, Mexico City: Grijalba.

Babington, B. (2001) (ed.) *British Stars and Stardom: From Alma Taylor to Sean Connery*, Manchester: Manchester University Press.

Babuscio, J. (1977) 'The Cinema of Camp (*aka* Camp and the Gay Sensibility)' in Cleto (ed) (1999) *Camp*, pp. 117–35.

Bach, S. (1992) *Marlene Dietrich: Life and Legend*, New York: Morrow.

de Baecque, A. (1998) *La Nouvelle vague: portrait d'une jeunesse*, Paris: Flammarion.

Bandyopadhyay, S. (1993) (ed.) *Indian Cinema: Contemporary Perceptions from the Thirties*, Jamshedpur: Celluloid Chapter.

Banga, I. and Jaidev (1996) (eds), *Cultural Reorientation in Modern India*, Simla: Indian Institute of Advanced Study.

Bard, C. (ed.) (1999) *Un Siècle d'antiféminisme*, Paris: Fayard.

Bardot, B. (1996) *Initiales B.B. Mémoires*, Paris: Bernard Grasset.

Bardot, B. (1999) *Le Carré de Pluton*, Paris: Bernard Grasset.

Barnes, R. and Eicher, J. B. (1993) *Dress and Gender: Making and Meaning*, Providence and Oxford: Berg.

Barthes, R. (1978) *De la mode*, Paris: Payot.

Basinger, J. (1994) *A Woman's View: How Hollywood Spoke to Women 1930–1960*, London: Chatto and Windus.

Baxter, J. (1971) *The Cinema of Josef von Sternberg*, London: Zwemmer.

de Beauvoir, S. (1960) *Brigitte Bardot and the Lolita Syndrome*, London: André Deutsch and Weidenfeld & Nicolson.

Bemberg, M. L. (1981) 'Interview' in *La Plata*, Buenos Aires, 29 November.

Bemberg, M. L. (1982) 'Interview' in *Los Andes*, Mendoza, 25 April.

Berry, S. (2000) *Screen Style: Fashion and Femininity in 1930s Hollywood*, Minneapolis: University of Minnesota Press.

Bhaumik, K. (2002) *The Emergence of the Bombay Film Industry, 1913–1936*, unpublished DPhil thesis, University of Oxford.

Bonfil Batalla, G. (1996) *México Profundo: Reclaiming a Civilization*, trans. Philip A. Dennis, Austin: University of Texas Press.

Bourdieu, P. (1990) [1980] *The Logic of Practice*, trans. Richard Nice, Cambridge: Polity Press.

Boyer, M. (1990) *L'Ecran de l'amour, Cinéma, érotisme et pornographie 1960–1980*, Paris: Plon.

Broccoli, C. (1998) *When the Snow Melts*, London: Boxtree.

Brunsdon, C. (1997) *Screen Tastes: Soap Opera to Satellite Dishes*, London: Routledge.

Bruzzi, S. (1997) *Undressing Cinema: Clothing and Identity in the Movies*, London: Routledge.

Bruzzi, S. and Church Gibson, P. (eds) (2000) *Fashion Cultures: Theories, Explorations, and Analysis*, London and New York: Routledge.

Burch, N. and Sellier, G. (1995) *La Drôle de guerre des sexes du cinéma français*, Paris: Nathan.

Chabria, S., Dharamsey, V. and Cherchi Usai, P. (1994) (eds) *Light of Asia: Indian Silent Cinema, 1912–1934*, New Delhi: Wiley Eastern.

Chadwick, W. and True Latimer, T. (2003) *The Modern Woman Revisited: Paris Between the Wars*, New Brunswick, NJ and London: Rutgers University Press.

Chaperon, S. (1999) 'Haro sur *le deuxième sexe*', in Bard (ed.) *Un Siècle d'antiféminisme*, pp. 269–83.

Chapman, J. (1999) *Licence to Thrill*, London: I.B. Tauris.

Chapuy, Arnaud (2001) *Martine Carol filmée par Christian-Jaque*, Paris: L'Harmattan.

Chatterjee, P. (1993) *The Nation and Its Fragments: Colonial and Postcolonial Histories*, Princeton, NJ: Princeton University Press.

Chenoune, F. (1993) *A History of Men's Fashion*, trans. Richard Martin, Paris: Flammarion.

Chenoune, F. (2000) 'Jalons pour une histoire culturelle de la mode. Une chronologie: 1952–1973', *Bulletin de l'Institut d'Histoire du Temps Présent* vol. 76, November.

Chinchore, P. (1990) 'Pandit Bhatkhande's Thoughts on Thumri', in Mehta (ed.) *Thumri: Tradition and Trends*.

Cleto, F. (ed.) (1999) *Camp: Queer Aesthetics and the Performing Subject*, Edinburgh: Edinburgh University Press.

Cocteau, J. (1979) *Mes Monstres sacrés*, Paris: Editions Encre.

Cohan, S. (1997) *Masked Men: Masculinity and the Movies in the Fifties*, Bloomington and Indianapolis: Indiana University Press.

Collins, A. F. (1995) 'When Hubert Met Audrey …', *Vanity Fair* (December), pp. 166–76, 180–3.

Comolli, J.-L. (1978) 'Historical Fiction: A Body Too Much', *Screen* vol. 19 no. 2, pp. 41–53.

Comolli, J.-L. and Narboni, J. (1985) [1971] 'Cinema/Ideology/Criticism', in Nichols (ed.) *Movies and Methods II*.

Cook, P. (1996) *Fashioning the Nation: Costume and Identity in British Cinema*, London: BFI.

de Cordova, R. (1990) *Picture Personalities: The Emergence of the Star System in America*, Urbana: University of Illinois Press.

Costantino, M. (1997) *Men's Fashion in the Twentieth Century: From Frock Coats to Intelligent Fibres*, London: B. T. Batsford.

Craik, J. (1994) *The Face of Fashion: Cultural Studies in Fashion*, London: Routledge.

Crane, D. (2001) *The Social Agenda of Clothing*, Chicago, IL: University of Chicago Press.

Crawley, T. (1975) *Bébé: The Films of Brigitte Bardot*, London: LSP Books.

Curry, R. (1996) *Too Much of a Good Thing: Mae West as Cultural Icon*, Minneapolis: University of Minnesota Press.

Dargis, M. (1996) 'A Man for All Seasons', *Sight and Sound* vol. 6 no. 12.

Dawson, A. S. (1998) 'From Models for the Nation to Model Citizens: *Indigenismo* and the "Revindication" of the Mexican Indian, 1920–40', *Journal of Latin American Studies* vol. 30, pp. 279–308.

Delbourg-Delphis, M. (1981) *Le Chic et le look: histoire de la mode féminine et des moeurs de 1850 à nos jours*, Paris: Hachette.

Delpierre, M., de Fleury, M. and Lebrun, D. (1988) *French Elegance in the Cinema*, Paris: Editions Paris-Musée et Société de l'Histoire du Costume.

Dietrich, M. (1987) *Marlene*, New York: Grove Press.

Doane, M. A. (1987) *The Desire to Desire: The Woman's Film of the 1940s*, Basingstoke: Macmillan.

Dore, E. and Molyneux, M. (2000) (eds) *Hidden Histories of Gender and the State in Latin America*, Durham, NC: Duke University Press.

Dowdy, A. (1973) *The Films of the Fifties: The American State of Mind*, New York: Morrow.

Dr No Pressbook, BFI microfiche.

Dwyer, R. (2000) 'Bombay Ishtyle', in Bruzzi and Church Gibson (eds) *Fashion Cultures*, pp. 178–204.

Dyer, R. (1979a) *Stars*, London: BFI.

Dyer, R. (1979b) *The Dumb Blonde Stereotype*, London: BFI.

Dyer, R. (1986) *Heavenly Bodies: Film Stars and Society*, London: BFI/Macmillan.

Eckert, C. (1991) [1978] 'The Carole Lombard in Macy's Window', in Gledhill (ed.) *Stardom: Industry of Desire*, pp. 30–9.

Edwards, T. (1997) *Men in the Mirror: Men's Fashion, Masculinity and Consumer Society*, London: Cassell.

Entwhistle, J. (2000) *The Fashioned Body: Fashion, Dress and Modern Social Theory*, Cambridge: Polity Press.

Entwhistle, J. and Wilson, E. (2001) *Body Dressing*, Oxford and New York: Berg.

Evans, C. and Thornton, M. (1989) *Women and Fashion: A New Look*, London and New York: Quartet Books.

Finch, C. and Rosenkrantz, L. (1979) *Gone Hollywood*, London: Weidenfeld Nicolson.

Flamini, R. (1994) *Thalberg: The Last Tycoon and the World of MGM*, New York: Crown Publishers.

Flashback, The Times of India Sesquicentennial (1990), Bombay: Times of India.

Flügel, J. C. (1930) *The Psychology of Clothes*, London: Hogarth.

Fouque, A. (1996) Interview on Bardot, *Arte*, June 1996.

Gaines, J. M. (1989) 'The Queen Christina Tie-Ups: Convergence of Show Window and Screen', *Quarterly Review of Film Studies* vol. x no. 4.

Gaines, J. M. (1990) 'Costume and Narrative: How Dress Tells the Woman's Story', in Gaines and Herzog (eds) *Fabrications*, pp. 180–211.

Gaines, J. M. (1992) 'Dorothy Arzner's Trousers', *Jump Cut* no. 37.

Gaines, J. M. (2000), 'On Wearing the Film', in Bruzzi and Church-Gibson (eds) *Fashion Culture*, London: Routledge.

Gaines, J. M. and Herzog, C. C. (1990) (eds) *Fabrications: Costume and the Female Body*, London and New York: Routledge.

Garber, M. (1993) *Vested Interests: Cross-Dressing and Cultural Anxiety*, Harmondsworth: Penguin.

George, N. (1992) *Buppies, B-Boys, Baps & Bohos: Notes on Post-Soul Black Culture*, New York: HarperPerennial.

Geraghty, C. (2000) *British Cinema in the Fifties: Gender, Genre and the 'New Look'*, London: Routledge.

Gledhill, C. (1987) (ed.) *Home Is Where the Heart Is: Studies in Melodrama and the Woman's Film*, London: BFI.

Gledhill, C. (1991) (ed.) *Stardom: Industry of Desire*, London: Routledge.

Golden, E. (with Kim Kendall) (2002) *The Brief, Madcap Life of Kay Kendall*, Lexington: University Press of Kentucky.

Gonzáles Casanova, M. (1995) *Los excritores mexicanos y los inicios del cine, 1896–1907*, Sinaloa, MX: El Colegio de Sinaloa.

Grant, B. (1995) (ed.) *Film Genre Reader II*, Austin: University of Texas Press.

Gutner, H. (2001) *Gowns by Adrian: The MGM Years 1928–1941*, New York: Harry N. Abrams, Inc.

Hall, M. (1930) *The New York Times*, 17 November.

Hall, S. (1980) 'Reformism and the Legislation of Consent', in National Deviancy Conference (ed.), *Permissiveness and Control*, New York: Barnes & Noble.

Hall, S. (1992) 'What Is This "Black" in Black Popular Culture?', in Dent (ed.) *Black Popular Culture*.

Hansen, K. (1999) 'Making Women Visible: Gender and Race Cross-Dressing in the Parsi Theatre', *Theatre Journal* vol. 51 no. 2.

Hanut, E. (1996) *I Wish You Love: Conversations with Marlene Dietrich*, Berkeley, CA: Frog Ltd.

Harper, S. (1987) 'Historical Pleasures: Gainsborough Costume Melodrama' in Gledhill (ed.) *Home Is Where the Heart Is*.

Haskell, M. (1997) *Holding My Own in No Man's Land: Women and Men and Film and Feminists*, New York and Oxford: Oxford University Press.

Hedetoft, U. (2000) 'Contemporary Cinema: Between Cultural Globalisation and National Interpretation', in Hjort and MacKenzie (eds) *Cinema and Nation*.

Herzog, C. C. and Gaines J. M. (1991) [1985] '"Puffed Sleeves before Tea-Time": Joan

Crawford, Adrian and Women Audiences', in Gledhill (ed.) *Stardom: Industry of Desire*.

Hjort, M. and MacKenzie, S. (2000) (eds) *Cinema and Nation*, London: Routledge.

Hollander, A. (1989) *Moving Pictures*, New York: Knopf.

Hollander, A. (1993) *Seeing through Clothes*, Berkeley and London: University of California Press.

Hollander, A. (1994) *Sex and Suits: The Evolution of Modern Dress*, New York: Knopf.

Hotchner, A. E. (1976) *Doris Day: Her Own Story*, London: W. H. Allen.

Hunt, L. (1991) 'The Many Bodies of Marie Antoinette', in Lynn Hunt (ed.) *Eroticism and the Body Politic*, Baltimore, MD: Johns Hopkins University Press.

Hunt, L. (1992) *The Family Romance of the French Revolution*, Berkeley: University of California Press.

Irigaray, L. (1985) *This Sex Which Is Not One*, trans. C. Porter and C. Burke, Ithaca, NY: Cornell University Press.

Jacobs, J. and Braum, M. (1977) *The Films of Norma Shearer*, Secaucus, NJ: Citadel Press.

John, Mr (1951–3) *Special Collection: Mr John Clippings*, New York: Fashion Institute of Technology.

Jones, D. (1999) 'Dressed to Kill', *Sunday Times Magazine*, 7 November.

Joseph, G. M. and Nugent, D. (1994) (eds) *Everyday Forms of State Formation: Revolution and the Negotiation of Rule in Modern Mexico*, Durham, NC: Duke University Press.

Karnad, G. (1980) 'Glorious Gohar', *Cinema Vision India* vol. 1 no. 1.

Kelly, R. D. G. (1996) 'Kickin' Reality, Kickin' Ballistics: Gangsta Rap and Postindustrial Los Angeles', in Perkins (ed.) *Droppin' Science*.

King, B. (1985) 'Articulating Stardom,' *Screen* vol. 26 no. 5.

Knight, A. (1980) 'Peasant and Caudillo in Revolutionary Mexico 1910–17', in D. A. Brading (ed.), *Caudillo and Peasant in the Mexican Revolution*, New York: Cambridge University Press.

Knight, A. (1994) 'Weapons and Arches in the Mexican Revolutionary Landscape', in Joseph and Nugent (eds) *Everyday Forms of State Formation*.

Kumar, N. (1988) *The Artisans of Banaras: Popular Culture and Identity, 1880–1986*, Princeton, NJ: Princeton University Press.

Lambert, G. (1990) *Norma Shearer: A Life*, New York: Knopf.

Landis, D. Nadoolman (2003) *Screencraft: Costume Design*, Burlington: Focal Press.

de Lauretis, T. (1987) *Technologies of Gender: Essays on Theory, Film and Fiction*, Basingstoke: Macmillan.

Laver, J. (1983) *Costume and Fashion: A Concise History*, New York: Oxford University Press.

Lever, E. (2000) *Marie Antoinette: The Last Queen of France*, trans. C. Temerson, New York: St Martin's Griffin.

Lewin, D. (1957?) Unidentified newspaper article on BFI microfiche system (from internal evidence it would appear to have been published in 1957).

Lipovetsky, G. (1994) *The Empire of Fashion: Dressing Modern Democracy*, trans. Catherine Porter, Princeton, NJ: Princeton University Press.

Lomnitz, C. (2001) *Deep Mexico, Silent Mexico: An Anthropology of Nationalism*, Minneapolis: University of Minnesota Press.

Macnab, G. (2000) *Searching for Stars: Stardom and Screen Acting in British Cinema*, London and New York: Cassell.

Maeder, E. (ed.) (1987) *Hollywood and History: Costume Design in Film*, New York: Thames and Hudson/Los Angeles County Museum of Art.

Mario, T. and Green, R. L. (1965) 'The Progressive Dinner Party', *Playboy*, January.

Martín Barbero, J. (1993) *Communication, Culture and Hegemony: From the Media to Mediations*, trans. Elizabeth Fox and Robert A. White, London: Sage.

Mehta, R. C. (1990) (ed.) *Thumri: Tradition and Trends*, Bombay: Indian Musicological Society.

Mercer, K. (1994) *Welcome to the Jungle: New Positions in Black Cultural Studies*, New York and London: Routledge.

Merck, M. (1994) *Perversions, Deviant Readings*, London: Virago.

Mohamed, F. (1933) 'Western Sex-plays and Indian Youths', *Varieties Weekly*, 15 July.

Molyneux, M. (2000) 'Twentieth-Century State Formations in Latin America', in Dore and Molyneux (eds) *Hidden Histories of Gender and the State in Latin America*.

Monaco, P. (1987) *Ribbons in Time: Movies and Society since 1945*, Bloomington: Indiana University Press.

Morin, E. (1972) [1957] *Les Stars*, Paris: Editions du Seuil.

Mort, F. (1986) 'Images Change', *New Socialist*, no. 23.

Mort, F. (1996) *Cultures of Consumption: Masculinities and Social Space in Late Twentieth-Century Britain*, London: Routledge.

Moseley, R. (2002) *Growing Up with Audrey Hepburn: Text, Audience, Resonance*, Manchester: Manchester University Press.

National Deviancy Conference (1980) (ed.) *Permissiveness and Control: The Fate of 60s Legislation*, Basingstoke: Macmillan.

Neal, M. A. (2002) *Soul Babies: Black Popular Culture and the Post-Soul Aesthetic*, New York and London: Routledge.

Neale, S. (1983) 'Masculinity as Spectacle: Reflections on Men and Mainstream Cinema', *Screen* vol. 24 no. 6, pp. 2–16.

Nichols, B. (1985) (ed.) *Movies and Methods II*, Berkeley: University of California Press.

Nixon, S. (1998) *Hard Looks*, London: Routledge.

O'Malley, I. (1986) *The Myth of the Revolution: Hero Cults and the Institutionalization of the Mexican State, 1920–1940*, New York: Greenwood Press.

Oxford English Dictionary (1989), Oxford: Clarendon Press.

Paranaguá, P. A. (1995) (ed.) *Mexican Cinema*, London: BFI.

Penley, C. (ed.) (1989) *The Future of an Illusion; Film, Feminism and Psychoanalysis*, London: Routledge.

Perkins, W. E. (1996) (ed.) *Droppin' Science: Critical Essays on Rap Music and Hip-Hop Culture*, Philadelphia, PA: Temple University Press.

Peyrusse, Claudette (1986) *Le Cinéma méridional. Le Midi dans le cinéma français, 1929–1944*, Toulouse: Eché.

Rajadhyaksha, A. (1987) 'The Phalke Era: Conflict of Traditional Form and Modern Technology', *Journal of Arts and Ideas* nos 25–6.

Rajadhyaksha, A. (1994) 'India's Silent Cinema: A "Viewer's View"', in Chabria, Dharamsey and Cherchi Usai (eds) *Light of Asia*.

Rao, V. (1996) 'Thumri and Thumri Singers: Changes in Style and Lifestyle', in Banga and Jaidev (eds), *Cultural Reorientation in Modern India*.

de los Reyes, A. (1996) *Cine y Sociedad en México, 1896–1930, Bajo el Cielo de México*, Volumen II (1920–4).

Rich, B. R. (1998) *Chick Flicks*, London and Durham, NC: Duke University Press.

Rihoit, C. (1986) *Brigitte Bardot. Un Mythe français*, Paris: Livre de poche.

Roach, M. E. and Eicher, J. B. (eds) (1965) *Dress, Adornment and the Social Order*, New York: John Wiley.

Roberts, Mary Louise (2003) 'Samson and Delilah Revisited: The Politics of Fashion in 1920s France', in Chadwick and True Latimer (eds) *The Modern Woman Revisited*.

Rosen, M. (1973) *Popcorn Venus: Women, Movies and the American Dream*, New York: Coward, McGann and Geoghegan.

Rubenstein, A. (1998) *Bad Language, Naked Ladies, and Other Threats to the Nation: A Political History of Comic Books in Mexico*, Durham, NC: Duke University Press.

Rubinstein, R. (1995) *Dress Codes: Meaning and Messages in American Culture*, Boulder, CO: Westview Press.

Ruffat, M. (2000) 'La Mode des années soixante entre artisanat et industrie?', *Bulletin de l'Institut d'Histoire du Temps Présent*, vol. 76, November, pp. 24–36.

Russell, D. A. (1983) *Costume History and Style*, Englewood Cliffs, NJ: Prentice-Hall.

Sarkar, T. (2001) *Hindu Wife, Hindu Nation: Community, Religion and Cultural Nationalism*, London: Hurst.

Saulquin, S. (1997) *La moda en la Argentina*, Buenos Aires: Emecé editores.

Schiro, A.-M. (1993) *The New York Times*, Obituary, 29 June.

Scott, A. (1979) 'The Milliner's Tale', *New York*, 26 February.

Sellers, R. (1999) *Sean Connery: A Celebration*, London: Robert Hale.

Sellier, G. and Vincendeau, G. (1998) 'La Nouvelle vague et le cinéma populaire: Brigitte Bardot dans *Vie privée* et *Le Mépris*', *Iris*, no. 26, Fall.

Servat, H.-J. (1996) *Les Années Bardot, L'Album Souvenir*, Paris: Editions No. 1.

Servat, H.-J. (2003) *In the Spirit of St Tropez*, New York: Assouline Publishing.

Shay, D. (1969) *Conversations: Volume 1*, Albuquerque, NM: Kaleidoscope Press.

Shih, J. (1997) *Fashionable Clothing from the Sears Catalogs, Late 1950s*, Atglen, PA: Schiffer Publishing.

Silverman, K. (1986) 'Fragments of a Fashionable Discourse', in Modleski (ed.) *Studies in Entertainment*.

Simpson, M. (1996) *It's a Queer World*, London: Vintage.

Smitherman, G. (1977) *Talkin' and Testifyin': The Language of Black America*, Boston, MA and New York: Houghton Mifflin.

Smitherman, G. (1994) *Black Talk: Words and Phrases from the Hood to the Amen Corner*, Boston, MA and New York: Houghton Mifflin.

Sobchack, V. (1995) ' "Surge and Splendor": A Phenomenology of the Hollywood Historical Epic', in Grant (ed.) *Film Genre Reader II*.

Sorlin, P. (1996) *Italian National Cinema, 1896–1996*, London: Routledge.

Soto, S. (1990) *Emergence of the Modern Mexican Woman: Her Participation in Revolution and Struggle for Modernity, 1910–1940*, Denver, CO: Arden Press.

Stacey, J. (1991) 'Feminine Fascinations: Forms of Identification in Star–Audience Relations', in Gledhill (ed.) *Stardom: Industry of Desire*, pp. 141–63.

Stacey, J. (1994) *Star Gazing: Hollywood Cinema and Female Spectatorship*, London: Routledge.

Steedman, C. (2002) *Dust: The Archive and Cultural History*, New Brunswick, NJ: Rutgers University Press.

Steele, V. (1988) *Paris Fashion, A Cultural History*, New York and Oxford: Berg.

von Sternberg, J. (1965) *Fun in a Chinese Laundry*, San Francisco, CA: Mercury House.

Street, S. (2001) *Costume and Cinema: Dress Codes in Popular Film*, London and New York: Wallflower.

Studlar, G. (1988) *In the Realm of Pleasure: Von Sternberg, Dietrich and the Masochistic Aesthetic*, New York: Columbia University Press.

Studlar, G. (1990) 'Masochism, Masquerade, and the Erotic Metamorphoses of Marlene Dietrich', in Gaines and Herzog (eds) (1990) *Fabrications*, pp. 229–49.

Stutesman, D. (1988) Interview with John P. John.

Stutesman, D. (2002) Interview with Juliet Polsca.

Sundar, P. (1996) *Patrons and Philistines: Arts and the State in British India, 1773–1947*, New Delhi: Oxford University Press.

Tabach-Bank, L. and Field, A. (2003) 'It's Reigning Men', *Vanity Fair*, April.

Tapert, A. (1998) *The Power of Glamour*, New York: Crown.

Turim, M. (1984) 'Designing Women: The Emergence of the New Sweetheart Line', *Wide Angle* vol. 6 no. 2; reprinted in Gaines and Herzog (eds) *Fabrications* (1990), pp. 212–28.

Vaughan, M. (2000) 'Modernizing Patriarchy: State Policies, Rural Households, and Women in Mexico, 1930–1940', in Dore and Molyneux (eds) *Hidden Histories of Gender and the State in Latin America*.

de la Vega Alfaro, E. (1995) 'Origins, Development and Crisis of the Sound Cinema (1929–64)', in Paranaguá (ed.) *Mexican Cinema*.

Veillon, D. and Denoyelle, F. (2000) 'Regard sur la mode des années soixante et sur l'arrivée de nouveaux acteurs', *Bulletin de l'Institut d'Histoire du Temps Présent* vol. 76, November.

Vincendeau, G. (2000) *Stars and Stardom in French Cinema*, London and New York: Continuum.

Vrljicak-Espain, C. (1992) *Mujeres de la imagen*, Buenos Aires: Editorial Planeta Argentina.

Wagner, J. (1959) 'Un Cinéma sous cellophane', *Cahiers du cinéma* vol. 99, September.

Ward Jouve N. (1991) *White Woman Speaks with Forked Tongue: Criticism as Autobiography*, London: Routledge.

Warwick, A. and Cavallaro, D. (1998) *Fashioning the Frame: Boundaries, Dress and the Body*, Oxford and New York: Berg.

West, C. (1993) *Race Matters*, Boston, MA: Beacon Press.

White, H. (1987) *The Content of the Form: Narrative Discourse and Historical Representation*, Baltimore: Johns Hopkins University Press.

Whitney, W. D. (1899) (ed.) *The Century Dictionary (Vol. III)*, London: *The Times*/New York: The Century Company.

Wilcox, R. (1942) *The Mode in Costume*, New York: Charles Scribner.

Wilson, E. (1985) *Adorned in Dreams: Fashion and Modernity*, Berkeley: University of California Press.

Wilson, E. (2001) *The Contradictions of Culture: Cities, Culture, Women*, London: Sage.

Wollen, P. (1969) *Signs and Meaning in the Cinema*, Bloomington: Indiana University Press.

Woodward, I. (1984) *Audrey Hepburn*, London: W. H. Allen.

Young, C. (1977) *The Films of Doris Day*, Secaucus, NJ: Citadel Press.

Zweig, S. (1933) *Marie Antoinette: The Portrait of an Average Woman*, New York: Garden City Publishing.

Further Reading

Bad Object Choices (eds) (1991) *How Do I Look? Queer Film and Video,* Seattle, WA: Bay Press.

Baillio, J. (1982) *Elizabeth Louise Vigée-LeBrun*, Fort Worth, TX: Kimbal Art Museum.

Barnard, M. (1996) *Fashion as Communication*, London: Routledge.

Bartra, A. (1994) 'Seduction of the Innocents', in Joseph and Nugent (eds) *Everyday Forms of State Formation*.

Blum, A. (1919) *Madame Vigée-LeBrun, Peintre des Grandes Dames du XVIII Siècle*, Paris: L'Éditions d'Art.

Bogle, D. (1989) *Toms, Coons, Mulattoes, Mammies and Bucks: An Interpretative History of Blacks in American Film*, New York: Continuum.

Brooks, G. (1968) [1904] *Dames and Daughters of the French Court*, New York: Books for Libraries Press.

Chierichetti, D. (1976) *Hollywood Costume Design*, New York: Harmony Books.

Delpierre, M. (1997) *Dress in France in the Eighteenth Century*, New Haven, CT: Yale University Press.

Dent, G. (1996) (ed.) *Black Popular Culture*, Seattle, WA: Bay Press.

Donahue, S. M. (1987) *American Film Distribution: The Changing Marketplace*, Ann Arbor: UMI Research Press.

Dyer, R. (1978) 'Resistance through Charisma: Rita Hayworth and *Gilda*,' in Kaplan (ed.) (1998) *Women in Film Noir*, pp. 115–22.

Dyer, R. (2000) 'Nice Young Men Who Sell Antiques: Gay Men in Heritage Cinema', in Vincendeau (ed.) (2001) *Film/Literature/Heritage*, pp. 43–8.

de Elia, T. and Quiroz, J. P. (eds) (1997) *Evita: An Intimate Portrait of Eva Perón*, London: Thames and Hudson.

Fine, E. A. (1978) *Women and Art: A History of Women Painters and Sculptors from the Renaissance to the 20th Century*, London: Allanheld & Schram/Prior.

Fontana, C. (1993) *María Luisa Bemberg*, Buenos Aires: Centro Editor de America Latina.

Forrest, E. (1951) 'Peck Reaches the Peak', *Picturegoer*, 3 November, pp. 13–14.

Fort, B. (1991) (ed.) *Fictions of the Revolution*, Evanston, IL: Northwestern University Press.

Fuss, D. (1991) (ed.) *Inside/Out*, London: Routledge.

Gledhill, C. and Swanson, G. (eds) (1996) *Nationalising Femininity: Culture, Sexuality and British Cinema in the Second World War*, Manchester: Manchester University Press.

Gray, F. (1994) *Women and Laughter*, London: Macmillan.

Gutwirth, M. (1992) *The Twilight of the Goddesses: Women and Representation in the French Revolutionary Era*, New Brunswick, NJ: Rutgers University Press.

Hall, E. B. (1969) [1926] *The Women of the Salon and Other French Portraits*, New York: Books for Libraries Press.

Harris, G. (1999) *Staging Femininities: Performance and Performativity*, Manchester: Manchester University Press.

Heller, N. G. (1987) *Women Artists: An Illustrated History*, New York: Abbeville Press.

Helm, W. H. (1915) *Vigée-LeBrun: Her Life, Works and Friendships*, London: Hutchinson.

Hobsbawm, E. (1996) *The Age of Revolution: 1789–1848*, New York: Vintage Books.

Hunt, L. (1984) *Politics, Culture, and Class in the French Revolution*, Berkeley: University of California Press.

Jacobowitz, F. and Lippe, R. (1992) 'Empowering Glamour', *CineAction!* nos 26/27, Winter, pp. 2–11.

Jallut, M. (1887) *Marie Antoinette et Ses Peintres*, trans. Philip Herbst, Paris: Editions A. Noyer.

Kaplan, E. A. (ed.) (1998) *Women in Film Noir*, London: BFI.

King, J. Whitaker, S. and Bosch, R. (eds) (2000) *An Argentine Passion; María Luisa Bemberg and Her Films*, London: Verso.

Knight, A. (1990) 'Revolutionary Project, Recalcitrant People: Mexico, 1910–1940', in Rodríguez O. (ed.) *The Revolutionary Process in Mexico*.

de Lauretis, T. (1991) 'Film and the Visible', in Bad Object Choices (eds) *How Do I Look?*, pp. 211–77.

Laver, J. (1992) *Costume and Fashion: A Concise History* (2nd edn), London: Thames & Hudson.

Leese, E. (1991) *Costume Design in the Movies: An Illustrated Guide to the Work of 157 Great Designers*, New York: Dover.

Ling, P. (1999) (ed.) *Gender and the Civil Rights Era*, New York: Garland Publishing.

Linville, S. (1998) *Feminism, Film, Fascism; Women's Auto/biographical Film in Postwar Germany*, Austin: University of Texas Press.

Mejia Barquera, F. (1989) *La industria de la radio y la television y la politica del estado mexicano (1920–1960)*, Mexico City: Fundación Manuel Buendia.

Meyer, J. (1976) *The Cristero Rebellion: The Mexican People between Church and State, 1926–1929*, London: Cambridge University Press.

Modleski, T. (1987) (ed.) *Studies in Entertainment: Critical Approaches to Mass Culture*, Bloomington: Indiana University Press.

Mulvey, L. (1975),'Visual Pleasure and Narrative Cinema' in Mulvey (1989) *Visual and Other Pleasures*, pp. 14–26.

Mulvey, L. (1989) *Visual and Other Pleasures*, Basingstoke and London: Macmillan.

Oliver, M. (1993) *Los Angeles Times*, obituary, 29 June.

Outram, D. (1989) *The Body and the French Revolution: Sex, Class and Political Culture*, New Haven, CT: Yale University Press.

Payne, B. (1965) *History of Costume from the Ancient Egyptians to the Twentieth Century*, New York: Harper & Row.

Peck, Gregory (1967) Interview with Peck, *Kaleidoscope* vol. 2 no. 3, pp. 4–18.

Perry, G. (1999) *Gender and Art*, New Haven, CT: Yale University Press.

Petersen, K. and Wilson, J. J. (1976) *Women Artists: Recognition and Reappraisal from the Early Middle Ages to the Twentieth Century*, New York: Harper & Row.

Puig, M. (1968) *Betrayed by Rita Hayworth*, trans. Suzanne Jill Levine (1992) London: Vintage.

Puig, M. (1969) *Heartbreak Tango*, trans. Suzanne Jill Levine (1992), London: Vintage.

Quinn, E. (1999) '"It's a Doggy-Dogg World": Black Cultural Politics, Gangsta Rap and the Post-Soul Man', in Ling (ed.) *Gender and the Civil Rights Era*.

Quinn, E. (2000) 'Who's the Mack?: The Performativity, Politics and Play of the Pimp Figure in Gangsta Rap', *Journal of American Studies* vol. 34 no. 1.

Revel, J. (1991) 'Marie Antoinette in Her Fictions: The Staging of Hatred', in B. Fort (ed.) *Fictions of the Revolution*.

Riva, M. (1992) *Marlene Dietrich by Her Daughter*, New York: Ballantine Books.

Riviere, J. (1929) 'Womanliness as Masquerade', *International Journal of Psychoanalysis* vol. 10, pp. 303–13.

Rodríguez O., J. E. (1990) (ed.) *The Revolutionary Process in Mexico: Essays on Political and Social Change, 1880–1940*, Los Angeles: UCLA Latin American Center Publications.

Salemson, H. J. (1947) 'Gregory Peck – Hollywood's Most Versatile Star', *Picturegoer*, 13 September, p. 10.

Schafer, J. O. (1981) 'The Souvenirs of Elizabeth Vigée-LeBrun: The Self-Imaging of the Artist and the Woman', *International Journal of Women's Studies* vol. 4.

Schreier, S. (1998) *Hollywood Dressed and Undressed: A Century of Cinema Style*, New York: Rizzoli.

Sheriff, M. D. (1996) *The Exceptional Woman: Elizabeth Vigée-LeBrun and the Cultural Politics of Art*, Chicago, IL: University of Chicago Press.

Simon, S. (1986) 'The Domestication of Majesty', *Journal of Interdisciplinary History* vol. 17.

Slatkin, W. (1985) *Women Artists in History: from Antiquity to the 20th Century*, Englewood Cliffs, NJ: Prentice-Hall.

Smith, V. (1996) 'The Documentary Impulse in Contemporary African-American Film', in Dent (ed.) *Black Popular Culture*.

Sweets, J. F. (1984) 'Vigée-LeBrun and Labille-Guiard Rivalry in Context', *Proceedings of the 11th Annual Meeting of the Western Society of French History*, University of Kansas Press.

Vigée-LeBrun, E. (1989) [1869] *The Memoirs of Elizabeth Vigée-LeBrun*, trans. S. Evans, London: Camden Press.

Vincendeau, G. (ed.) (2001) *Film/Literature/Heritage: A Sight and Sound Reader*, London: BFI.

Wollen, P. (1993) 'Out of the Past: Fashion/Orientation/the Body', in *Raiding the Ice Box*, Bloomington: Indiana University Press.

Worsley, H. (2000) *Decades of Fashion*, London: Hulton Getty Picture Collection.

List of Illustrations

Whilst considerable effort has been made to correctly identify the copyright holders, this has not been possible in all cases. We apologise for any apparent negligence and any omissions or corrections brought to our attention will be remedied in any future editions.

Shanghai Express, Paramount Publix Corporation; *Morocco*, Paramount Publix Corporation; *Spellbound*, © Vanguard Films; *Pillow Talk*, © Arwin Productions; *Ocean's Eleven*, © Warner Bros.; *Pulp Fiction*, Miramax Films/Band Apart/Jersey Films; *Jackie Brown*, Miramax Films/Band Apart; *Anarkali*, Imperial Film Company; *Indira M.A.*, Imperial Film Company; *Allá en el Rancho Grande*, Bustamente and De Fuentes; *Breakfast at Tiffany's*, © Paramount Pictures Corporation; *Sabrina*, © Paramount Pictures Corporation; *Les Girls*, Loew's Incorporated/Sol C. Siegel Productions/MGM; *The Reluctant Debutante*, Avon Productions/Loew's Incorporated/MGM; *Une Parisienne*, Films Ariane/Cinétel/Filmsonor/Rizzoli Editore; *Voulez-vous danser avec moi?*, Francos Films/Vides Cinematografica; *Dr No*, © Eon Productions; *Goldfinger*, Danjaq/Eon Productions; *De eso no se habla*, Oscar Kramer Films/Aura Film.

Index

Page numbers in **bold** indicate detailed analysis; those in *italic* denote illustrations; *n* = endnote.